'30

'30

Major League Baseball's Year of the Batter

RAY ZARDETTO

McFarland & Company, Inc., Publishers
Jefferson, North Carolina, and London

All photographs are courtesy of the National Baseball
Hall of Fame Library, Cooperstown, New York.

LIBRARY OF CONGRESS CATALOGUING-IN-PUBLICATION DATA

Zardetto, Ray.
 '30 : Major League Baseball's year of the batter /
Ray Zardetto.
    p.   cm.
 Includes bibliographical references and index.

 ISBN 978-0-7864-3666-8
 softcover : 50# alkaline paper ∞

 1. Batting (Baseball)—History—20th century.
 2. Baseball—United States—History—20th century.
 I. Title. II. Title: Thirty. III. Title: 1930. IV. Title:
 Major Leage Baseball's
 year of the batter.
 GV869.Z37   2008
 796.357'64—dc22   2008023099

British Library cataloguing data are available

©2008 Ray Zardetto. All rights reserved

*No part of this book may be reproduced or transmitted in any form
or by any means, electronic or mechanical, including photocopying
or recording, or by any information storage and retrieval system,
without permission in writing from the publisher.*

On the cover: Jimmie Foxx at bat in the 1930 World Series

Manufactured in the United States of America

*McFarland & Company, Inc., Publishers
 Box 611, Jefferson, North Carolina 28640
 www.mcfarlandpub.com*

Table of Contents

Acknowledgments	vi
Warming Up	1
1 Spring Training	5
2 Opening Day	23
3 April	37
4 May	54
5 June	82
6 July	108
7 August	131
8 September	162
9 October and the World Series	195
Afterword	211
Chapter Notes	223
Bibliography	229
Index	231

Acknowledgments

There is nothing like the drama of a baseball season. It is a six-month marathon that tests the physical and mental endurance of its athletes like no other sport. How these athletes respond on a day-to-day basis and how the fortunes of their teams rise and fall during the course of this six-month gauntlet is what makes each baseball season so different and so interesting.

To re-create the day-to-day world of baseball in 1930, I was fortunate to have a treasure trove of contemporaneous material to work from, most written by sportswriters of the time. I am indebted to their eloquent descriptions of games and vivid portrayals of the men who took the diamond. Without their great work, it would have been impossible to bring a human dimension to this story.

I would like to give a nod of thanks to my colleagues at the Society for American Baseball Research (SABR), who institutionalized the notion that every aspect of baseball should be covered, cataloged and celebrated. I am equally indebted to baseball's modern keepers of the flame — those who have spent immeasurable time and resources creating websites which preserve every aspect of the game for posterity. These fans have created a digital Library of Alexandria just for baseball — an electronic depository of virtually everything known about the game. There are many incredibly rich and entertaining sites, foremost among them www.baseball-almanac.com, www.baseballlibrary.com, www.retrosheet.org and www.baseball-reference.com.

I would also like to acknowledge the assistance offered to me by the National Baseball Hall of Fame in Cooperstown, New York. They are on the front lines of preserving and promoting the sport, and their work is unparalleled.

Most of all, I want to thank my grandfather. A decorated veteran of World War I who was seriously wounded at the Argonne, he would sit with me on our porch as Yankee games poured out of the radio on warm summer nights, and regale me with stories about the players of his younger years. It was he who turned my interest in the game into an unrelenting passion undiminished today.

Warming Up

There has never been a baseball season like 1930.

Restrictions on pitchers during the prior decade and the game's first generation of sluggers moved baseball away from low-scoring, pitching-oriented games and toward contests of long wallops and higher scores. The 1930 season represents the apex of the pendulum's swing in this direction. Never before or since have major league hitters pounded pitchers, dented outfield walls and scored runs at the pace they did that season.

The offensive carnage was widespread and deep: Nine of the 16 teams hit better than .300; The entire National League hit .303; the American League, .288; The New York Giants hit a staggering .319; The Philadelphia Phillies hit .315, yet lost 102 games; Sixty percent of the starting players—76 in all—hit better than .300; An unprecedented seven pairs of teammates hit .350 or better; The National League batting champion hit .401; Twenty players had 200 or more hits; two reached the 250-hit plateau; Six players had over 150 RBIs; Thirty-two players had 100 or more RBIs; A still-standing single-season record of 191 RBIs was set; Three of the top seven and four of the top ten single-season RBI totals were achieved; A record number of runs were scored; Thirty-six players scored 100 or more runs; Two teams scored over 1,000 runs—the first time that milestone had ever been achieved—and the only time more than one team did it in the same season; A record number of home runs were hit; The Chicago Cubs set a record for home runs by one team in a season; Only two pitchers in the major leagues had ERAs under 3.00; Only one team had an ERA under 4.00.

All eight regulars for the St. Louis Cardinals hit over .300. Six of eight regulars for the Yankees, Senators, Giants and Pirates hit .300. Five regulars did it for the Phillies, Dodgers, Cubs, Indians and Athletics, while four regulars with the Reds, Braves, Tigers and White Sox achieved the feat. The Browns had two .300-hitting regulars, and the poor Red Sox had but one.

On top of this unprecedented offensive barrage, the National League staged a madcap, down-to-the-wire pennant race involving four teams, the winner of which staged a miraculous late-season comeback equal to any in the history of the game. The American League offered its own pennant drama, as an upstart and lightly regarded Washington team overcame incredible obstacles to play David to the league's Goliath — the Philadelphia Athletics.

Many of the game's true hitting immortals walked the ball fields of 1930 — Babe Ruth was still in his prime, batting with Lou Gehrig and Bill Dickey in the Yankee lineup. In Philadelphia, Jimmie Foxx, Mickey Cochran and Al Simmons racked up big numbers. Charlie Gehringer held court in Detroit, Earl Averill in Cleveland and Heinie Manush in St. Louis, while Joe Cronin roamed Washington's infield and Goose Goslin and Sam Rice the outfield.

In the National League, the Cubs marched out heavy artillery in the persons of Rogers Hornsby, Hack Wilson, Kiki Cuyler and Gabby Hartnett. John McGraw's Giants matched them with Mel Ott, Freddie Lindstrom and Bill Terry. The Cardinals had Frankie Frisch, Chick Hafey and Jim Bottomley, the Pirates boasted Pie Traynor and the Waner brothers, the Dodgers had Babe Herman, Cincinnati had Harry Heilmann, and even the lowly Phillies had Chuck Klein and Lefty O'Doul.

Then there were players who turned in great seasons in 1930 and seemed ticketed for stardom, only to have bad fortune intervene and cut short their careers. These players include Johnny Hodapp, Lew Fonseca, Dick Porter and Eddie Morgan of Cleveland, Dale Alexander of Detroit, Adam Comorosky of Pittsburgh, Charlie Gelbert of St. Louis, and Riggs Stephenson of the Cubs.

What caused baseball's offensive EKG to spike to unparalleled heights in 1930? Much of it may have been caused by an accident of manufacturing. After introducing a more tightly wound and compact baseball in 1920 that helped increase the offensive production associated with that decade, a thicker cover was sewn on the ball for the 1930 season, presumably to deaden it. However, this thicker coat buried the stitches, making it difficult for pitchers to grip the ball properly and throw pitches with any bite. The result was a season of fat batting practice fastballs and flat, hanging curveballs — nirvana for hitters and pure misery for pitchers.

It would also be fair to say that pitching was in a transitional phase in 1930. Many of the superstar names of the prior decade (and in some cases earlier) were coming to the end of the line, including Grover Cleveland Alexander, Herb Pennock, Sad Sam Jones, Ray Kremer and Eppa Rixey. At the same time, many of the next generation of great pitchers were rookies or had yet to come of age, among them Red Ruffing, Mel Harder, Carl Hubbell, Lefty Gomez and Dizzy Dean.

What remained in 1930 was one bona fide superstar pitcher in the American League — Philadelphia's Lefty Grove, perhaps the best southpaw in AL history. Grove was supported by a couple of solid, if not superstar hurlers like

George Earnshaw and Rube Walberg. Cleveland had 20-game winner Wes Ferrell and Chicago had future Hall of Famer Ted Lyons in his prime. The Yankees had such successful pitchers as Waite Hoyt and George Pipgras, but they were showing signs of significant wear and tear.

The National League did not have a hurler equal to Grove but came close with Dazzy Vance of Brooklyn, even though he was 39 years old. There were solid stalwarts like Burleigh Grimes, who started the season with Boston and finished with St. Louis; Jesse Haines and Bill Hallahan, also with the Cardinals; Fred Fitzsimmons with the Giants; and Pat Malone, Guy Bush and Charlie Root with the Cubs. Few names beyond that caused National League hitters to lose much sleep.

Whatever the reasons for it, 1930 was a spectacular, one-of-a-kind season that offered white-knuckle pennant races and hitting feats the likes of which had never been seen and were not likely to be seen again. It was a year that fans hoped they would live long enough to tell their children and grandchildren about.

1

SPRING TRAINING

It was the morning of March 8, 1930, and Babe Ruth had come to the Jungle Club resort by the serene waters of Florida's Boca Ciega Bay in preparation for the rite of renewal that was spring training. For the first time since joining the Yankees in 1920, he had come to camp without a contract.[1]

Ruth was bothered by the lack of respect shown to him by the team for which he had done so much. He did things on a ball field no one had ever accomplished. He had already won ten home run titles while raising the single-season touchstone from 29 to 54 to 59 to the Holy Grail of 60 homers, which he hit three years earlier. Only last August, he clubbed his 500th career round-tripper, giving him more than twice as many as the next player on the list (Cy Williams with 237). He led the American League in runs scored eight times and RBIs six times. Now, at age 35, the Babe had added a few pounds around the middle and had lost much of his leg speed, but he remained the reigning home run champion, having rapped 46 in 1929 to go with 154 RBIs and a .345 batting average.

He was the game's greatest drawing card, and his slugging had elevated the Yankees to prominence — they were now New York City's premiere franchise, drawing over one million fans per year — and there was no doubt who the patrons were coming to see. To make his case, all the Bambino had to do was point to 1925, when he played only 98 games and the Yankees drew a decade-low 697,000 fans. His biographer, Robert W. Creamer, summed up Ruth this way:

... a unique figure in the social history of the United States ... more than any other man, Babe Ruth transcended sport, moved far beyond the artificial limit of baselines and outfield fences and sports pages. Every day, certainly several times a week you read and heard about him. When Willie Sutton was released from jail, *Time* Magazine reminded us he was the "Babe Ruth of bank robbers." A caption in the *New York Times* under a photograph of Enrico Caruso dubbed him "the Babe Ruth of operatic tenors" ... glutton, drunkard, hell raiser but beloved by all — except the Japanese during World War II. The Japs shouted "To hell with Babe Ruth," the ultimate insult, to GIs on Guadalcanal.[2]

Despite this resume, Ruth had been rebuffed in his desire to manage the Yankees. Their long-time skipper, Miller Huggins, died near the end of the 1929 season and Ruth saw himself as the natural successor—a veteran player who knew how to win. The Yankee brain trust, however—the regal German beer baron Colonel Jacob Ruppert and his no-nonsense general manager Ed Barrow—still saw Ruth as the big, barrel-chested and undisciplined kid who ate too much, drank too much and caroused too much. To them, there was no way he could manage others when he could barely manage himself. To replace Huggins, they turned to coach Bob Shawkey, one of the team's former pitching stars. Ruth accepted their decision grudgingly and reported to spring training ready to play.[3]

Now, a week into spring training, Ruth was torn between the competitive fire that had him participating in team workouts even though he had no contract, and his business sense, which told him to sit out spring training until a contract was done. In a practice game just a few days earlier, Ruth had suffered a nasty gash on a slide into third base. That injury was a bit of a caution light for the Bambino, for he knew the Yankees would not pay him a cent if he were injured before he signed.[4]

Ruth wanted a three-year deal from the Yankees with a raise from his present $70,000 salary to $85,000 per year. Ruppert and Barrow insisted that $80,000 per year for two years was the best the club could do.

"I don't see why the Colonel should quibble over a mere $5,000,"[5] Ruth told the scrum of reporters that followed him virtually everywhere he went. But Ruppert was doing just that, and Ruth could take it no longer. He knew the seasons were getting longer, the opposition younger, and the seasons of glory fewer. He wasn't going to squander one of them sitting in a hotel room over the "mere $5,000."

With his wife Claire in tow, Ruth made his way over to the Princess Martha Hotel, which, like the Jungle Club, was one of a new line of St. Petersburg hotels recently constructed in response to the burgeoning winter tourist trade. It was new, freshly furnished, and Ruppert had a suite among the 2,000 rooms in the building. Ruth's fame transcended the game, and as he entered the lobby of the Princess Martha, he was recognized by men, women, baseball fans and non-baseball fans alike. He waved and flashed the era's most recognized grin at everyone who called his name. When a few children gasped in recognition, he went out of his way to spend a few moments with each of them, talking baseball and signing autographs. Ruth always made time for the kids.

With fans gawking and reporters watching, Ruth paced and dawdled away an hour until Ruppert returned from a morning visit to the Yankees' practice field. When the white-haired owner of the Yankees saw Ruth, the two greeted each other warmly, Ruth bellowing a bearish hello, Ruppert replying softly in

Bob Shawkey (center) with his prized sluggers Lou Gehrig (left) and Babe Ruth. Shawkey, a veteran of 13 seasons as a Yankee pitcher, became their manager in 1930 much to the disappointment of Ruth, who wanted the job. Shawkey's downfall may have been his familiarity with his teammates.

his princely Germanic accent. The occasional business differences between the two had not cooled their personal relationship.

Ruppert invited Ruth to his suite, and about 15 minutes later, word reached the reporters in the lobby that they should make their way quickly to Ruppert's room. Reporters entered to the news that the deal was done. Ruth had agreed to a contract that would pay him $80,000 per year for the next two years. Expressing satisfaction and support for new manager Shawkey, Ruth pledged to "try and hit a home run for each of the thousand dollars the club has laid on the line."[6]

He started living up to his promise two hours later, when he whacked a home run in the Yanks' exhibition game against the Boston Braves before a sellout crowd. Barrow, known for his business acumen if not his prescience, famously said afterward that "no ballplayer will ever be paid as much as Ruth."

Ruth's annual $80,000 salary was beyond the comprehension of most Americans at the time. Baseball commissioner Kenesaw Mountain Landis made $65,000 annually and President Herbert Hoover made $75,000, leading to a mythically legendary Ruth wisecrack that he made more than the president because he had a better year than Hoover. All of those salary figures were incomprehensible to most families in the United States, where the average annual salary in 1930 was $1,368. The average "Joe" working an assembly line made about $17 a week and an educated professional such as a doctor might make about $3,000 per year.[7]

The players gathering for spring training in 1930 played in a country of 123 million people, most of whom were nervous and concerned. They had seen the black economic clouds roll over the country, beginning with a recession in August of 1929 that seemed to stop economic production in its tracks. Over the next three months, production declined at an annual rate of 20 percent, prices fell by seven and one-half percent, and business inventories became stagnant. Whether it was cause or effect, the stock market crashed at the end of October and wiped out over $16 billion in wealth. By the end of 1930, the Gross National Product declined almost nine and one-half percent and unemployment skyrocketed to nine percent. Over the next two years, as the country dropped into the free-fall of the Great Depression, manufacturing output would drop 54 percent, stocks would lose 80 percent of their value, the GNP would plummet another 13.4 percent, and unemployment would touch 25 percent.

As Ruth signed and the players practiced, an American artist named Grant Wood put an apt face to the consternation of 1930 when he unveiled the stark and rigidly stoic farm couple of his classic "American Gothic" painting at the Art Institute of Chicago.

The American League

Eight of the 16 major league teams had new managers going into 1930, divided evenly with four in each league. Three of the new American League skippers were with perennial second-division teams—Bob Killefer with the St. Louis Browns, Donie Bush with the Chicago White Sox and Heinie Wagner with the Boston Red Sox.

Bob Shawkey was the only new American League manager who inherited a squad expected to win. Shawkey was in a very tough position, replacing Miller Huggins, who had guided the Yankees through their first dynastic run and garnered the respect of the entire veteran club—including Ruth, which was not easy to do. Shawkey, who had played with or coached most of the men he would now manage, was expected to lead the Yanks back to their gloried heights of 1928, when they won their third straight pennant and second consecutive World Series. They had enough hitting with Lou Gehrig, Bill Dickey and Tony Lazzeri behind Babe Ruth, but their aging pitching staff had begun to fray in 1929. No one knew if the younger replacement arms were major league caliber.

Conversely, Connie Mack's Philadelphia Athletics dethroned the Yankees rather easily in 1929 with a vibrant pitching staff led by Robert "Lefty" Grove and a lineup that matched the Yankees muscle for muscle with Al Simmons, Jimmie Foxx and Mickey Cochran. Mack's situation could not have been more different from Shawkey's. The 67-year-old beanpole of a former catcher was the only manager the Athletics had ever known in their 29-year history, and by 1930, he was the unquestioned czar of Shibe Park. On the field, he managed the in-game strategy, ranging from handling pitchers to making the lineup to positioning his defense batter after batter. Off the field, he controlled all aspects of the business, from player scouting and contract negotiations to the price of hot dogs sold in the grandstand.

Mack's team had rolled over a formidable Chicago Cubs squad in five games to win the 1929 World Series, and the manager quickly set a stake in the ground for his players as they gathered for spring training

"We've proven we're a fine ball club," he said. "But I have always maintained that no team is entitled to call itself 'great' unless it repeats. By that I mean we won a pennant and a World Series last year. If we take the Series [again], then my boys deserve to be ranked as a great team."[8]

To most experts, the American League race came down to whether the Yankees had enough steam to overtake the talent-rich Athletics. The Associated Press released a preseason poll of 65 sportswriters; 60 picked the A's to repeat. In fact, a number of the sportswriters expected New York to have a tough time fending off Detroit and Cleveland, teams that showed measurable improvement in 1929. The oddsmakers agreed with the sportswriters, making the

Athletics an overwhelming 3-to-5 favorite and the Yankees an 8-to-5 bet. The next best odds went to Detroit at 10-to-1 and St. Louis at 15-to-1. Chicago and Cleveland were both 20-to-1. The Boston Red Sox were at the bottom of the list at 1,000-to-1, and just one notch above them stood Washington at 100-to-1.

The odds seemed a bit steep for a Washington team that had made consecutive World Series appearances in 1924–25 and had been a first-division team in the four ensuing years. One of the main reasons they had become competitive was the man the *Washington Post* called "Washington's answer to Babe Ruth." Leon "Goose" Goslin, also known as "the Wild Goose of the Potomac," was like Ruth in that he had not come to terms with his club by the start of spring training. Unlike the hyper-energetic Ruth, Goslin was content to stay on his farm in rural southern New Jersey rather than join his fellow ball players at their spring training facility in Biloxi, Mississippi. Called "Goose"—some said because of his bird-like facial features and others because of the way he flapped his arms when running after fly balls—Goslin broke into the American League at the age of 21, hitting .324 in his rookie year (1922). Since then, he had posted six consecutive seasons of .300 or better, including a league-leading .379 batting average in 1928. He did not hit as many home runs as Ruth—few could in cavernous Griffith Stadium—but he was Washington's middle-of-the-order RBI guy, driving in a league-leading 179 runs in 1924, part of a string of five straight years in which he drove in more than 100 runs.

Where Ruth's early years had been molded in a tough Baltimore slum, Goslin was raised on a wide-open spread of New Jersey farmland. Where Ruth seemed to be energized by the fame and the spotlight, Goslin remained a simple farm boy with little regard for the attention he received from playing baseball.

"It was all a lark to me," Goslin said about his big league career in *The Glory of Their Times*. "I never feared a thing, never got nervous. I was just a big country kid from South Jersey who didn't know better."[9]

The most famous story told about Goslin centered on the last day of the 1928 baseball season. Goslin was battling St. Louis' Henry "Heinie" Manush for the batting title, and the two teams were playing each other in the final game. Manush stroked two hits to move within a breath of Goslin for the batting lead. If Goslin sat out his last at-bat of the game, he would be assured the batting title. If he took the at-bat and did not get a hit, Manush would win the crown. With the game's outcome secondary at this point, Washington manager Bucky Harris left the decision up to Goslin, and the Goose opted out of hitting. His teammates, however, refused to accept his decision and goaded the Goose into taking the at-bat. Reluctantly, Goslin came to the plate with the batting title on the line and took two quick strikes. He complained loudly to the home plate umpire in the hope of being thrown out of the game. When that did not work, Goslin hunkered down and slapped the next pitch into right field for a single to nose out Manush by one point. Coming through with clutch hits became one of Goslin's trademarks, and he would do it for both Washington and Detroit in World Series play.

At this point, however, Goslin had to face the unpleasant reality of his nightmarish 1929 season. Various aches and pains plus a lingering shoulder injury had limited Goslin to a .288 average and 91 RBIs. His team had an equally disappointing season, and much of the blame was put on the Goose's shoulders. Detractors said Goslin had stopped taking care of himself physically, claiming he was an "old" 29. Owner Clark Griffith wasn't happy with his star and let it be known in his contract offer for 1930, which cut Goslin's salary from $16,000 to $10,000. Claiming he had never been so insulted in his life, Goslin turned it down, and responded by asking for $17,000. Both sides became entrenched.[10]

Meanwhile, in Biloxi, Walter Perry Johnson had gathered his troops for spring training. Two things about Johnson were legendary — his fastball and his gentlemanly demeanor. As to the first, Ty Cobb called Johnson's right arm "the most powerful ever turned loose in a ball park."[11] As to the second, sportswriters had dubbed Johnson "Sir Walter" and "White Knight" as sincere compliments and the high regard in which they held him and his character.[12]

The 1929 season had been as difficult for Johnson as it had been for Goose Goslin. It was his first season as a manager and he knew what the whisperers said, mostly that he was too nice a guy to be an effective manager and the team should have done better than a 71–81 record and a fifth-place finish.[13] Of course, the whisperers were just that, because no one in Washington, D.C., criticized Johnson openly. There was no athlete more beloved in any city than Johnson in the nation's capital, where he had toiled for 22 years.

"Let there be no misunderstanding, no delusion that Walter Johnson is, or was, a baseball legend. Not only inaccurate is that description, it demeans him," wrote long-time *Washington Post* sportswriter Shirley Povich in trying to explain the lofty regard in which Johnson was held.[14]

Called the "Big Train" in honor of his incomparable fastball, Johnson's career numbers remain staggering to this day. He won 417 games, second all-time to Cy Young. He registered a career ERA of 2.17, won 20 or more games ten times, and led the league in ERA five times and strikeouts 12 times. He won the pitcher's Triple Crown (wins, strikeouts, ERA) three times. His record of 110 shutouts remains untouched, and he finished his career with a then-record 3,508 strikeouts while walking only 1,405.

Having watched his team close out the 1929 season by surrendering meekly to the last-place Boston Red Sox, 2–1, Johnson silently vowed things would be different in 1930. From the first day of spring training, they were.[15] Players were drilled in the fundamentals of bunting, base stealing and defense each day. News dispatches from training camp spent as much time describing the diet and exercise regimen put together by Johnson and the team trainer as they did describing the team's play in exhibition games. Johnson's work ethic was so impressive that a number of his players urged him to come out of retirement and pitch for the team once again. Johnson laughingly declined. The focus and the work paid off in a team sharp and focused from the get-go. Johnson's boys won 17 of 19 exhibition games and made only 11 errors. When Johnson declared his team ready for the regular season, few doubted him.

The only fly in the ointment was Goslin's holdout. Johnson and Griffith both knew that without Goslin, Washington's offense could not compete with the rest of the American League. One of Goslin's teammates anonymously told the *Washington Post* that, "If the Goose has a good year at all, it is likely to mean the difference to us between a first division and a second division berth."[16]

As the first two weeks of March passed, the stalemate between Griffith and Goslin held fast, with each expecting the other to make the first move toward opening a negotiation. The situation became more complicated when word emerged that Goslin blamed his poor performance in 1929 on Johnson for riding him too hard and too often. Press reports at the time quoted Goslin as saying he would not play for Johnson. Griffith responded by saying that Goslin must not only accept the team's salary terms, he also must make a statement that he could and would unhesitatingly play for Johnson. With no response forthcoming from southern New Jersey, Griffith had some preliminary discussions with the Tigers and Browns about a possible trade, although he later told reporters he had discouraged those teams from continuing the dialogue.[17]

The first sign of a thaw came when Goslin sent a telegram on March 18 denying the harsh words he reportedly said about Johnson, although he gave no indication he was ready to sign a contract. Five days later, Griffith announced he had no choice but to slap Goslin with the penalties usually applied to AWOL players: Goslin was placed on the suspended list and, whenever he arrived in camp, he would train at his own expense and continue to do so until the team was satisfied that he was in playing shape.

Like all of the players in the age before free agency, Goslin had little choice but to show up on the club's terms or risk not playing, which meant not being paid for the entire season. Goslin finally sent word to the club on March 31 that if the club would pay his travel expenses, he would join them in Chattanooga, where they were scheduled to play a few exhibition games. Griffith readily agreed. Goslin arrived on April 1 and signed his contract the next day for the $10,000 proposed by Griffith. It wasn't a total loss for the Goose — Griffith gave him an incentive clause in the contract which, depending on his performance, could earn Goslin as much as $6,000 in bonuses, thereby equaling his 1929 pay. Goslin also agreed to train at his own expense.[18]

The little training he required became evident two days later, when Goslin was in the lineup for two exhibition games against the Birmingham Barons. The Barons likely wished Goslin had held out a few more days. The Nationals won both games, with the Goose smacking a three-run home run and two other hits while throwing a Barons runner out at the plate in the first game. He then collected three more hits, including a home run, and drove in four runs in the second game, again throwing out a Barons runner on the base paths in the ninth inning to squelch Birmingham's late comeback attempt.

If Johnson had any lingering doubt or animosity toward Goslin for what the outfielder said during his holdout, the manager did not reveal it.

"I'm tickled to death," Johnson said of Goslin's return.[19]

Johnson's euphoria lasted only until a special telegram arrived at camp. It was not good news. Johnson's 15-year-old son Walter Jr. had been struck by a car while riding his bicycle, and he was hospitalized with two broken legs. Suddenly all of the training, all of the preparation, and all of the strategizing about baseball meant nothing to the intensely devoted family man. Johnson headed north ahead of his team to hold a bedside vigil with his wife. They were told by the doctors that one of his son's legs might need to be amputated. It was a harbinger of the tumultuous and personally trying season that lay ahead for the Washington manager.

One other American League slugger was giving his manager a holdout headache as the final hours of spring training ebbed away. The Athletics' star left fielder Al Simmons, considered by many to be the best overall player in the game, refused to sign a contract. Connie Mack had confidently reassured the press and the fans that Simmons' holdout would be resolved before the season began. Now, two days away from the season opener against the Yankees, Mack sat in his cramped office at Shibe Park and publicly conceded he was wrong about Simmons. Privately, he realized that without his left fielder, the A's would have a very tough time repeating as American League champions. Simmons knew it, too, and figured that fact gave him powerful leverage. Mack had less than 48 hours to resolve the situation if he wanted Simmons in the lineup for Opening Day against New York.

The National League

The National League also had four new managers in 1930, and, as in the American League, three of them were with second division clubs: with Bill McKechnie of the Boston Braves, Dan Howley of the Cincinnati Reds and Jewel

Ens of the Pittsburgh Pirates). The fourth new skipper was with a team of recent championship vintage and eager to return to it. Cardinals owner Sam Breadon had given St. Louis fans a World Series team in 1926 and again in 1928, and following an off-year in 1929, he wanted his team back on top again. He felt he had the necessary talent to do it with Frankie Frisch, Jim Bottomley and Chick Hafey in the batting order and Jesse Haines and Bill Hallahan leading the pitching staff. To pull it all together, the impulsive Breadon, who had burned through five managers in the previous five seasons, turned to a former army top-sergeant, catcher and minor league manager named Charles "Gabby" Street. The talkative Street had not managed at the major league level before, but he had done something 22 years earlier that forever etched his name in American sports lore.

As was usually the case, August was hot and muggy in Washington, D.C. A crowd gathered around the base of the Washington Monument on this particularly soupy day of August 21, 1908, to watch a unique exhibition of athleticism. Two local sportsmen, John Biddle and Preston Gibson, had taken a sack of baseballs and climbed to the top of the monument, 505 feet above the ground. Standing below them at the base of the obelisk was Gabby Street, bedecked in street clothes, his shirt sleeves rolled up while he wore his catchers mitt. Street was going to attempt something that Biddle had bet Gibson could not be done—catch a baseball dropped from the top of the monument. It had been tried before without success, most prominently by Hall of Fame catcher Buck Ewing.[20]

Street was the current catcher for the Washington Nationals baseball club with tough hands and quick reflexes—both requirements for catching the Nationals' newest pitching dynamo, Walter Johnson. But not even the Big Train could throw the ball as fast as it would be coming at Street this morning—about 135 feet per second (one-eighth the speed of a rifle bullet).[21]

Street looked up into the haze of the Washington sky and indicated he was ready. Standing in the small observation room one-tenth of a mile above, Gibson put the first ball on a grooved wooden chute and let it roll out the window and into its free fall. Almost immediately, the ball began to flutter like a knuckleball as it plummeted through the air. Street picked up the flight of the ball about halfway down, took a few quick steps and lunged desperately before the ball hit the ground and bounded away. A second ball came down and fell further from Street's reach. A third fell with the same unsatisfactory result. A few spectators, all of them fans of the Nationals, became concerned that Street could be seriously hurt after seeing the velocity of the baseball. A few urged him to quit; Street politely declined. One ball after another came down, some hitting the monument during descent, others falling too close to it for Street to safely attempt a catch. At one point, the wily catcher moved to a different side of the

Walter Johnson (left) and Gabby Street as battery mates with the Senators. Street's handling of Johnson's peerless fastball may have helped him do what most thought impossible — catching a ball dropped from the top of the Washington Monument.

monument, hoping the wind currents might be more favorable, but it did not help. He missed ten in a row.

    Up above, Gibson decided to stop rolling the balls down his chute and instead began tossing them out the window by hand to ensure they cleared the monument by a safe distance. Street missed the first one of these tosses by a few feet. Gibson then tossed out the twelfth ball and Street seemed to have it gauged. He quickly snapped at it with his glove but missed it by a hair. More determined than ever, Street raised his arms in anticipation of his thirteenth try. The next ball began to fall, starting as a little gray speck against the sky, then looking larger as it approached. This time, when Street reached out with the glove at eye level, a tremendous crack echoed across the monument mall. One witness said it sounded like a rifle shot. Amazingly, Street had caught the ball and was holding it up proudly for all to see.[22]

"I could not see the ball until it was halfway down," Street said. "The ball before the one I caught I could see very plainly but I guess I was a bit timid about closing my hands on it for it struck the edge of my glove. The ball I caught hit my mitt with terrific force, much greater than any pitched ball I have ever caught. The force of the ball benumbed my hand. I made the catch just as if it were an easy fly at a ball game, only that I held my arms more rigid so as not to have them knocked apart by the force of the ball."[23]

Street played for a few more years before he coached and managed, and later used his naturally loquacious manner to become a popular broadcaster. However, regardless of his achievements on the playing field, in the dugout or in the broadcast booth, he would always be remembered as the guy who caught a baseball tossed from the top of the Washington Monument.

The fraternity of major league catchers was well aware of Street's gravity-defying catch, including Wilbert Robinson, who in 1915 was entering his sophomore year as manager of Brooklyn's National League team. Having been one of the game's top catchers during the 19th century, Robinson was convinced that anything Gabby Street could do, he could do as well.[24]

It had rained on March 13, 1915, and the scheduled spring training practice game had been cancelled. The fun-loving Robinson arranged for the team trainer to get on an airplane, fly over the field and drop a baseball to him from 500 feet in the air. Many Brooklyn players gathered around their manager to make sure they had a good vantage point. Some of them were destined to become legends themselves, Casey Stengel was present, as was Jack Coombs and Zach Wheat.

Robinson stood on the grass portion of the infield when the plane buzzed overhead. Everyone looked up at the same time and, from the back of the plane it came, small and round, seemingly suspended in the air for a second before beginning its fall. Robinson moved slightly toward the pitcher's mound, following the flight of the ball, and then quickly realized he needed to take a step back. He raised his glove as quickly as he could but he was not fast enough. The sphere struck Robinson on his shoulder and seemed to explode on contact, with streams of liquid spattering in all directions. The force of the blow dropped Robinson flat on his back. He felt the liquid covering him and cried out in a moment of blind panic, assuming it was his own blood. Only when he recovered his senses and saw the hysterical laughter of his players did he realize that he had tried to catch a grapefruit instead of a baseball. The trainer later said he had forgotten to bring a baseball on the plane, and substituted the grapefruit instead. A faction of Brooklyn's players remained convinced that Casey Stengel had put the trainer up to the prank.[25] Robinson joined in the laughter; he always loved a good joke — even if it was on him.

In 1930, Robinson was about to enter his 17th year managing the Brooklyn team, and he still loved a good joke. Now 67 and pleasingly rotund, "Uncle Robbie" maintained the same jocular and warm nature that endeared him to most everyone he knew. He had slowed a bit with age but he was still respected for his baseball mind and for his colorful and impressive baseball lineage. He was born on June 29, 1863, just two days before the Battle of Gettysburg. Robinson loved baseball from an early age, playing for a minor league in New England and Philadelphia of the American Association before making it to the majors. He became catcher and captain of the National League's Baltimore Orioles in the 1890s, a team that had attained legendary status to Robinson's contemporaries. Considered one of the nastiest teams of all time, this Oriole franchise was an aggregation of gritty, pugnacious players as prone to hit with their fists as with their bats. They won three straight pennants and perfected an ultra-aggressive style of play that included breaking rules and inciting riots in the stands. The Orioles were a walking Hall of Fame of 19th century stars, beginning with Robinson, who was the field leader of the team, and continuing with manager Ned Hanlon, Hugh Jennings, Dan Brouthers, Wee Willie Keeler, and an overly obnoxious firebrand of a third baseman named John McGraw.

If Robinson was the heart and soul of the Orioles, McGraw was the bile. Most every biography and contemporary account of McGraw uses the word "fiery" to describe his demeanor both on the field and off. Born in New York in 1873, he worked his way out of poverty by playing baseball, and he became a decent offensive third baseman — good enough to join Hanlon's rowdies. McGraw epitomized the Orioles' attitude. He would do anything to win, and hardly a day went by when he wasn't fighting, or challenging to a fight, an opposing player, an umpire, a fan, or one of his own teammates.

McGraw finished his playing career as the 20th century dawned, and he fashioned his hard-nosed tactical mind for managing. He became the manager of the New York Giants in 1902, a seminal moment in the history of that franchise as well as New York baseball. He became the National League's most prominent personality, ruling the Giants with an uncompromising iron fist for the next three decades.

McGraw and Robinson developed a personal bond during their years playing together in Baltimore, no doubt forged from their similar on-field competitiveness and desire to win at any cost. They became business partners and the best of friends despite their polar-opposite personalities off the field. Where Robinson was "Uncle Robbie," the guy everyone wanted seated at their table, McGraw was "Little Napoleon," the dictatorial chief who needed to be in charge, and just as importantly, needed for everyone to know he was in charge.

"With my team, I am absolute czar," he once said, "and my men know it. I order plays and they obey. If they don't, I fine them."[26]

The way the two were perceived is clearly evident in things said by those who knew them:

> It is doubtful that baseball ever produced a more colorful figure than the esteemed Wilbert Robinson. Like Falstaff, not only was he witty himself, but the cause of wit in others.—John Kiernan, the *New York Times*[27]
>
> He was a great catcher, but to my mind, his greatest quality was his personality.

John McGraw (left) and Wilbert Robinson during their playing days with the legendary Baltimore Orioles of the 1890s. Despite polar-opposite personalities, they became close friends and business partners until an argument in 1913 destroyed their friendship and ignited a feud still festering in 1930.

His good nature was a sure way to drive away the blues and he drew us together as a social and harmonious club.—Bill Prince, Robinson's manager in 1885.[28]

Contrast that to these observations about McGraw:

I have seen him walk onto ball fields where he is about as welcome as a man with the black smallpox.—Pitcher Christy Mathewson[29]
His very walk across a field in a hostile town was a challenge to the multitude.—Sportswriter Grantland Rice[30]
McGraw eats gunpowder every morning and washes it down with warm blood.—Giants coach Arlie Latham[31]

Robinson had been out of baseball for a few years when, in 1911, McGraw invited him to join the Giants as a coach. Uncle Robbie came on board to handle the pitchers and worked with such talent as Christy Mathewson, Rube Marquard and Hooks Wiltse. McGraw's team won three straight National League pennants, but they came up short in each of the World Series, losing to the Athletics in 1911 and 1913, and the Red Sox in 1912. When Connie Mack's team outpitched and out-hit the Giants in 1913 for an easy five-game series win, McGraw was furious. It probably did not help that Mack called his series victories a "stick in John McGraw's eye." Mack was still stinging over McGraw's dismissive attitude about the entire American League when it formed in 1901 and the disrespect he had shown to the Athletics by arrogantly referring to them as "white elephants."

The night after the 1913 World Series ended, McGraw hosted a reunion party for his former Baltimore teammates. The tall tales, jokes and the liquor flowed freely—perhaps too freely. At one point in the evening, a heavily liquored McGraw snarled at Robinson, and blamed his inept coaching as the reason they had lost to Philadelphia. An equally liquored Robinson, agitated at McGraw's provocations, began evaluating McGraw's managing in equally unflattering terms. The two lunged at each other but were separated by former teammates, just as they might have been on the ball field decades earlier. McGraw then had the last word by firing Robinson on the spot. Robinson replied by throwing a stein of beer in McGraw face and leaving the party. He replied more fully the next month when he took the job managing the Brooklyn club.[32]

The feud was still festering in 1930 as McGraw prepared for his 28th full year as Giants manager and Robinson began his 17th at Brooklyn's helm. The two had not spoken a word to each other since the incident in 1913, yet both managers were of a like mind. They each prepared their teams to win the championship, but if that was not to be, then at least their teams needed to be good enough to prevent the other from winning the pennant.

Meanwhile, with a by-the-book efficiency for which he would best be known, Cubs manager Joe McCarthy was gathering his troops in California and getting them ready to defend their National League crown. Joseph Vincent

Rogers Hornsby (left), Hack Wilson, Al Simmons and Jimmie Foxx meet before the 1929 World Series. The Cubs' painful five-game loss to the Athletics in that series would come back to haunt manager Joe McCarthy before the 1930 season ended.

McCarthy was beginning his fifth season as boss of the Cubs. He became the manager of the last-place Cubs in 1926 and brought them in fourth twice and third once before grabbing the National League's brass ring in 1929. It was the first of many successes that would allow McCarthy to retire with the highest winning percentage of any manager in history. A man of quiet authority and self-restraint, McCarthy seemed to blend the best elements of his managerial contemporaries.

"He didn't have McGraw's violent pugnacity, though Joe was pugnacious. He controlled it better," said Yankee general manager Ed Barrow, who would later partner with McCarthy to lead the Yanks through one of their most dominant eras. "He was a man of constant self-restraint but he drove his players as hard as McGraw did. He had tenacity rather than pugnacity, and although he was a harder and more aggressive personality than Connie Mack, he had a deep understanding and sympathy for his players as Connie did."[33]

1 Spring Training

The Cubs had dominated the senior circuit in 1929 with a lineup of mashers, including Rogers Hornsby, Hack Wilson, Gabby Harnett and Kiki Cuyler. They lost the World Series to Connie Mack's A's in five games, most famously melting down in the seventh inning of Game Four when they lost an 8–0 lead by giving up 10 seventh-inning runs.

Along with their formidable offense, they had the National League's deepest rotation with veterans Charlie Root, Guy Bush, Sheriff Blake and Pat Malone. Despite this bevy of talent, McCarthy knew the key to managing the club was handling the temperamental Wilson and especially the acidic Hornsby. Rogers Hornsby was a great hitter — the greatest right-handed hitter in an era of great hitters — but his talents came at a heavy price. Hornsby was humorless, single-minded and outright obsessed with baseball, and he publicly heaped scorn on teammates he thought less dedicated. His tactless honesty and negativism did not sit well in the clubhouses and front offices where Hornsby played, which explained why he was moved so frequently despite a resume that included the second highest lifetime batting average in history (.358), three .400 seasons capped off with the century's highest mark of .424, a span of five magnificent seasons where he *averaged* .402, and a Triple Crown.

Reporting for spring training in 1930, "the Rajah" had a problem. He had been bothered by a sore heel the season before and it noticeably limited his base running and fielding ability. During the offseason, the ailment was diagnosed as a bone spur and surgically repaired. However, as the Cubs limbered up during the first few days of camp, Dr. F.C. Early, who was keeping an eye on Hornsby's recovery, told McCarthy that the growth on Hornsby's heel bone had returned and the 34-year-old slugger should seriously consider retirement.

To this point, McCarthy's relationship with Hornsby had been professional and free of problems, but the manager knew his superstar second baseman was not very popular in the clubhouse. Regardless of McCarthy's thoughts about the equation — lose Hornsby's peerless hitting ability but cleanse the clubhouse of his negativism — he kept silent about it while Hornsby preempted further discussion of the matter. The Rajah declared to the doctors and the Cubs that he could and would play and that his heel would get better once he had some time to stretch it out.

As spring training progressed in the California sunshine, Hornsby's swing remained tentative, and his limp revealed the pain. McCarthy had no idea how much pain Hornsby's heel would cause the entire club by the end of the season.

The Associated Press sportswriters tabbed McCarthy's Cubs as favorites, with 54 of 66 picking them to repeat. To their way of thinking, no National League team had improved itself enough to make up the 10½-game spread by which the Cubs had won the year before. The oddsmakers agreed and made

Chicago even money to win, while the New York Giants were 3-to-1, Pittsburgh 4-to-1 and St. Louis 5-to-1. Cincinnati and Brooklyn were 12-to-1, and, the Boston Braves were 1,000-to-1. While the oddsmakers did not think much of Philadelphia, making them a 40-to-1 long shot, a few reporters tabbed the usually putrid Phillies as a dark horse in the race, suggesting that if some of their unproven pitching came through, they had more than enough hitting to win. Little did they realize what a unique and lasting niche this Phillies team would carve for itself.

Each team broke camp, and for the first two weeks of April, worked toward the destination city where it would start the regular season. For the Nationals, it meant returning to the nation's capital. Baseball gave the first day of its schedule to Washington so the president of the United States could throw out what was genuinely the first ball of the season. The Boston Red Sox came to town to provide the opposition.

Commissioner Kenesaw Mountain Landis was happy to dismiss the prognosticators and the gamblers who had all but handed the pennants to Philadelphia and Chicago. It was his responsibility to promote the game, and as the first crowd of the regular season gathered in Washington, he declared, perhaps conscious of the deteriorating economic situation, that "the pennant races are as wide open as a beggar's hand."[34]

2

OPENING DAY

An excited assemblage of fans filed through the turnstiles of Griffith Stadium to greet their team for the new season. For reasons of nostalgia or habit, most fans called their team the Senators after a popular 19th century franchise that played in the area, but officially the team was known as the Washington Nationals. It would be another two decades before ownership relented to the popular will and officially changed the team's name to the Senators.[1]

The team name may have generated confusion, but it was crystal clear who was in charge of it. Clark Griffith emerged from the Nationals' dugout like a king surveying his dominion. His castle—a two-tier, 32,000-seat ballpark bearing his name—was rapidly filling with fans and they were eager to see Griffith's legions in flannel uniforms and stirrups attack the invading Red Sox from Boston. Goose Goslin, who crammed a month of spring training into half as much time, was ready to go, and he would lead an attack that featured an impressive array of professional hitters:

- Sam Rice, who in 20 seasons never hit below .293, had seven 200-hit seasons, and finished 13 hits shy of 3,000
- Joe Judge, a slap hitter who had nine .300 seasons and was a great defensive first baseman despite standing only 5 feet 8 inches tall
- Ossie Bluege, an equally adept third baseman and solid hitter with a lifetime .272 mark over 18 seasons
- Buddy Myer, a hard-nosed and aggressive second baseman whom Griffith traded in 1927 and then, after calling it the dumbest trade he ever made, swapped five players to get him back
- Joe Cronin, the one-time bank clerk about to blossom into the League's best offensive shortstop. He would hit over .300 and drive in more than 100 runs in eight seasons, splitting his 20-year career between Washington and Boston. He would become player-manager for both teams and later president of the American League and a Hall of Famer. He also married Griffith's niece in 1934.

Clark Griffith (right) greets his manager Walter Johnson and wishes him luck for the upcoming season. Johnson was looking to revitalize a team that had underperformed in 1929.

Griffith rushed onto the field to greet Walter Johnson, with whom he had always had a warm relationship, and asked for an update on Johnson's injured boy. Johnson's smile was that of a relieved parent. The outlook for his son had turned refreshingly sunny. After some early concerns, both legs were now healing properly and the prognosis was good. In fact, as it turned out, Walter, Jr. would be out and playing baseball in a few months.

Griffith, pleased by the good news, excused himself. It was almost three o'clock. Griffith made his way through the grandstand, stopping to say hello to Charles Curtis, the white-haired vice president of the United States, and Andrew Mellon, the secretary of the treasury. Working his way through the aisles, the somewhat lordly Griffith, who always seemed bigger than his five-foot, six-inch frame, stopped to shake hands with the various senators and congressmen scattered about the lower-tier seats.

Griffith was entering his second decade as owner of the Washington Nationals, and his face was among the most recognizable in Washington. He was a true pioneer of the game, having pitched with legends like Cap Anson and "Old Hoss" Radbourne in the 19th century prior to jumping to the nascent American League in 1901. He pitched for 23 years, won 20 or more games seven times, and finished with 237 wins. He also earned his nickname "Old Fox" for both his cunning as a player on the field and for his business acumen off of it. Before joining the Senators, Griffith was the first manager of the New York Highlanders (later Yankees), a franchise he now despised for their cavalier spending habits; it was the team he always wanted to beat more than any other.[2] Griffith had limited financial resources in Washington and had to carefully weigh the spending of each dollar. His players would say that when it came to salaries, he weighed the spending much too carefully.[3]

Not that he wasn't a kind soul. Over time Griffith brought back favorite players past their prime for a last go-round with the Senators, and he and his wife, who had no children of their own, adopted the seven kids of Mrs. Griffith's brother after his untimely death. But his kindness would not deter a compelling business decision when it needed to be made, which is why, in 1935, he did not flinch at trading Joe Cronin to Boston even after the prized shortstop had married into the family.

Griffith made his way outside the park and waited for the president of the United States. During hard times, Griffith had earned money in vaudeville, so he knew how to draw a crowd. Griffith used the idea of the president throwing out the first ball as a way to bring publicity and prestige to the Nationals; he developed it into a tradition for the sporting and the political world.[4]

It must have been quite satisfying for Griffith, who was born in the modest surroundings of a Midwestern log cabin, to rub elbows with the last five presidents of the United States. His trek began with the bulbous William

Howard Taft, a genial and intelligent man who, even though he tipped the scales at over 300 pounds, appreciated the athleticism of the game. Taft said baseball "summons to its presence everybody who enjoys clean, straight athletics." After Taft, Griffith had also come to know the following presidents:

- Woodrow Wilson, an avid and high-brow fan who, according to Al Schacht, a former player and long-time observer of the game, "stayed right until the end of games and I would say he knew baseball better than the average fan."
- Warren Harding, a "man's man" who loved cigars, card games and baseball to the point where he would keep detailed scorecards and brood over Washington's losses. "He was the sort that gloomed and did not enjoy his supper if he had seen the Washington team lose," said one of his friends. "On the contrary he felt it was a pretty good world and that things would come out all right in Europe or elsewhere if he had seen the Senators win."
- Calvin Coolidge, cool and impersonal with little regard or knowledge of the game, unlike his wife Grace, who may have been the most rabid baseball fan to ever live in the White House. "She knew a lot more about baseball than he did, but so did everybody else," wrote sportswriter Shirley Povich.[4]

A hundred miles to the north of Washington, Connie Mack and Al Simmons continued their standoff. Coming off a season in which he hit .357 and led the league with 157 RBIs, Simmons wanted a Babe Ruth–type of salary rather than the $30,000 Mack was offering. Despite the high regard in which Simmons held Mack, this was a business negotiation and, like everything Simmons did, he went at it with almost demonic energy.

To the pitchers of his era, Simmons was probably the most feared batter when the game was on the line. Simmons posted 11 consecutive seasons in which he batted over .300 and drove in more than 100 runs. "Jimmie Foxx was a pain," pitcher Red Ruffing once said about facing the Athletics' two biggest hitters with men on base, "but Al Simmons was a plague." Even non-pitchers admitted they were intimidated by his presence in the batters box. "When he'd grab hold of a bat and dig in, he'd squeeze the handle of that doggone thing and throw the barrel toward the pitcher in his warm-up swings. He looked so mad — and this was batting practice," recalled Yankee outfielder Tommy Heinrich, who played against Simmons for years.[5] "I hate pitchers," Simmons would say frequently.

Born Aloysius Szymanski, he took his Anglican sounding surname from a paint store in his native Milwaukee. He was a wicked line drive hitter instead of a pure power hitter; still, he hit 307 career home runs in 20 seasons to go along with a lifetime .334 average. Simmons retired 73 hits short of 3,000, hold-

Despite a reputation for orneriness, Al Simmons (left) maintained a warm regard for Connie Mack throught his life. The feeling was mutual. Mack kept a picture of Simmons on the wall of his office until he retired.

ing the American league record for most hits by a right-handed batter until Al Kaline broke it almost forty years later. He joined Foxx, Grove, Mack and Cochran in the Baseball Hall of Fame in 1953.

Connie Mack had a respect for Simmons that never faded. Of all the players that passed through Shibe Park during Mack's half-century of managing the

Athletics, the only player's picture he kept on the wall of his office was that of Al Simmons.⁶

"If I could only have nine players named Simmons," Mack once sighed.⁷ However, like his swaggering left fielder, Mack had to put his personal feelings aside during a business negotiation, something he once admitted he had to force himself to do.

"After all my years," he once said, "there are two things I never got used to—haggling with a player over his contract and telling a boy he's got to go back [to the minor leagues]."⁸

With Simmons threatening to go home and sit out the season, Mack issued a public statement warning fans who planned to attend the season opener against the Yankees the next day that Simmons most probably would not be in the lineup. There was also the chance Mack was looking to get a leg up in the public perception war that might follow a lengthy holdout by one of his superstars.

The lines in the sand were drawn. Simmons was ornery and nasty; Mack was calm and much more patrician. But they both had an equally stubborn competitive streak, and there was no telling how long this stalemate might last.

Herbert Hoover emerged from his car to the respectful applause of the surrounding crowd, his cherubic face forcing a steely smile, his right hand waving and then self-consciously combing his dark hair, which had not yet been overtaken by the gray that would come over the next few years (he was only in the 13th month of his administration). Hoover had amassed more electoral votes than any other candidate in history (up to that time) despite the fact he was a shy and reserved man of Quaker heritage. An engineer by trade, he had a strong sense of public service, which began when he organized food and relief efforts that saved millions of European lives during and after World War I.

Griffith was a bit surprised to see the president decked out in an overcoat on such an agreeably warm day, but he happily greeted Hoover and escorted him into the stadium and down to the presidential box. Hoover responded more animatedly than usual, obviously happy to enjoy a brief respite from the extreme schedule he had been keeping the past few weeks in response to the economic reversals battering the country.

Despite the modern perception that he was a laissez-faire president who took little or no action in response to the growing economic crisis, Hoover had just proposed a $160 million tax cut to help stimulate the economy. He also had secured a promise from business executives to invest $1.8 billion in new projects and a pledge to maintain wages. In fact, Henry Ford had just announced he would raise his workers' daily wage from six to seven dollars. In response, Hoover won a concession from union leaders to withdraw current wage-increase demands. Just a few days earlier, he told his federal department heads to speed up construction projects and made appeals to all 48 governors to do the same. This whirlwind of action prompted the *New York Times* to say of Hoover that "no one in his place could have done more and very few of his predecessors could have done as much."[9]

The president took his place in the box next to the Nationals' dugout and stood attentively as the U.S. Army marching band played *The Star Spangled Banner*, the song that in one year would become the national anthem of the United States. When the band concluded, the American flag was raised to the top of the center field flag pole. All eyes then turned to the presidential box, where some 7,000 photographers prepared to record Hoover's season-initiating toss. While some presidents liked to milk the moment by holding the ball aloft to create a sense of anticipation, Hoover threw the ball almost as soon as Griffith handed it to him. By his own admission, Hoover was not much of an athlete, having once played shortstop, "where I was no good"[10] and his throw this day displayed that lack of ability. It went high and wide of the players set to catch it, but the crowd cheered nonetheless and then turned its attention to the playing field.

The first game was a close but fairly typical game and served no notice of the mayhem that was to follow for the rest of the season. The Nationals picked up where they left off in spring training, jumping to a 1–0 lead in the bottom of the first. With one out, Sam Rice singled to center and Goose Goslin, looking to forget the flak he took for his poor 1929 season and his spring holdout, slammed a single to right. After Buddy Myer was hit by a pitch to load the bases, Joe Cronin dropped a bloop hit into shallow right field to score Rice. Goslin held up at third base to keep the bases full. With Joe Judge at the plate, the Nationals had a chance to blow the game open, but Judge hit a foul pop that Boston catcher Johnnie Heving caught. Inexplicably, Goslin danced too far off of third and Heving whipped a throw down in time to cook the Goose for the third out, spiking the rally and beginning a season of silent tension between Goslin and Walter Johnson.

After Boston first baseman Phil Todt doubled in a run to tie the score in the fourth, Washington starter Fred "Firpo" Marberry excited the crowd with a two-out, two-run double to left in the sixth, giving the Nationals a 3–1 lead. Marberry gave one run back to Boston in the seventh and reliever Garland Braxton surrendered the lead when the Sox scored two in the eighth to go ahead, 4–3. Boston reliever George Smith was entrusted to protect the one-run lead and seemed about to lock it up when, with two out in the bottom of the ninth, he left too much of a fastball over the plate and outfielder Sam West brought the still-hopeful crowd to its feet with a ringing double off the distant right field wall. That brought up Goslin, who now had a chance to redeem himself for his base running blunder in the opening inning. Goslin got a fastball he liked and took his mighty hack. At the instant the ball met the bat, the crowd erupted, thinking the Goose had tagged one—which he had—but directly at center fielder Tom Oliver, who caught it for the final out of the game. Considering their torrid spring and heightened expectations, the 4–3 loss was a disappointment to Washington, but the setback would be very temporary.

The rest of major league baseball took to the stage on Tuesday April 15. Overcoats, hats and gloves were the order of the day at cathedral-like Shibe Park in Philadelphia, where cold and gray had replaced the balmy temperatures of the day before. The A's were on the field for their pre-game batting practice with many eyes on a young, unknown outfielder named Spencer Harris, whom Connie Mack had tabbed to replace the unsigned Al Simmons.

A buzz began generating when the 36,000 pairs of eyes in the stands caught sight of a tall, square-shouldered but almost sickly pale player emerging from the A's dugout. His white-as-moonlight skin was a distinct giveaway for anybody who had been around Shibe Park long enough. Only one player on the Athletics never tanned—even in the sunniest of summers—and that was Al Simmons. As more and more fans realized Simmons was on the field, in uniform and limbering up, the sporadic cheers meshed into one loud grandstand-shaking roar. Word quickly spread through the press box that old man Mack had pulled off a miracle. In a final last-ditch meeting only two hours earlier, Mack had signed his recalcitrant outfielder to a three-year deal valued at $100,000.

Sam Murphy, later reporter for the *New York Sun*, that "Simmons could not bring himself to go home with his team about to play the Yankees in front of a huge crowd. Simmons contacted Mack on the morning of Opening Day and the two had a conversation, after which Simmons rushed to Shibe Park, signed the deal and rushed into uniform to get a greeting from the crowd equal to the one Ruth gets from his public in New York."[11]

The crowd cheered as Simmons took his place at the plate for batting practice and walloped a few fat fastballs across the outfield. The fans went into delirium after the pre-game ceremonies when Simmons ran to his usual perch in left field. With Simmons back in the fold, Mack had all four of his superstars on the field for Opening Day—Simmons, Mickey Cochran behind the plate, Lefty Grove on the mound and the hefty Jimmie Foxx at first base.

Cochran was one of the premier personalities in the game and considered by his contemporaries to be the best catcher in baseball (he was voted the catcher on Baseball All-Time Centennial team named in 1969).

"Greatest catcher of them all, Cochran was," said battery mate Lefty Grove. "A great ballplayer, all around; good hitter, good runner, good arm, smart."[12]

"Cochran was great—a great inspirational leader," recalled Charlie

Gehringer, the Detroit Tigers' Hall of Fame second baseman who played against Cochran for nine years before they spent five seasons together in Tiger uniforms. "Cochran was always in charge on the field." In years to come, Gehringer would select Cochran as the best catcher he ever saw. "He could do more things to beat you." Gehringer said.[13]

Cochran had a fiery temperament that often resulted in trashed clubhouses after tough losses and unrefined, often vulgar repartee with the opposition during games. In his autobiography, Cochran recounted how he was warned by Commissioner Landis during the 1929 World Series to clean up his verbal act. Cochran started the next game by shouting to the Cubs, "Hello, sweethearts, we're going to serve tea this afternoon during the game. Come on out and get your share!"

After that game, according to Cochran, Landis visited the Athletics' locker room in Chicago and approached Cochran.

"Hello sweetheart," the usually dour commissioner said. "I'm here for my tea. Will you pour?"[14]

Cochran's on-field presence transcended his statistics, but his numbers should not be overlooked. He had nine .300 seasons and compiled the highest career average ever for a catcher, batting .320. He was coming off a .331 season in 1929 with 113 runs scored and about to embark on his greatest hitting season ever.

When it came to tantrums and trashing clubhouses, Robert Moses "Lefty" Grove did not take a back seat to Cochran or anyone else in baseball. He had his own hair-trigger volcanic temper and it was easily ignited by a turn of bad fortune on the field, whether it be a bad bounce of the ball or a misplay by a teammate. Humorless and high-strung, Grove was once asked to name the funniest thing that ever happened to him in the game. He replied, "I never saw anything funny about the game."[15]

In his book describing baseball in the 1930s, author Thomas Gilbert called Grove "a tough, unsentimental competitor long on talent and short on charm. Grove was focused on winning in a way that almost seemed to have nothing to do with his team. Famous for dark moods and a quick temper, Grove was the kind of pitcher who would throw at his own teammate if he hit him too hard in batting practice."[16]

Connie Mack and the Athletics put up with Grove because he was the best pitcher in baseball at the time and arguably the best left-hander in the history of the game. His fastball was the stuff of legend in the American League.

"It was so fast that by the time you made up your mind whether it would be a strike or a ball, it just wasn't there any more," Charlie Gehringer recounted in *When the Grass Was Real* by Donald Honig. "He'd just fire the ball and defy you to hit it."[17]

Connie Mack (center) with his prized battery Mickey Cochran (left) and Lefty Grove. Both Hall of Famers were ultra-intense competitors known to tear up locker rooms or tear into teammates after tough losses.

"Lefty was really a good-natured fellow when the pressure of the game was off," said Mickey Cochran. "He was a tough loser and I'll take that sort of competitor any time in preference to the chap who loses with a high heart."[18]

Grove led the American League in wins four times, in ERA nine times and in strikeouts seven consecutive years. In 1930, he was in the midst of an incredible four-year run of excellence in which he posted a record of 103–23. Seven straight years and in eight out of nine he was a 20-game winner, and by the time he retired, a somewhat mellower Grove had won exactly 300 games over 17 years. He was elected to the Baseball Hall of Fame in 1947.

At the tender age of 21, Jimmie Foxx had a breakout year in 1929. The even-keeled half of the A's slugging tandem clubbed 33 home runs, drove in 117 runs and racked up a .354 average hitting behind Al Simmons in the lineup. Those numbers would prove to be no fluke for the hulking six-foot slugger whose 195 pounds seemed to be distributed mostly in his huge shoulders and arms.

Ted Lyons, the ace left-hander for the Chicago White Sox who faced Foxx many times during his career, said Foxx's biceps looked as thick as car tires.

The easy-going Jimmie Foxx had 37 home runs, 156 RBIs and hit .335 behind Al Simmons in the Athletics' lineup. Yankee pitcher Lefty Gomez once observed of the brawny Foxx, "He had muscles in his hair."

"How much air you carrying in those arms, Jimmie?" Lyons said he once asked the slugger, to which the good-natured Foxx replied, "About thirty-five pounds."[19]

"He wasn't scouted, he was trapped," was the famous and popular quip from Yankee pitcher Lefty Gomez about Foxx's size. He also famously claimed that Foxx "had muscles in his hair."

"Double X" as he came to be known in the local press would become the most prolific slugger of the 1930s, winning four home run titles, a Triple Crown and three MVP awards. He drove in more than 100 runs 13 times.

"He was a great hitter," said Wes Ferrell, another pitching adversary of Foxx's. "I'd strike him out three times and then he would hit a home run so far out of Shibe Park that you just had to stand there and admire it. Foxx was a wonderful guy, too. Always smiling and looking to have a good time."[20]

No slugger in the 20th century reached the 500-home run plateau as quickly as Foxx. His final seasons were hampered by diminished vision, the result of a nagging sinus infection, but he managed to finish his career with 534 career home runs, at the time the most ever hit by a right-handed batter and second all-time only to Babe Ruth. He was an easy Hall of Fame choice in 1951.

Like all championship teams, Simmons and Foxx had a stellar supporting cast.

George "Mule" Haas was a solid outfielder, a lifetime .292 hitter and one of the best bench jockeys in the league.

Jimmy Dykes, another wickedly effective bench jockey, played all infield and outfield positions well, while hitting better than .300 in four of his last six seasons—leading to a lifetime .280 mark.

Ed "Bing" Miller, another top-notch defensive outfielder, who compiled a lifetime .312 average and posted nine .300 seasons—his best being .324 in 1924.

Max Bishop, the eagle-eye second baseman and leadoff hitter who had 100 or more walks in eight seasons, was considered the best defensive second baseman of the era, leading the league in fielding four times.

The Yankees were the first team to challenge the defending world champions. They arrived in Philadelphia for Opening Day and new manager Bob Shawkey tabbed 30-year-old veteran George Pipgras, an 18-game winner in 1929, to face Lefty Grove.

After the Yankees went out quietly in their half of the first inning, Pipgras retired Bishop, walked Haas and retired Cochran in the bottom of the first. That brought up Simmons, with the roar of the crowd again signifying its approval of his having signed in time to play the game. Simmons wielded one of the longest bats in the game, which compensated for a swing that tended to step "in the bucket," that is, as a right-handed hitter, he stepped more toward third base than directly toward the pitcher. "Bucketfoot Al" zoned in on Pipgras' second pitch and launched a high fly to right field. Ruth started back a few steps but quickly realized it would be a futile chase. The ball disappeared over the right field wall and into the street beyond, sending the crowd into delirium and sending Grove back to the mound with a 2–0 lead.

The Yanks tried to counter in the third. With a man aboard, Ruth uncorked his pinwheel swing and launched a moon shot well above the right–center field fence. The slugger started his famous home run trot, unaware that his ball had struck the public address loudspeaker. Although it was above the home run fence, the speaker jutted into the field of play and therefore was ruled a double by the umpires. The Yanks lost two runs on the ruling but regained them quickly when Foxx misplayed Gehrig's ensuing grounder for an error. That was all Grove would allow. He took command from that point, allowing no more runs and a total of six hits while striking out nine. The A's posted four more

The swing that earned Al Simmons a .381 average and the 1930 batting title. He beat out Lou Gehrig by such a razor-thin margin, the contest was not decided until after the season ended.

runs and prevailed, 6–2, to start the year ahead of the Yankees, just as they had in 1929.

"If I had disappointed that crowd," said Simmons after the game, "I would never have had the nerve to face them again. I'll never forget that greeting. I thought the stands were coming down."[21]

In the National League, the current and former National League kings—the Cubs and Cardinals—inaugurated the season facing one another in St. Louis. The game began ominously for the Cubbies. In the top of the first, Rogers Hornsby rapped a two-out single to center and Chicago's cleanup hitter, Hack Wilson, drilled a sizzling double to the left field corner. Normally Hornsby would have scored, but the bone spur jabbing at his heel caused him to limp around the bases. He was thrown out at the plate on a close play after he decided not to slide in deference to his injury. Although Wilson lost the RBI, he recorded one with a sacrifice fly later in the game, his first of an unprecedented total for the season.

The Cubs broke out to a 5–1 lead after six innings, but when starting pitcher Sheriff Blake hurt his leg while running the bases, reliever Guy Bush came in and gave up six runs, four hits, four walks and two wild pitches over the next two innings. Fortunately for Bush, the Cubs plated four runs in the top of the eighth and held on for a 9–8 victory.

The most ironic Opening Day game took place in Brooklyn. The Phillies, who would set a major league record by being involved in only six shutouts in 1930 (they would pitch two and be victimized by four), whitewashed Wilbert Robinson's flock, 1–0. If shutouts were a rarity for the Phillies in 1930, the sight of Chuck Klein driving in a run was not. He had the only RBI in the game on his way to the second highest season total in National League history.

Despite the growing economic concerns across the country, 205,112 fans attended the seven Opening Day games (the Indians and White Sox were rained out in Chicago). The cumulative Opening Day attendance in 1929 for eight games had been 169,500.

3

APRIL

The chilly weather of April 15 was the precursor of a stubborn wintry cold front that locked the Northeast in a grip of freezing temperatures and rain. It also wrecked havoc with the schedule in both leagues. The Yankees and A's lost the remaining two games of their opening series to the weather, and both had the first games of their next series postponed as well. On April 23, the entire American League schedule was wiped out, and the Pittsburgh Pirates has to halt their home opener in the third inning because of heavy snow. Brooklyn had three straight games postponed. However, no team was as bedeviled by the weather as the New York Giants. By April 25, when the cold front finally relaxed, McGraw's men had seen seven of their eleven scheduled games postponed.

The American League

After losing its Opening Day game, Washington headed north to Fenway Park and gained a measure of revenge by beating the Red Sox two straight. After two off-days—one scheduled and one forced by the weather—the Nationals arrived in Philadelphia on April 17 to begin a critical test. Over the next ten days, they were going to play the A's six times. The world champions had bullied their way to 16 wins in the 20 meetings with Walter Johnson's team in 1929.

"Last year, the Athletics had but to scowl at Washington and the poor team in the nation's capital bowed in meek submission," wrote the *Sporting News*.[1]

After bad weather cancelled the scheduled opener of the series, the two teams squared off on April 19. The game started promisingly for the Nats when they placed two runners aboard in the first inning, but the middle of the order failed to bring them around against Rube Walberg, Philadelphia's number three starter. Washington starter Myles Thomas matched zeroes with Walberg through four innings, but in the bottom of the fifth with two outs, Mickey Cochran reached him for a single and Al Simmons followed with a laser-like home run over the fence in center field. Jimmie Foxx then singled and Bing Miller doubled Foxx home; suddenly the score was 3–0. The shell-shocked visitors never recovered. Simmons hit a second home run to help his teammates hang a 9–0 drubbing on Washington. Demonstrating how little he needed spring training, Simmons closed out the month of April leading the AL with a .432 batting average.

Washington returned home the next day to take on the Yankees and starting pitcher Tom Zachary, who was carrying a 12-game winning streak that extended back to 1929. The game was tied 3–3 in the bottom of the eighth when Zachary walked leadoff hitter Joe Cronin. Manager Bob Shawkey went to the bullpen, a move he soon regretted when his decision begat a single, wild pitch, walk, throwing error, and a Sam Rice two-run single. Washington won, 6–3, and the Yankees, who had lost a pair of games to the Red Sox after their Opening Day loss to Philadelphia, were 0–4.

Walter Johnson brought his boys back to Philadelphia on April 21 for a single-game shot at the Athletics. The game startled poorly for Washington when starter Bump Hadley gave up two first-inning runs, but he held his ground for the rest of the game. Keyed by a two-run Joe Cronin home run, Washington won, 6–3.

After another win against Boston (their third straight), the Nationals were primed to host Connie Mack's defending champions for three games, on April 25–27. Although they trailed at some point in all three games, the Nationals swept the series. The first win was a 6–4 decision behind Goose Goslin's three hits, one of which was a game-deciding two-run homer in the eighth. The second win was an 8–4 final, with Buddy Myer's three-run shot highlighting a scoring spree over the seventh and eighth innings. The third win was an 11–6 margin, with Goslin whacking another home run and two more singles.

The Nationals piled on two more victories against the visiting Yankees, outscoring them 6–5 in the first game, and in their most stirring game of the season to date, took the next contest 11–8 after trailing 7–0. Suddenly, the Nationals had won eight in a row, had whipped Philadelphia four straight times, and were leading the American League.

"Last season, the Washington Senators were so low that none would do them reverence," wrote John Kiernan of the *New York Times*.... They took the field this season and trampled all over the well-known Athletics.... The Senators may skid again, but what they have already accomplished is considered a favorable omen in Washington and a positive outrage in Philadelphia."[2]

"The team that beats Washington would be the one to win the pennant," Mack said after watching his champions take three on the chin.[3]

Meanwhile, the Yankees were an edgy bunch. With four losses in their first four games, the first Yankees team since 1922 to go 0–4, questions regarding rookie manager Shawkey's decisions—such as his hook of Tom Zachary in the Washington game—were cropping up.

The Yanks took their 0–4 record into their home opener against the Athletics and Lefty Grove on April 22 before 66,000 fans. Despite his team's slow start, Shawkey still put a lethal lineup on the field every day. It featured five future Hall of Fame players, beginning with Babe Ruth. Although no longer a spring chicken, Ruth was still the unchallenged home run king in baseball and a brutal offensive force. In the past four seasons, he had hit 46, 54, 60 and 47 home runs, averaged 145 runs scored, and his lowest RBI total during that stretch was 142.

Batting behind Ruth, Lou Gehrig may have been the best RBI man in the history of the game, even though Ruth's frequent home runs often cleared the bases by the time Gehrig came to the plate. In the last three seasons, his RBI totals had been 126 (1929), 142 (1928) and 175 (1927)—the last mark representing the league record for RBIs in a season to that point. He later re-set the American League RBI record to 184, where it still stands. Gehrig was in the midst of a streak that would see him score 100 times and drive in 100 runs for 13 straight seasons. During this stretch he averaged scoring 139 runs and driving in 148 per season. He was also in the midst of another streak that would bring him some notoriety. Heading into the 1930 season, Gehrig had played in 732 consecutive games, about one-third of the way to his famous 2,130 consecutive games played. Sportswriter Stanley Frank assessed Gehrig's position among the pantheon of Yankee legends, stating, "Lou was the most valuable player the Yankees ever had because he was the prime source of their greatest asset—an implicit confidence in themselves and every man on the club."[4]

The other Hall of Famers-to-be for the Yanks included Tony Lazzeri, considered one of the best clutch hitters in the game. He had driven in more than 100 runs in four of his first five seasons, missing only in 1928 because of injuries. He would register four more 100+ RBI seasons, including 121 in 1930; Bill Dickey, who was starting his first full season as catcher, hit well over .300 for six straight years and in nine of the next ten seasons on his way to a career .313 mark. He also would drive in over 100 runs in the next four seasons. Dickey quickly earned the reputation as a great defensive catcher with a cannon arm, and although he was not the charismatic on-field leader that Mickey Cochran was, their playing skills were considered equal; Earle Combs, the smooth leadoff hitter with great base running skills, was a career .325 hitter over 12 seasons. He had five years of 190 or more hits, collecting 202, 191 and 231 hits in the last three campaigns, while scoring 119, 118, and 137 runs. That was part of a streak of eight consecutive years in which Combs scored 100 or more runs.

The Yanks also had Hall of Fame pitchers Waite Hoyt and Herb Pennock on the roster, but Manager Shawkey gave the ball to 23-year-old sophomore hurler Roy Sherid for the home opener to face Lefty Grove.

The Yankees' offense gave the home fans a lot to cheer about as they solved Grove for six runs in the first three innings and knocked him out of the game. However, Sherid was hit equally hard by the A's batters, and the Yanks' lead was only 6–5 after three innings. George Pipgras relieved Sherid and held the lead until the A's scored once to tie the game in the eighth and took a 7–6 lead in the top of the ninth when Bing Miller hammered a drive into the lower left field grandstand. Earle Combs tried to rally the Yanks by leading off the bottom of the ninth against Rube Walberg with a walk. Combs was sacrificed to second, which brought up Babe Ruth, who had to be drooling at the chance to get at Walberg. The Bambino nailed the Philadelphia southpaw for 17 of his career homers (including four in his 60-homer season of 1927), meaning Walberg, who gave up 163 home runs in his career, surrendered 10 percent of them to the Babe.

Sure enough, Ruth put his signature upper-cut swing on a pitch and sent the ball soaring toward the bleachers in right-center, but an untimely and unfriendly breeze caught the ball at the apex of its arc, which slowed it just enough for Miller to catch it with his back pinned against the bleacher barrier for the second out. Combs tagged from second base and raced for third, then made the turn and kept coming for the plate. An alert Miller relayed to Max Bishop, who gunned a strike to Cochran. The ball and the runner arrived at the same time as Cochran moved to block the plate and, in a photo finish, Combs was called out. The A's improved their record to 4–1, while the Yanks dropped to 0–5.

Two days later, on April 25, Ruth whacked his first home run of the season and the Yankees finally won their first game, beating Boston, 3–2, in 10 innings. Even with this victory, the Yanks shared last place with the Detroit Tigers, who were in the midst of their own seven-game losing streak.

"The Yankees are in the cellar," reported the *New York Times*' John Kiernan. "Of course this can't go on. The ... Yankees are so unaccustomed to the cellar that they haven't yet discovered where the staircase is."[5]

The *Sporting News* pointed out some of the Yankees' problems: "Shawkey has a team feeling the autumn wind. His pitchers are not frisking merrily on the lawn.... Babe Ruth ... is not batting home runs with the vigor of early youth.... Shawkey has many things to tame that are more annoying than cold soup at dinner."[6]

Ruth pooh-poohed the notion that the Yankees were feeling their age, and he told the press his simple remedy for what ailed his team.

"What we need," said the Babe, "is some of those big innings we used to have.... We'd pile up six, seven, eight runs in an inning; we wouldn't miss one day in four at it.... We'll have to get back to our old habits."

"The sooner the better," agreed Combs.[7]

American League Notes for April

The St. Louis Browns wowed their fans with a five-game winning streak, vaulting into second place on April 27 with a 6–4 record. It proved to be the high-water mark for the season as they proceeded to lose their next five in a row and drop to the second division, where they would stay for the rest of the campaign.

Bud Clancy of the Chicago White Sox managed to do something no first baseman had accomplished in 39 years. On April 27, he went an entire game without a chance in the field.

Jimmie Reese made his major league debut with the Yankees on April 19. Reese, who played two years with New York and roomed with Babe Ruth, started as a bat boy in the Pacific Coast League in 1919 and stayed in the game for 75 years, right up until his death in 1994 at age 92 while coaching for the California Angels (who subsequently retired his uniform number 50).

American League Standings on April 30, 1930

	W	L	PCT.	GB
Washington	10	3	.769	—
Cleveland	8	4	.667	1.5
Chicago	6	4	.600	2.5
Philadelphia	6	5	.545	3
St. Louis	6	7	.462	4
Boston	5	8	.385	5
Detroit	5	10	.333	6
New York	3	8	.272	6

The National League

The only thing that seemed capable of stopping the New York Giants in April was the weather. They won their Opening Day game at the Polo Grounds, 3–2, over Bill McKechnie's Boston Braves, only to have their next three scheduled games postponed. After sweeping a three-game series from the Phillies at the Polo Grounds on April 19–21, the Giants had four more consecutive games postponed due to the winter-like weather. New York sportswriter John Drebinger noted humorously that "the Giants ... are developing a very fine game, but it is bridge, not baseball."[8]

"It's like going from the North Pole to the South Pole,"[9] quipped first baseman Bill Terry of the Giants' travels to the frigid and rainy towns of Boston and Philadelphia, where his team did not play a single inning.

Terry, an introspective and extremely intense personality, had registered a .372 batting average and 226 hits in 1929, and would post six 200-hit seasons, six 100-RBI seasons, and nine straight years hitting better than .320 on his way to the Baseball Hall of Fame. To Terry, baseball was not a game; it was a serious business, and he was not out to fulfill a boyhood dream by playing it.

"I played baseball because I could make more money doing that than I could doing anything else," he once explained.[10]

Terry's lack of respect for the men who ran the game was legendary. "Baseball," he once said, "must be a great game to survive the fools who run it. No business in the world has ever made more money with poorer management."[11]

Terry's stark attitude did not win him many friends among the players or the sportswriters (which might help explain his not being elected to the Baseball Hall of Fame until 1971, a full 35 years after he stopped playing). He had a cool and contentious relationship with John McGraw. They were constantly throwing darts at each other, much of the time over business matters.

"Terry can ask for more money in the winter and do less in the summer than any ballplayer I know," McGraw once said.[12]

In *The Glory of Their Times*, Bob O'Farrell, a catcher with the Giants in 1930, told a story that illustrated the contentious nature of their relationship. McGraw let Terry swing away with a count of three balls and no strikes. The sweet-swinging Terry smacked a home run. When Terry returned to the dugout, McGraw exclaimed loudly that "I'll take half of that one!" referring to the fact he gave Terry the green light. "You can have it all!" an annoyed Terry responded sharply.[13]

"McGraw will call every move and every pitch, till the count is three and two and the bases are loaded and then all of a sudden he leaves the pitcher to fend for himself," Terry once said of McGraw. Another time, Terry exploded after the "Little Napoleon" blamed a loss on one of his players. "You've been blaming other people for the mistakes you've been making for 20 years!" he shouted.[14]

Ironically, two years later, a burnt-out McGraw turned the managerial reigns over to his first baseman.

"Memphis Bill" Terry was one of six active players on McGraw's 1930 roster destined for enshrinement at Cooperstown. Four of them — Terry (14 years), Mel Ott, (22 years), Carl Hubbell (16 years), and Travis Jackson (15 years) — would play their entire careers exclusively in a Giants' uniform.

The diminutive Ott (5 feet 9 inches and 170 pounds) used a distinctive high leg kick to generate a quick, powerful swing. He slugged 42 homers with 151 RBIs in 1929 at the ripe age of 20. By the time he retired, he would win six home run titles and be the first National Leaguer to hit 500 home runs. At the time of his retirement, his final tally of 511 homers would be a full 200 more

John McGraw (right) on the day in 1933 when, wracked by ill health, he ended his storied run as manager of the New York Giants and handed the reins to Bill Terry. Theirs was always a frosty relationship, but McGraw agreed Terry was a suitable replacement.

than any other National League player and third all-time behind Ruth and Foxx.

Hubbell perfected a nasty screwball that permanently disfigured his pitching arm but made him one of the toughest pitchers of his era. "The screwball's an unnatural pitch," he said. "Nature never intended a man to turn his hand like that throwing rocks at a bear."[15] Dubbed "The Meal Ticket" by teammates for his tough performance in big games, the chronically thin left-hander caught everyone's attention with an 18-win season in 1929. By the time he ended his career, he had 253 wins, five straight 20-win seasons, and three times led the National League in wins and ERA.

Jackson was known primarily as a defensive shortstop. He earned the nickname "Stonewall" for his ability to keep batted balls in the infield. He batted over .300 six times, and was coming off a 1929 season in which he poked a career-best 21 home runs.

The other two eventual Hall of Famers on McGraw's team were Fred Lindstrom and Dave Bancroft.

Lindstrom posted four straight .300 seasons, including a 231-hit, .358 effort in 1928. He was a fierce competitor, an independent spirit, and one of McGraw's favorite players, even though Lindstrom never hesitated to bark right back at McGraw when the manager spewed verbal abuse at him. Despite their tiffs, Lindstrom swore loyalty to McGraw — the only Giants manager he ever knew. Lindstrom did not play his entire career with New York. When McGraw resigned, Lindstrom was upset — he was not particularly fond of Terry, and he claimed McGraw had promised him the manager's job.[16] His wish to be traded was honored and he spent two years with the Pirates, one with the Cubs, and his last season with Brooklyn. Lindstrom would be a controversial Hall of Fame choice, having played more than 100 games in only eight of his 13 seasons.

Bancroft was a 39-year-old shortstop who was reaching the end of a career, which he split between the Phillies and Giants. He would only play 10 games in 1930 before retiring to become one of McGraw's full-time coaches.

The weather finally relented and allowed the Giants to play baseball again on April 26 in Philadelphia. Over 25,000 fans squeezed into the Baker Bowl, an outdated and ancient facility that was built in 1887, to see the Giants sweep the Phils again, this time by scores of 13–2 and 7–5. They saw Jackson and Terry homer in each game, the Giants hammer out 16 hits in both contests, and the Phils make three errors in each outing.

It was a cocky group of Giants that boarded their train back to New York with a 6–0 record. John McGraw's team was headed to Flatbush. It was time for his first showdown of the season with Wilbert Robinson.

The Brooklyn team that awaited the undefeated Giants was known not as the Dodgers, but as the Robins in tribute to the man who had managed them since 1914. Wilbert Robinson's Flatbush flock was off to a tough 2–6 start, the most troubling aspect of which was the fact their competition had been only Boston and Philadelphia, two of the league's acknowledged also-rans.

"Aside from the poor pitching," reported the *Sporting News*, "the lack of a will to win seems to have been the main defect of the team."[17]

However, there was no pressure felt in the Brooklyn dugout under the guidance of the benevolent Robinson. He insisted his boys have fun — a dictum they followed too enthusiastically at times, leading to their being known as the "Daffiness Boys" for the unintentionally zany way they sometimes played the game.

Sportswriter Frank Graham explained that the "Daffiness Boys" "were not normally of a clownish nature, and some of them were very good ballplayers, indeed, but they were overcome by the atmosphere in which they found themselves as soon as they put on Brooklyn uniforms."[18]

One look at the distorted action Giants ace Carl Hubbell forced on his arm in order to throw his wicked screwball and it was no wonder he could not lift his arm later in life.

The crown princes of "daffiness" were pitcher Arthur "Dazzy" Vance and outfielder Floyd "Babe" Herman.

Vance was a remarkable story in that arm trouble prevented him from starting his major league career until he was 31. Despite this late start, he still blazed his way into the Baseball Hall of Fame. Vance, a colorful character and a free spirit, had a very high leg kick and exaggerated windup, which he embellished by slicing the sleeves of his shirt into twirling ribbons to provide an additional distraction for the hitter. Vance combined a paralyzing curve ball with a searing fastball to lead the National League in strikeouts seven straight seasons (1922–28) while twice leading in wins and three times in ERA.

"He was wicked," outfielder Rube Bressler said of Vance. "He had a curve ... you couldn't see it. It was like an apple rolling off a crooked table." Bressler later joined the Robins and roomed with Vance, calling him very funny and a great storyteller.[19]

Babe Herman was a five-sport star from Glendale, California. Known in New York as "the other Babe," he had a reputation as a clumsy fielder, reinforced by his leading the league in errors at first base in 1927 and in the outfield in 1928.

"His fielding was the despair of his teammates," the *Sporting News* said.[20]

"He wore a glove for one reason," a teammate chimed in anonymously, "because it was a league custom."[21]

"If I put him in the lineup everyday, he can hit .400 if he sets his mind to it. But he'll lose the club 2–3 games a week with his glove," remembered Otto Miller, who managed Herman in the minor leagues.[22]

Even the scout who signed Herman conceded, "He's kind of funny in the field, but when I see a guy go six-for-six, I've got to go for him."[23]

A tall left-handed hitter described as "lanky, blue-eyed and blond, with a perpetual schoolboy air" by the *Sporting News*,[24] Herman always seemed to be in the middle of strange plays, sometimes his fault and sometimes not. Twice during the 1930 season, Herman committed the same base running *faux pas* by stopping to watch a home run hit by a teammate, only to get passed on the bases by that teammate, reducing the homer to a single.

Herman recounted in *The Glory of Their Times* by Lawrence Ritter that Wilbert Robinson was a sound baseball man and a good manager, although he did have some "idiosyncrasies" that helped fuel the legend of the "Daffiness Boys." Herman related that Robinson once wanted to put a new catcher in the starting lineup for a game, but because he didn't know how to spell the new catcher's name, he didn't play him. According to Herman, Robinson would sit

Opposite top: Giants shortstop Travis Jackson, who had his best season in 1930, hitting .339. Jackson, Carl Hubbell, Bill Terry, and Mel Ott all played their entire careers with the Giants and later became Hall of Famers. Three other Giants on the 1930 roster would also make it to Cooperstown — Dave Bancroft, Fred Lindstrom and manager John McGraw. *Bottom:* Wilbert Robinson (left) showers appreciation on his ace left-hander Dazzy Vance. A classic late bloomer, the Brooklyn southpaw did not start his major league career until he was 31 years old. He wound up leading the National League in strikeouts seven times, and in 1930, the 39-year-old Vance's 2.61 ERA led the league.

3 April

on the bench during a game and start reminiscing about the good old days of baseball or about his favorite pastime of hunting and fishing to the point where he would lose track of the game and forget to give signs to the third base coach.

Not that giving signs to third base coach Joe Kelley would have made any difference, according to Herman. Kelley, a former teammate of Robinson's on the 19th century Baltimore Orioles, was getting on in years and suffering from failing eyesight, as described by Herman:

> One day I hit a line drive over first base and the ball caromed into the Brooklyn bullpen and got tangled up under the benches. As I was coming into second, I saw Kelley motioning for me to hold up. But then I saw the right fielder was still scrambling around under the benches so I headed for third. Coming into third, he stopped me again or I could have scored. "Gee, Joe, what's going on?" [Herman asked]. "Babe," he whispered, "without my glasses, I can't even see who is pitching."[25]

Perhaps the play that best encapsulates the "Daffiness Boys" occurred in Ebbets Field on August 15, 1926. Brooklyn had the bases loaded with Hank DeBerry on third, Vance on second, and Chick Fewster on first. Herman socked a pitch off the right field wall. DeBerry scored, but when Vance got to third, he slowed down, not sure if the ball had been caught. Meanwhile, Fewster was chugging full speed into third, so Vance lit out for the plate. Problem was, the ball got to the catcher quickly, and Vance was caught in a rundown between third and home. Herman, who slid into second, saw the rundown. Thinking Vance had already scored and Fewster was in the rundown, Herman took off for third base. Within a few moments, Herman slid into third from one side while Vance slid back into the base from the other side, all while Fewster stood motionless on top of the base.

The cherubic and beloved Wilbert Robinson was in his 17th year managing Brooklyn in 1930. "Uncle Robbie" brought a casual approach to discipline and fundamentals, creating the legend of the "Daffiness Boys" in Brooklyn.

"That's the first time the men on this club have gotten together on anything," Manager Robinson is said to have shouted.

Amid the shouting and chaos around third base, according to Bressler as he remembered it in *The Glory of Their Times*, Vance lifted himself from the dirt and shouted in a way only he could, "Mr.

Umpire, fellow teammates and members of the opposition, if you carefully peruse the rules of our national pastime, you will find there is one and only one protagonist in rightful occupancy of this hassock, namely yours truly, Arthur C. Vance."[26]

The umpires agreed with Vance and called Herman and Fewster out.

"Everybody blames me," Herman later complained in *The Glory of Their Times*. "Actually it was Dazzy Vance who caused the whole mess. If there was any justice, Vance would have been the one declared out because he's the one that caused the traffic jam in the first place. But down through history, for some strange reason, it's all been blamed on me."[27]

The reputation as the man who doubled into a double play followed Herman the rest of his career. Other stories did as well, such as ones that said he put lit cigars in his pocket and frequently got hit in the head with fly balls. He steadfastly denied the latter had ever happened and he once supposedly confronted a group of sportswriters about it.

"If a fly ball ever hits me on the head, I'll quit," Herman is said to have promised.

"How about on the shoulder?" a sportswriter asked him.

"The shoulder doesn't count," Herman replied.

Casey Stengel, who managed Brooklyn after Robinson retired, always maintained that Herman's reputation as a clown was undeserved, adding that his main problem was that he played on bad teams.[28] Certainly there was nothing clownish about his hitting prowess.

"I wasn't the world's greatest fielder as a lot of stories will attest, but I was always a pretty fair country hitter,"[29] Herman once said of himself. On that point there is little debate. Herman was coming off a .381 season in 1929 and would post a .393 batting mark in 1930. He would hit over .300 in nine of his 12 seasons (not counting the one season he played for Brooklyn during World War II after an eight-year retirement), hit for the cycle three times, and finish with a career .314 batting average. His off-field claim to fame is that he doubled for the painfully uncoordinated Gary Cooper in the hitting scenes filmed for the Lou Gehrig biopic "Pride of the Yankees."

Herman had some high quality teammates in 1930.

Glenn Wright was considered one of the best shortstops in the game even though he was already experiencing the shoulder trouble that would eventually ruin his throwing arm. The 1930 season proved to be a good rebound year for him after being limited to 25 at-bats in 1929.

Johnny Frederick burst on the scene as Brooklyn's new center fielder in 1929, hitting .328, scoring 127 runs and slapping out 206 hits, 52 of them doubles, to set a rookie record. His career was relatively brief—five seasons—and 1930 would be his high-water mark.

Adelphia Louis Bissonette, better known as Del Bissonette, hammered a Brooklyn rookie record 25 home runs in 1928. Like Frederick, he had a short five-year career ruined by injuries, and 1930 was his best major league season.

Alfonso Ramon Lopez became Brooklyn's starting catcher in 1930 after a short stint with the team (three games) in 1928. Al Lopez was a marginally good hitter, but excellent at handling pitchers and playing defense. He would play 19 years and retire having played more games as a catcher than anyone in history. He then put together a stellar career as a manager.

After losing 1–0 to the Phillies in their season opener, the Robins were rained out of three straight games. They were then twice pounded by the Braves, 10–8 and 7–2, before they pasted Boston, 15–8, on April 21 for their first win of the season. With a win finally under their belt, the Robins arrived in Philadelphia. Whenever the Robins and Phillies got together in the hitter-friendly Baker Bowl, they usually turned the national pastime into a game more akin to pinball. For example, in a doubleheader played the previous May, the teams combined to score 50 runs, with the Robins winning one game, 20–16, and the Phillies the other 8–6.

More than 10,000 fans were on hand for the first game and they saw the Phils break a tie with a run in the bottom of the ninth to win, 6–5. Chuck Klein went four-for-four and hit his second home run of the season. Les Sweetland, who authored the 1–0 Opening Day shutout of the Robins, was the winning pitcher again. He was now 2–0, with both wins coming against Brooklyn. He finished the season with a record of 7–15 and a 7.71 ERA in 35 games.

The two teams outdid themselves the next day, a frigid Wednesday afternoon. The Phils scored five runs in the first and built a 7–2 lead after three innings. The Robins scored seven in the fourth and fifth innings combined to go ahead 9–7, but the Phils plated five more in their half of the sixth. The Robins promptly answered with six in the top of the seventh for a 15–12 lead. The Phils scored two in the eighth and two in the ninth to win the game, 16–15. The teams banged out a combined 38 hits, one of them Klein's third home run. Despite the prolific offenses, the game was decided when Brooklyn second baseman Jake Flowers botched a routine two-out ground ball with a Philly runner at third base.

This type of game proved typical at the Baker Bowl in 1930. A record total of 1,187 runs were scored at the ballpark during the season, an average of more than 15 runs per game. After splitting two more games with Boston to post six losses in eight games, the Robins came home to face their intra-borough rivals from Manhattan.

The first game between the Giants and Robins in 1930 took place at Ebbets Field on April 27. The Giants sprang into action with three runs in the second inning, but the Robins tied it in the third. The Giants scored two in the fourth and the teams traded single tallies in the eighth to make it 6–4. Reliever Johnny Morrison came in to pitch the top of the ninth for Brooklyn, trying to hold the deficit to two runs. He retired two batters quickly, and then walked three in a row. McGraw let Andy Reese, a utility player who was in the starting lineup as the left fielder, hit for himself, and Reese launched a Morrison's pitch into the left field seats for a grand slam, sealing a 10–4 victory, the Giants' seventh straight without a loss. Bill Terry had a run-scoring double for New York while Babe Herman and Glenn Wright homered for Brooklyn.

The Giants also received a complete game from Fred Fitzsimmons. He was a stalwart on the mound, having won 14, 17, 20 and 15 games in the previous four seasons, and, was currently in a streak that would see him pitch more than 200 innings for nine consecutive years. He pitched well into his 40s and finished his career with 217 wins.

Leo Durocher, in his biography, *Nice Guys Finish Last*, described Fitzsimmons' delivery this way: "He would turn his back completely to the batter as he was winding up, wheel back around and let out the most god awful grunt as he was letting the ball go — rrrrrhhhhhooooo! — like a rhinoceros in heat."[30]

The scene shifted to the Polo Grounds for the next three contests, and the host Giants moved ahead quickly 3–0 behind Travis Jackson's home run. In the fifth, against Giant left-handed veteran starter Willie Walker, the Robins loaded the bases with no outs. At this point, Uncle Wilbert shocked everybody by rolling the platoon dice and sitting the left-swinging Herman, his best hitter, in favor of utility player and right-handed hitter Eddie Moore. Moore responded with a sacrifice fly, and an ensuing ground out cut the lead to 3–2. Al Lopez hit an RBI triple in the next inning to tie the game, but Terry singled in the bottom of the eighth, stole second, and scored on a single by outfielder Wally Roettger to send the Giants to the ninth with a 4–3 lead.

Walker, still on the mound, hit the first two batters he faced and walked Moore to load the bases with no outs. With the undefeated season on the line, McGraw brought in thirty-three-year-old right-hander Joe Genewich. The batter was Rube Bressler, who hit a slow tap to first. Terry nabbed it and threw home for the force play and the first out. Next up was part-time outfielder Harvey Hendrick, who caught a fastball and drove it into right field, out of the reach of Mel Ott, for a double, allowing all three runners to score. Suddenly, the Robins had a 6–4 lead. Their starter, Clise Dudley, retired the Giants in the bottom of the ninth and New York's undefeated streak was over. McGraw spent the night chewing on the fact his team blew a ninth-inning lead and lost its first game of the year to a Wilbert Robinson team that had its best hitter on the bench for the second half of the game.

The next game of the series, on April 29, was described by the *New York Times*' John Drebinger as follows:

There was a little baseball but it was quickly followed by an amazing display of football, a dash of soccer, a bit of cricket, and wound up with a score that would have done credit to a billiard match.[31]

The Robins plated a pair of runs in the top of the first and then scored 11 runs in the top of the second, with every member of the lineup getting at least one hit. The Giants countered with two in their half of the second, but the Robins added three more in the top of the third to make the score 16–2. The Giants then responded with a nine-run rally in bottom of the third, during which every member of their lineup got a hit. After three innings, the score was 16–11. Though they never looked at each other across the field, both McGraw and Robinson had to be wondering what had happened to the game they knew, where pitching and defense was king and runs came at a premium. When the dust settled and the final six innings were completed, the Robins had a 19–15 victory. The teams had 41 hits between them; Herman had a three-run home run, a three-run triple, and joined Robins third baseman Wally Gilbert with seven RBIs in the game. Ott had two home runs and Terry one for the Giants.

The Giants and Robins were not the only ones abusing pitchers on April 29. There were a total of 123 runs scored in the seven major league games that day, an average of 17 runs per game.

The Robins were flying high after back-to-back wins against the McGraw-men and went for a sweep, with ace Dazzy Vance on the mound against Carl Hubbell. "King Carl," as it turned out, had a bad day, allowing nine hits and two walks; he hit a batter and made a wild pitch. The Robins scored four runs in the first inning and, with Vance pitching well enough, coasted to an easy 9–4 decision. Herman hit his fourth home run and drove in four runs. As a reflection of the bad blood between the two teams, twice in the game Vance was decked by fastballs as he batted, and the newspapers reported afterward that the Robins accused the Giants of egging on one of their young pitchers to hit Vance in the head.

The games drew over 50,000, "the largest turnstile count for this time of year in a long time," reported the *Sporting News*.

The Brooklyn sweep at the Polo Grounds not only ended the Giants' undefeated season, it knocked the New Yorkers out of first place. The preeminent perch was now held by the Pittsburgh Pirates, fresh off a seven-game win streak against Chicago (two wins), St. Louis (four wins), and Cincinnati (one win).

After losing to the Cubs on Opening Day, it was feast or famine for the Cardinals as they took two of the three remaining games in the series with Chicago. They smashed Cubs starter Charlie Root for seven hits in the first two innings and 20 hits overall in a 13–3 victory on April 16, then racked up 16 more hits against an ineffective Guy Bush and a couple of relievers for an 11–1 victory on April 18. In between those two games on April 17, Chicago's Pat Malone pitched a masterful three-hitter for a 3–0 win in a contest shortened to six innings by rain.

The Cards' early hitting star was outfielder George Fisher. In one game he went four-for-four at the plate, in each of two others he went three-for-three and four-for-five in another.

The Cardinals came north to Chicago to resume the rivalry and help the Cubs open their home season on April 22. The Redbirds proved to be rude guests in spoiling the Cubs' home debut, 8–3. St. Louis' winning pitcher was Wild Bill Hallahan, who lived up to his moniker, walking nine and striking out eleven while allowing only one hit.

The Cubs could not hold a 5–0 lead the next day, but scored a run in the bottom of the ninth to win 6–5. More miserable Cub pitching helped the Cards win the rubber game, 9–2.

If ineffective starting pitching wasn't enough to worry the Cubs, Hornsby's tender heel was, forcing him to miss five of the seven games against St. Louis. The Rajah had hoped the heel would repair itself as he started playing regularly. To the contrary, the heel was not getting any better at all.

National League Notes for April

Jake Flowers of Brooklyn led the National League in hitting at the end of April with a gaudy .469 average. George Fisher of St. Louis and Riggs Stephenson of the Cubs both posted .462 marks, and Paul Waner of the Pirates was hitting .455.

National League Standings on April 30, 1930

	W	L	Pct.	GB
Pittsburgh	9	3	.750	—
New York	7	3	.700	1
Chicago	8	8	.500	3
Boston	5	5	.500	3
St. Louis	6	8	.429	4
Brooklyn	5	7	.417	4
Philadelphia	5	7	.417	4
Cincinnati	4	8	.333	5

4

MAY

He sat slumped by himself in a corner of the Philadelphia Phillies' dugout, arms folded, his lead lowered, giving his teammates the mistaken impression he was asleep. Grover Cleveland "Pete" Alexander kept quiet and to himself. He had little to say and less in common with the pitchers he sat alongside — anonymous talents such as Harry Smythe, Claude Willoughby, Hap Collard, Hap Elliott, By Speece and Snipe Hansen — all of whom were in diapers when Old Pete reigned supreme in the National League, and was better known as "Alexander the Great." He assumed they knew nothing of his baseball pedigree. Six times he led the National League in wins, strikeouts and shutouts; six times his ERA was under 2.00, and five times he led the league in that category. He won 190 games for the Phillies from 1911 to 1917, including seasons of 31, 33, and 30 wins from 1915 to 1917, respectively. He won 128 games for the Cubs and 55 for the Cardinals, giving him 373 for his career, one more than the venerated Christy Mathewson and the most ever by a National League pitcher. He sensed none of his teammates cared about his accomplishments — after all, what modern player had any appreciation for the players that came before him?

On the afternoon of May 28, 1930, the Boston Braves crossed swords with the Phillies at Braves Field. The Braves scored two early runs off Phillies starter Phil Collins, then added a third run in the sixth. Manager Burt Shotton decided to pinch-hit for Collins in the top of the seventh, and he called for Alex to get his arm ready for some relief work. Pete responded with his usual Midwestern stoicism and shuffled out to the bullpen mound, his every move silently tracked by the curious eyes of his fellow Phillies still unsure of what to make of their unfriendly and sphinx-like teammate. They knew the old man had a world of baseball experience to share, but he had never given the slightest indication that he wanted, or was willing, to share it.

Alexander steadied himself on the bullpen mound, a feat that took a lot more concentration that it once did. As he went into his windup and threw, his pitches had only a fraction of their former bite, and he did not place them with the precision that had been his bread and butter. Still, he had the guile and smarts earned from 20 major league seasons and 695 games that he confidently believed would see him through.

The Phils got a run back in their half of the seventh and trailed 3–1 as they took the field. Alexander the Great ambled toward the pitching mound with an indifferent shuffle. The Phils brought him back after all these years hoping he could be a steady, veteran influence on an unproven pitching staff. The results thus far had been disappointing. His three starts had all resulted in no-decisions, although he gave a good account of himself in two of the games. His five relief appearances were considerably rougher and were responsible for his 0–3 record and 9.00 ERA.

Pete toed the rubber, digging a small hole alongside it from where he would anchor himself, grabbed the ball with his shorter-than-normal fingers and began his warm-up tosses. His mind began to wander, taking him back to a place not far from here, a day that to Alex seemed like yesterday, but in baseball's measure of time, was an eternity ago. Pitching at the now-demolished South End Grounds on the crisp afternoon of September 7, 1911, Alex used an array of baffling curves and off speed pitches to defeat the Boston club, 1–0, and hold them to one hit — a measly ground ball single. That victory, his 28th of the season, still stands as a record for rookie pitchers, and he bested the legendary Cy Young in doing it. In 1911, Young was a grizzled 44-year-old veteran in his 22nd season, just trying to hang on a little bit longer.

"When the kids beat you, it's time to get out," Young said, announcing his retirement after that game. "The kid" Young referred to was Alexander, then a square-shouldered, sandy-haired 24-year-old farm boy from Elba, Nebraska. Now, looking considerably older than his 43 years, Alex was the grizzled veteran trying to hang on a little bit longer.

The intervening years had been difficult and downright cruel. Alex suffered concussions and double vision on the ball field. He interrupted his career to serve in World War I, lost the hearing in one ear from an exploding artillery shell, had an ear torn by shrapnel, and damaged permanently the muscles of his pitching arm from pulling the lanyards of the artillery pieces. He was also diagnosed with, and treated for, shell shock.

But more terrible than any of these ailments was the epilepsy. In an era when most people shunned those afflicted because they believed it to be caused by the "touch of demons," Alexander followed the lead of many of his fellow sufferers by turning to alcohol.[1] He drank to dull the traumatic memories of war. He drank to lessen the severity of the terror, if not the effects, of his disease. And he drank to be more socially acceptable — in this American era, it was more palatable to be drunk in public than to have an epileptic seizure.[2]

His biographer Jack Kavanagh wrote that "Old Pete knew he had a problem with alcohol. The traumas of front-line service had changed him from a cold-beer-after-the-game casual drinker to one who would hide bottles of booze and drink to ward off epilepsy. It was his opinion that an alcoholic edge held the sneak attacks of his ailment at bay."[3] John Kiernan of the *New York Times* said Alex was "not what could be called an ardent prohibitionist at all stages of his career."

The shadow of his epilepsy was never far from Alex, and while he never suffered a seizure on the field, he did occasionally fall victim in the dugout.

"He took epileptic fits two or three times a season," said former teammate Hans Lober in *The Glory of Their Times*. "He'd have a seizure on the bench. He'd froth at the mouth and shiver all over and thrash around and sort of lose consciousness. It was awful. We'd hold him down and pour some brandy down his throat and in a while he would be all right."[4]

After the war, Alexander toiled for the Chicago Cubs, and while he was a lesser pitcher than he had been with Philadelphia, he had two 20-win seasons, averaged fifteen wins per year for his six full years there, and always posted a winning record. But the taunting demons in his mind sent Alexander off on drinking binges that would last for days. He was in and out of sanatoriums and he eventually ran afoul of manager Joe McCarthy, who sold him to player-manager Rogers Hornsby in St. Louis. Alex won 21 games for the Cards at the age of 40 in 1927 and 16 more at the age of 41 in 1928, but it was the 1926 World Series that forever etched him in baseball lore.

Alexander had bested the Yankees in Games Two and Six, and in the seventh game, with the Cardinals leading by one run in the bottom of the seventh, Hornsby called on Alex to pitch to the Yankees' young slugger Tony Lazzeri (ironically also an epileptic) with the bases loaded and two out. Whether Alex was feeling the after-effects of a celebratory night of drinking at this point is open to debate. Alexander always insisted he was sober and alert.

"Some people say I celebrated the night before and had a hangover when Hornsby called me from the bullpen to pitch to Lazzeri. That isn't the truth. On Saturday, I'd beaten the Yankees 10–2 to make the Series all even. In the clubhouse after that game, Hornsby came over to me and said, 'Alex, if you want to celebrate tonight, I wouldn't blame you. But go easy for I may need you tomorrow.' I said, 'Okay, Rog. I'll tell you what I'll do. I'll ride back to the hotel with you and I'll meet you tomorrow morning and ride out to the park with you.' Hell, I wanted to win that series and get the big end of the money as much as anyone."[5]

Alexander's condition never mattered much to Hornsby. "I'd rather him pitch a crucial game for me drunk than anyone I've ever known sober. He was that good," Hornsby said.[6]

Against Alexander, Lazzeri managed to whack one pitch long and foul. ("One more foot the other way and he would have been the hero and I would

The 1930 season was the end of the line for pitching immortal Grover Cleveland Alexander. He retired with the most wins in National League history but he was ravaged by alcoholism, epilepsy and twenty-two years of major league pitching when the Phillies released him.

have been the bum,"[7] Alex said afterward.) Then in one of the World Series' most memorable moments, Alex struck out Lazzeri and then held the Yankees at bay for the final two innings. Although he was saluted as a hero in St. Louis and joined baseball's pantheon of World Series stars, it did not make his life any more tolerable.

"He was a loner," said Wild Bill Hallahan, his teammate in St. Louis. "He would go off by himself and do what he would do, which was drink, I suppose."

Alex always pitched efficiently and rapidly and when asked why, he responded "What do you want me to do? Let those sons of bitches [batters] stand up there and think on my time?"[8]

He also had a nice, easy sidearm motion that was the envy of his profession. Much of the time he "looked like he was hardly working at all, like he was throwing batting practice," according to one teammate.[9]

"I used more effort winding up than he did in pitching nine innings," marveled one-time teammate Burleigh Grimes. "He threw a sinker and a curve — always kept them down. He was fast, too. That thing would come zooming in there and then kick in about three inches on a right-handed batter. He'd throw you that curve, and you couldn't tell which was which because they didn't do a thing until they were right on top of you."[10]

Babe Ruth, who as a rookie with Boston watched Pete pitch in the 1915 World Series before facing him in the Fall Classic eleven years later, also talked of his easy manner on the mound.

"Just to see old Pete out there on the mound, with that cocky old undersize cap pulled down over one ear, chewing away at his tobacco and pitching baseballs as easy as pitching hay is enough to take the heart out of a fellow."[11]

Unfortunately, it was a different Pete Alexander pitching on May 28, 1930. Guile and experience were not enough. In two innings of work, he allowed two hits and two runs while striking out one. He had now allowed 22 earned runs in 22 innings. The few thousand fans at Braves Field who watched Alex walk off the mound after the bottom of the eighth inning were unaware that an era of the game was passing before their eyes. Alexander was leaving a major league baseball field for the last time. A few days later, on June 3, the Phillies gave Alexander his unconditional release.

"I'm just going to sit tight and see what turns up," Alex said after getting the news. "I think I would like to play in the west. I guess I'm kind of used to it out there."[12]

"It will be a tough fight ahead for old Alex," editorialized the *Sporting News*, "and all the worse because the man Alex has got to lick is himself. He has disappointed the fans ... and he has disappointed his friends and those who have tried to render ... assistance...."[13]

The rest of Alexander's life seemed to get more difficult as he grew older. He played for barnstorming teams like the House of David, and he was featured in a sideshow in which he spoke about his famous strike out of Lazzeri. But, because his reputation as a drinker preceded him, he never found his way back into the major leagues despite his stated desire to be a coach. To add insult to injury, a few years after he retired Alex had to surrender sole possession of his perch as the winningest pitcher in National League history when a researcher found that Christy Mathewson was not properly credited with a win in 1902, leaving both men tied for the most career wins in the National League at 373.

Alex was unable to hold a job and he had to scrounge for money. The one remaining piece of good news in his life was his election to the Baseball Hall of Fame in 1939. Upon hearing the news, his response was, "I'm in the Hall of Fame and I'm proud to be there, but I can't eat the Hall of Fame."[14]

The one light in Alex's life was Amy Arrants, an Omaha girl he met on a blind date and whom he married in 1918. That they were in love was never in question, but his mounting difficulties with alcohol after World War I caused Amy to divorce him in 1929. He won her back and they remarried in 1931, only to be divorced again in 1941. As a testament to Alex's inherent good nature and his sincere attempts to right himself, she remained on good terms with her ex-husband, talking with him, encouraging him and helping him whenever she could. His additional problems included a heart attack he suffered in 1947, and shortly thereafter, the amputation of his right ear due to a cancerous growth.

Through it all, Pete hoped to win Amy back again. Shortly after mailing her a letter on November 4, 1950, the destitute Hall of Famer suffered another heart attack and died in St. Paul, Minnesota, at the age of 63.

Alex had just come back from a humiliating visit to the East Coast, where he attended the World Series games between the Yankees and Phillies at Yankee Stadium. Although invited as a guest of the Yankees, he entered the stadium unrecognized and had to stand in the back of the mezzanine level for half the game, forgotten. Finally, a veteran writer recognized him and offered him a chair in the press box. With that exception, the greatest pitcher in the history of the Phillies and the most prolific winning pitcher in the history of the National League went completely unnoticed and uncelebrated.

The American League

If Grover Cleveland Alexander looked like hell in the 1926 World Series, Cleveland manager Roger Peckinpaugh lived through hell in the World Series of a season earlier. The normally smooth-fielding shortstop, who backboned Washington's consecutive pennant winners in 1924-25 and built his career on defensive excellence, committed eight errors in the seven games of the 1925 Fall Classic and helped the Pittsburgh Pirates rebound from a 3–1 deficit in games to snatch the championship trophy. It was a bitter end to a great season in which Peckinpaugh was named the American League MVP for his stellar play at shortstop and his .294 batting average.

Peckinpaugh never shied away from or made excuses for his nightmarish performance. Instead, he weaved a solid professional career as a thinking man's player — so smart and mature, in fact, he was made manager of the New York Yankees in 1914 at the age of 23. There had never been a younger manager in the history of the game. Now, with his playing spikes hung in retirement, the 39-year-old Ohioan had come home to the shores of Lake Erie to put his baseball brain to work for a team that had been directionless since winning the world championship in 1920.

Peckinpaugh arrived in Cleveland in 1928, just as the Indians were producing an unusually talented crop of young players, and he did not hesitate to throw them right into the caldron of big league competition.

"We weren't going anywhere," he explained. "It didn't matter if we finished fifth or seventh. We wanted to know which among our youngsters were likely to do us any good."[15] The result was a jump from seventh place in his first season to a surprisingly strong third place in 1929, the biggest leap any team made that season.

Expectations for 1930 were high — in fact, too high for a group that turned out to be as unlucky as it was spirited and as fragile as it was talented. The Indians consisted of several star-crossed players.

Johnny Hodapp reached the major leagues as a 19-year-old prodigy with stardom written all over him. He could play every infield position and had a strong arm. In his first two full seasons, he hit .327 and .323 (1928–29). His most memorable game occurred on July 28, 1929, when he became the first player to get two hits in one inning twice in the same game. Hodapp solidified his place as one of the best hitters in the game in 1930, posting a .354 average, 225 hits (leading the AL), 51 doubles (also a league-high), 111 runs scored and 121 RBIs. Less than a year later, his career would be essentially over. A severe knee injury limited his defensive mobility and destroyed his swing. He was traded to the White Sox in 1932, moved to the Red Sox in 1933 and was out of baseball by 1934, taking with him a lifetime .311 average.

Lou Fonseca, whose .369 average in 1929, made him the defending American League batting champion. He hit over .300 six times in his 12 major league seasons but rarely competed for a full year because of serious injuries, which included a broken leg in 1928, a broken arm (limiting him to 40 games) in 1930 and a torn ligament in his leg, which ended his career two years later. He would fade away with a lifetime .316 average.

Eddie Morgan became the Indians' first baseman in 1930 and responded by hitting .349 with 26 homers and 47 doubles. His slugging percentage of .601 was fifth-best in the league. The next year he hit a career-high .351 but inexplicably lost his power stroke, hitting only 11 home runs, and the next year he managed to hit only four homers with a .293 average. Two seasons later, he was out of the major leagues, retiring with a lifetime .314 batting average.

Lew Fonseca was one of Cleveland's highly talented but incredibly unlucky players of the era. The 1929 batting champion (.369), Fonseca was limited to 40 games in 1930 because of a broken arm. Severe injuries plagued Fonseca his entire career and forced him from the game prematurely.

Dick Porter played in the minor leagues until he was 28, then after a limited role in 1929, he burst on the scene in 1930, hitting .350. A promising career was derailed when he was beaned after 119 games. The next two years he hit .312 and .308 before fading out of the game with a lifetime .308 average.

Wes Ferrell immediately became one of the best right-handed pitchers in the game, recording a 21–10 record in his rookie campaign of 1929. The hot-tempered right-hander would win 25, 23, and 22 games in the next three seasons, the only man to win 20 or more games in each of his first four campaigns. A sore arm derailed him in 1933 and his Cleveland career abruptly ended. He rebounded to post two 20-win seasons for the Red Sox later in the decade and hung around long enough to win 193 games. Ferrell may be the best hitting pitcher in history. His lifetime .280 average is tops among pitchers, as are his nine homers in one season and 38 career round-trippers.

Not all of the Indians were derailed by bad luck. Two notable exceptions to the Indians' class of hard knocks were pitcher Mel Harder and outfielder Earl Averill.

Harder debuted with Cleveland as an 18-year-old in 1928 and stayed in uniform as a player or coach for 36 years. He went 11–10 in 1930 and finished his playing career with 226 wins, second most for the Indians' franchise behind the great Bob Feller. As a coach, he groomed seven different 20-game winners, turned outfielder Bob Lemon into a buzz saw of a starting pitcher, and handled one of the greatest rotations of all-time — the 1954 Indians staff of Lemon, Feller, Mike Garcia and Early Wynn.

Averill joined the team in 1929 and immediately became a star, hitting .332, .339 and .333 his first three seasons. He still holds the club record for runs scored (1,054) and RBIs (1,024). He became one of the most beloved players in Cleveland history and won a place in the Baseball Hall of Fame. His defensive prowess as a center fielder was so well regarded that in the three All-Star Games they played together Joe DiMaggio moved to right field.

The Indians quietly put together a 7–4 April and entered May in the middle of a six-game winning streak, taking three straight from the Browns in St. Louis and the first three of a four-game series against the Red Sox at Fenway. Although their win streak ended with a horrendous 18–3 loss to Boston the next day (May 5), they still shared first place with Philadelphia. Now they faced their first real challenge of the season by heading on an eight-game road trip into New York (two games), Philadelphia (four games) and Washington (two games).

Ferrell and Harder combined to get the Indians off on the right foot, holding the Yanks at bay, 7–6, on May 6. Ed Morgan hit his first of three home runs during this eight-game stretch and Harder sewed up the win when Babe Ruth's drive with a man aboard in the bottom of the ninth fell a few feet short of the

Hall of Famer Earl Averill hit .339 in 1930 and would patrol Cleveland's outfield for another decade. His defense was so well regarded that Joe DiMaggio moved to a corner outfield position in the All-Star Game so Averill could play center field.

bleachers. Ruth did find the range the next day, parking a three-run shot to help the Yanks forge an early 8–2 lead. The Tribe charged back by scoring five in the eighth, the last pair on Morgan's long triple, but the Indians failed to bring him home and fell short, 8–7.

Philadelphia provided little brotherly love to the Indians as the Athletics won three of the four games, although the game Cleveland won left quite an impression on the overflow Sunday afternoon crowd of 29,000. The Indians hammered the A's, 25–7, while banging out 25 hits, nine of which were two-baggers, and scoring in every inning but the eighth. Everybody in the starting lineup had at least one hit, one run scored and one RBI (except Fonseca, who did not drive in a run). Ferrell put in six innings of work to walk away with his fifth win (he also had two hits, three runs scored and an RBI). A part-timer named Bibb Falk had the game of his life with five hits, five runs scored, and five RBIs.

Continuing their trek southward, the Indians squared off against the

Nationals, and scored five first-inning runs and six third-inning runs to win the opener, 11–6, but the next day they lost to the Nationals, 4–2.

All in all, the Indians won only three of the eight games against New York, Philadelphia and Washington. Add in the three of four they won from Boston beforehand and they managed a .500 trip to the East Coast.

"A 50–50 break on an eastern journey is not an entirely unsatisfactory record," said the *Sporting News*, "but it is a little disappointing in view of the fact the Indians started with three victories in Beantown and that the hitting was powerful enough to win in all 12 games."[16] The Indians were still a flawed young team but they showed that their potent lineup, described as "slam-bang and slashing" by the *Sporting News*, could hit with the big boys. Cleveland was second in the league in runs scored with 153 (to Philadelphia's 167). Their team average was an impressive .320, well ahead of Philadelphia's .294, Washington's .292 and the Yankees' .278. They started this stretch tied with the A's for first place and ended it in third, three games behind. They would be heard from again before the race was done.

The Athletics opened May by winning six in a row and ten out of twelve games. The streak started with a merciless 19–2 pounding of the Tigers in which the offense scored in every inning but two and strafed four Tiger pitchers for eighteen hits including five home runs (two each by Jimmie Foxx and Max Bishop and one by Al Simmons), three doubles and two triples. It ended with a 14–7 pasting of the White Sox, in which the offense scored in every inning but two, and bombarded three Chicago pitchers for 17 hits, including five doubles and one home run. In the last six games of the twelve-game run, the A's scored 56 runs (9.3 per game). They also jumped back into first place by one game over the Nationals as the two teams prepared for a four-game weekend showdown in mid–May — two games at Shibe Park and two at Griffith Stadium.

The two games in Philadelphia were played as a doubleheader on Friday, May 16. In the opener, Washington scored twice in the second and fourth innings and held on for a 5–3 win. Part-time outfielder George Loepp, Washington's leadoff hitter, had four hits and two RBIs while Joe Cronin contributed three hits. In the nightcap, neither team managed a scoring threat in the first five innings. Washington struck for the first run in the sixth when both Sam West and Goose Goslin doubled. The lead held into the eighth when West walked and Goslin singled him to third. Joe Judge cracked a two-strike pitch over the right field wall to up the score to the eventual final of 4–0. Washington had now won six straight from the A's and leapfrogged them into first place.

To add to Connie Mack's misery, he had a pair of wisdom teeth extracted after the games and subsequent painful complications kept him off the field for the next two weeks.

The series moved to Washington and the third game was as painful for the

Athletics as a tooth extraction, with the Nationals winning, 16–5. West continued his torrid hitting with a homer and four hits.

The Nationals sent Lloyd Brown to the mound to try to seal the sweep. He kept his end of the bargain, allowing only three hits, no two of which were in the same inning. In the sixth, the A's reached him for a run when Bishop walked, went to second on a sacrifice by Mule Haas, and advanced to third as Jimmy Dykes grounded out. Simmons walked, and Foxx hit what looked like a double-play grounder to Cronin at short, but Simmons, again showing his overall value to his team, barreled into second baseman Buddy Myer before he could complete the relay to first. Foxx was safe and Bishop crossed the plate with what turned out to be the only run of the game. Lefty Grove was a touch better than Brown, shutting out the Nationals on five hits and breaking Washington's win streak against his team at seven.

Notably, one Senator who did not get a hit in this game was Sam Rice. It ended the veteran outfielder's 28-game hitting streak which dated to the third game of the season.

Meanwhile, the Yankees, who ended April with a dismal 3–8 record, evened their season record with an 8–3 spurt, mostly at the expense of Chicago and Detroit. When they followed that by taking two of three from Boston on May 16–18, they were 13–12 and only four game out of first place.

More importantly, the Yanks made a key transaction on May 6. They sent seldom-used utility man Cedric Durst to the Boston Red Sox in exchange for right-handed pitcher Charley "Red" Ruffing. The trade had a minimal impact on the 1930 race, but it soon set up the Yankees for their next run of dominance. Ruffing had toiled six years with Boston, compiling a frightful 39–96 career record and .289 winning percentage. After joining New York, he won 231 games and 65 percent of his decisions, reversing a career record that was 57 games under .500 to one that was 48 over. He pitched for seven Yankee pennant winners, won 20 or more games four times, and won more games than any other hurler in the 1930s.

Ruffing was the latest rider on the one-way talent train between Boston and New York that wrecked the Red Sox and midwifed the Yankees' dynasty. Babe Ruth was the first and most prominent player on this train, but the most important passenger may have been Ed Barrow, the severe and unflinching general manager who left Boston to run the Yankees' business operations in 1921. Barrow had a dependable eye for talent, and when he could not find it for the Yankees in the minor or independent leagues or among the country's sandlots, he fleeced the hapless and eminently pliable Red Sox. In a fairly short span of time, the Red Sox sent to New York, without adequate talent compensation, such star players as Ruth, pitchers Waite Hoyt, Herb Pennock, Carl Mays, "Bullet" Joe Bush and George Pipgras, infielders Joe Dugan and Everett Scott.

The Red Sox, once an envied and dominant franchise, had shriveled to a perennial American League doormat. The 1930 season would be their sixth consecutive finish in last place and seventh in eight years. It was truly "the Boring Twenties" for Sox fans, as their team managed to win only 36 percent of its games during this time, going 448–778. The nadir was reached from 1926 to 1928 when the team posted records of 47–105, 46–107 and 51–103.

Management hoped new manager Charles "Heinie" Wagner could instill a winning attitude, having been the shortstop for Boston's 1912 world championship team when he hit a career-high .274. Considered a level-headed and dependable player, Wagner was designated by Red Sox management to watch over Babe Ruth during the slugger's last years in Boston where, as his fame grew, so did his predilection for women and drink.

But Wagner had little talent to pencil into the lineup on a day-to-day basis. Few Boston hitters took part in the offensive clambake of 1930. Their top run producer was outfielder Earl Webb, who hit 16 homers and drove in 66 runs — meaning Hack Wilson drove in 125 more runs than Boston's top RBI man. Webb, at least, was a major league talent. In this, his first full year, he would hit .323 on his way to a lifetime .306 average. In 1931, he set the still-standing record of 67 doubles in one season. The Sox also had Phil Todt, a consistent but not great hitter and a leading defensive first baseman. Starting pitcher Jack Russell, only 24, would suffer through a 9–20 season, but in three years, he became one of the first top-flight relief pitchers while helping Washington win a pennant. The rest of the team was an eclectic and thinly talented bunch that included shortstop Hal Rhyne, who would hit only .203 in this year of the hitter (though he improved to .272 the next year); pitcher Milt Gaston, who went 13–20, the second time he would lead the league in losses (18 for the Browns in 1928); and pitcher Hod Lisenbee, who as a rookie with Washington in 1927 beat the "Murderer's Row" Yankees five times, but then became a journeyman pitcher, winning only 32 more games over his remaining eight seasons.

The Sox enjoyed some satisfaction in the month of May, patching together a five-game winning streak that actually propelled them as high as fourth place on May 10. They also won a close-fought 5–4 victory over the hated Yankees on May 16, but that would be their last win for the entire month. They lost their next fourteen straight, dropping them to 12–28 and to their familiar berth in the American League cellar.

Thanks to the awful April weather, the Yankees, Athletics, Nationals and Red Sox were about to have their stamina and pitching staffs tested. The Red Sox were in Washington and the Yankees traveled to Philadelphia for back-to-back doubleheaders on May 21 and 22.

The Nationals started a seven-game win streak by sweeping both doubleheaders from Boston on the strength of solid starting pitching and timely hitting. On May 21, they bashed out 16 hits, with Sam Rice getting four of them, to win the first game, 10–2. Joe Cronin had two hits and two RBIs to win the nightcap, 6–1. The next day, the Nats took a close first game, 3–2, and a 13–1 laugher in the second game. Rice had four hits on the afternoon, raising his league-leading average to .404.

Baseball had to dust off the record books for the two doubleheaders between the Yankees and the Athletics.

The Yanks got off to a good start in the first game on May 21. Babe Ruth clobbered a two-run home run in the first inning, and then walloped a three-run shot in the third inning — a tape measure drive that cleared the right field wall, continued over the street behind the wall, and landed in the yards behind the first row of houses. Ben Chapman also homered for the Yanks, giving them a 6–0 lead in the fourth inning. Ruth slugged his third home run of the game in the eighth inning, but by this time the Yanks were in no mood to celebrate. Between Ruth's second and third clouts, the New York pitching staff collapsed. The A's scored two in the fourth, two in the fifth on a Jimmie Foxx home run, and nine in the seventh, relegating Ruth's third homer to a meaningless seventh run in a 15–7 drubbing. In the second game, Rube Walberg went all the way, pitching a five-hitter, while Al Simmons hit a two-run smash and Jimmy Dykes a solo shot as the A's completed the sweep, 4–1.

By losing both games, the Yanks dropped six back of the A's. Another Philadelphia sweep would leave them eight games behind, a daunting gap to make up against a quality team like Philadelphia, even though the season was still young.

Again, it was the Sultan of Swat, Babe Ruth, who ignited a firestorm of long balls on May 22 with two shots in the first game — one in the third inning and one in the fourth — as the Yankees' pitching held fast for a 10–1 win. Chapman also homered, as did pitcher George Pipgras. Both teams flexed their muscles in the second game to the tune of ten home runs, with Lou Gehrig hitting three of them, including a grand slam (and eight RBIs). Babe Ruth hit his sixth in two days during the nightcap, giving him 12 home runs for the season and a share of the major league lead with Hack Wilson. With Gehrig hitting his bases-loaded smash in the first inning, the Yanks scored seven times and then added two in the second inning for a 9–0 lead. The Yanks' pitching staff floundered again, and by the sixth inning the game was tied, 12–12, but the New York bats smashed their way to eight runs in the last three innings and settled the game in their favor, 20–13. Tony Lazzeri hit New York's other home run, while the A's five were hit by Foxx (two), Dykes, Simmons and Max Bishop.

Over the course of the two doubleheaders, Ruth hit six home runs; he and Gehrig each had a three-home run game — their first in regular-season play (Ruth had done it twice in the World Series). The combined ten home runs hit by both teams in the nightcap of the May 22 doubleheader tied the all-time record set by the Cardinals and Phillies in 1923.

In all, there were 26 home runs hit in the ten major league games played that day.

The Yankees and Athletics, however, were not through yet.

They took their long-ball circus north to New York for another doubleheader at Yankee Stadium on May 24. Before a packed house of 65,000, Ruth homered in both games again; his two-run shot capped a five-run fifth inning in the first game as the Yanks prevailed, 10–6. He connected again in the nightcap as the Yanks waltzed to an 11–1 victory. With this pair of home runs, Ruth once again took baseball into uncharted home run territory. He became the first player to hit eight home runs in six games (and produced 16 percent of his output for the 1930 season).

"Just to show the young fellows what an old master can do, Babe Ruth lashed out six homers in two days," marveled John Kieran of the *New York Times* after the first two doubleheaders in Philadelphia. Some say Hack Wil-

The classic "from-the-heels" uppercut swing of Babe Ruth that revolutionized the game. Despite turning 35, Ruth was still a major force in 1930, hitting 49 home runs to win his 11th home run title, and driving in 153 runs.

son will beat him out. Others nominate Chuck Klein or Lou Gehrig. The only one who will beat Babe Ruth out of the home run championship is Father Time."[17]

With the back-to-back sweeps, the Yankees were in third place, only one game behind second-place Philadelphia. Washington, thanks to their double sweep of the Red Sox, had opened up a four-game lead, the largest seen by any team so far in the season.

The Yanks' momentum was blunted the next day when the A's clobbered them, 10–3, and then came to a complete standstill when they lost two of their next three games at home to Washington. The Nationals showed they could play long ball with the Yankees as Goose Goslin and Joe Judge twice hit back-to-back home runs in the first game, a 10–7 Washington win. With the Yankees again in their rearview mirror, the Nationals headed to Shibe Park for a three-game set that would close out the month of May.

It began with a morning-afternoon doubleheader on May 30. The Nationals built a 6–3 lead in the morning game, an advantage starting pitcher Adolph Liska protected until two were out in the bottom of the ninth. Spencer Harris should have been the last batter of the game when he lifted a foul pop behind the plate, but catcher Muddy Ruel saw it too late. The ball dropped only a few feet away from him. Harris cashed in his second chance with a single and pinch-hitter Dib Williams walked. The next batter was Al Simmons, who mashed Liska's first pitch into the left field seats to tie the game. Foxx whacked the next pitch for a double, and manager Walter Johnson brought in Fred Marberry, who recorded the third out.

In the tenth, Marberry stranded two A's runners, and in the eleventh, with one out, he gave up singles to Simmons and Foxx. Walter Johnson ordered Bing Miller intentionally walked to load the bases, bringing up Jimmy Dykes. With Simmons breaking for the plate on the suicide squeeze, Dykes fouled a pitch off. Ruel next called for a pitchout, and he was correct. Simmons, breaking for the plate again on another suicide squeeze attempt, reversed his course and desperately tried to get safely back to third as Ruel whipped a throw to Ossie Bluege. The throw was a shade off-target and Bluege's tag came down a split-second after Simmons had grabbed the bag. He was safe. Marberry recovered and struck out Dykes and coerced Eric McNair, a solid reserve player, to fly out to end the threat. Marberry walked the tightrope again in the bottom of the 13th inning. Simmons doubled with one down. Foxx rapped a single, with Simmons putting on the brakes at third. Again, Johnson ordered Miller intentionally passed, loading the bases for Dykes. This time there was no suicide squeeze attempt. Dykes swung away, but he flailed at three of Marberry's pitches and missed. Now there were two outs and McNair up again. This time the super-sub ripped a liner to left-center field for a hit and the Athletics were 7–6 winners.

Connie Mack decided to rest Simmons in the second game—that is, until his squad was trailing 7–5 in the bottom of the fourth inning. With the bases loaded, Mack sent up his star left fielder, who promptly tagged a Garland Braxton pitch into the left-center field seats for a grand slam. Later, a three-run Goslin home run would help the Nationals rally, but the Mackmen won, 15–11.

Gordon McKay of the *Philadelphia Record* marveled at Simmons' performance, calling him the most feared hitter in the American League. "His power rests in a pair of tremendous shoulders. His swing ... really means something when he hits that ball."[18]

Simmons provided his own reason for his success at the plate. "Every time I get up to the plate, I'm gripping the bat to take a cut with everything I have. When the team is ahead by a lot of runs or behind a lot, you get a bit careless ... and you don't ... bear down. It's different with me this season."[19]

The A's followed up their stunning twin-bill sweep with another victory, 7–3, the next day, May 31. The four-game lead Washington enjoyed only a week earlier was suddenly gone. The two teams were tied for first place again.

"We find that Washington leading the American League..., is a good thing," crowed the *Sporting News*. "The result has confounded the prophets and paralyzed the skeptics. Philadelphia has been unable to run away from their league. They can be beaten."[20]

American League Notes for May

Joe Sewell of Cleveland sat out a game on May 2 against Boston because of the flu, ending his consecutive game playing streak at 1,013. He came up short of Everett Scott's then-record of 1,307 consecutive games played. The longest active streak now belonged to Lou Gehrig, who had played in 755 straight games. Pointing out that the Yankee first baseman would have to play 552 more games in a row to surpass Scott, the *Sporting News* said "the odds were against him."

A.M. Wheeler, who believed to be the oldest living professional ballplayer at the time, celebrated his 89th birthday on May 13. He had known Cap Anson and recalled a particular game he played in the 1860s for the Buffalo Niagrans, which they won, 200–10.

John Stone, a young outfielder with the Tigers, hit four doubles and two home runs in a doubleheader on May 30, making him the first player in major league history to have six extra-base hits in a doubleheader in which no extra innings were played.

Sam Rice (.403), Al Simmons (.386) and Babe Ruth (.374) were the top three hitters in the American League at the end of May.

Sam Rice was also the league's top base stealer, with a paltry eight. His teammate George Loepp had six. No one else had more than five.

Lefty Grove and Sam Jones were 6–0 for Philadelphia and Washington, respectively, while Mel Harder was 5–0 for Cleveland.

American League Standings on May 31, 1930

	W	L	PCT.	GB
Philadelphia	27	14	.659	—
Washington	27	14	.659	—
New York	22	17	.564	4
Cleveland	23	18	.561	4
Detroit	18	24	.429	9.5
St. Louis	17	23	.425	9.5
Chicago	15	23	.395	10.5
Boston	12	28	.300	14.5

The National League

May was a good month for the Brooklyn Robins. They won 20 of 28 and finished the month on top of the National League by two games over St. Louis. Brooklyn set the tone by opening May with two wild wins over the Cardinals at Sportsman's Park. On May 3, they broke a 6–6 tie with five runs in the top of the ninth and then hung on to win 11–10 as the Cards scored four in the bottom of the inning. The next day they won by the same score, this time getting three in the top of the thirteenth while snuffing a Redbird rally in the bottom of the frame.

On May 18, Brooklyn took over first place by sweeping Philadelphia at Ebbets Field by the relatively mild scores of 3–0 and 7–5. When the teams met again at the Baker Bowl two days later, it was a more typical Robins-Phils game, with Brooklyn prevailing, 16–9. Babe Herman rocketed a home run among his five hits and collected six RBIs. May proved to be a great month for Herman. He closed the month leading the league with a .411 average and he was second in RBIs with 38 — one behind Hack Wilson and Chuck Klein. In fact, all of the Robins enjoyed May. The team was hitting .325 at the end of the month with Jake Flowers (.372), Johnny Frederick (.371), Al Lopez (.359) and Del Bissonette (.357) providing ample backup to Herman.

On May 30, during the first game of a doubleheader at Ebbets Field against Philadelphia, the Daffiness Boys struck again. First baseman Del Bissonette rapped a shot over the right field wall with two men on in the fifth inning. Babe Herman, the runner at first, held up thinking the ball might be caught. He loitered long enough that Bissonette, already in his home run trot, passed Herman and was called out, reducing his three-run homer to a two-run single. Despite this, the Robins swept the Phils, 11–1 and 11–9. Herman hit his tenth home run of the season and Klein hit two, bringing his season total to 12.

While Uncle Wilbert placidly guided his minions through May, chaos reigned across the National League landscape as the other contenders battered each other's pitching staffs to a pulp.

The Giants spent the first half of May on a 13-game road trip. They started in Cincinnati, where they traded 9–8 decisions with the Reds before losing the rubber game of the series, 8–4. Next, they headed into Forbes Field for four games with the first-place Pittsburgh Pirates.

The Pirates represented perhaps the bluest of blue-collar cities in 1930; therefore, it was a bit ironic that their manager had the most noblesse sounding of names—Jewel Winklemeyer Ens. A former utility infielder, it would be his job to corral the rich hitting talent that always blessed the Pirate franchise and turn it into a contender.

While the nearby mills produced the steel to build America's cities, the Pirates churned out the heavy lumber to build a legacy of batting championships. The Pirates won almost one-quarter of the batting titles awarded in the 20th century (24), beginning with Honus Wagner's seven before his retirement in 1917. Three years later, the Pirates introduced a cat-like third baseman with a thick New England accent that would become at third base what Wagner was at shortstop—the acknowledged greatest player at his position according to Baseball's Centennial Committee vote in 1969.

Harold "Pie" Traynor played 17 years for the Pirates. He then managed the team from 1934 to 1939 and became a member of the Baseball Hall of Fame in 1948. He also became a legendary and beloved figure in the Pittsburgh community by doing radio and TV sports commentary for three decades after his playing days. During his career, he hit .320, the peak of which was from 1925 to 1930, when he hit .342. Although he never won a batting title, he hit over .300 ten times. A top-notch contact hitter, Traynor struck out only 278 times in a career spanning 7,559 at-bats. He was considered a defensive whiz at the hot corner, leading his league in assists three times, putouts seven times, and double plays four times.

"Pie had the quickest hands, the quickest arm of any third baseman," said former teammate Charlie Grimm. "And from any angle he threw strikes."

The Cubs' Billy Herman agreed.

"Most marvelous pair of hands you'd ever want to see."[21]

Although he missed the first six weeks of the 1930 season with an eye infection, Traynor returned in late May and compiled the highest batting average (.366) and on-base percentage (.423) of any season during his career. If the Pirates were once Honus Wagner's team, they were now Pie Traynor's club.

Traynor's Pirates were so talented offensively that a team batting average over .300 became commonplace. They hit .305 in 1927, .309 in 1928 and .303 in 1929 (they would make it four in a row with a team .303 mark in 1930).

Traynor's most prominent teammates were the Waner brothers, Paul and Lloyd. They patrolled the Pittsburgh outfield together for more than a decade and, between them, registered 5,611 hits, still the major league record for brothers (the three Alou brothers are second with 5,094). Heinie Groh, a long-time veteran infielder, closed out his career with the Pirates just as the Waner brothers were starting out.

"It sure was a delight to watch those two play baseball," he said in *The Glory of Their Times* by Lawrence Ritter. "Could they ever hit! All line drives! And both of them fast as antelopes."[22]

Only 5 feet 8 inches and 150 pounds, Paul Waner joined the Pirates in 1926 and amassed three batting titles (1927, '34, '36), a lifetime .333 average and 3,152 career hits. In 1930, he would bat .368 with 217 hits, one of eight seasons he would surpass 200. He was known to play hard and celebrate harder, with contemporaries saying Paul had the sharpest bloodshot eyes in baseball.

"He had to be a graceful ballplayer," Casey Stengel once said, "because he could slide without breaking the bottle in his hip."[23] During one season while Traynor was the Pirate skipper, Waner swore off alcohol, only to find his season average dip to .250. Traynor, with a twinkle in his eye, said he personally escorted Waner to the nearest watering hole, and within a few weeks, Waner was again hitting well over .300.[24] Conceding his reputation as a hard drinker, Paul once explained that playing baseball after a few drinks made the ball a bit fuzzier, and therefore a bit bigger and easier to hit.[25]

Younger brother Lloyd explained that "Paul thought you played best when you relaxed and drinking was a good way to relax."[26] Lloyd had a tamer reputation, and an even smaller physique.

"Too small, too thin and too scrawny," was Pie Traynor's reaction the first time he saw the 5 foot 6 inch 135-pound outfielder.[27]

"Nobody thought he [Lloyd] could ever make the team," Paul Waner recalled in *The Glory of Their Times*. "He only weighted 130 pounds then and was 20 years old. Our outfield that season [1927] was supposed to be Kiki Cuyler, Clyde Barnhart and me. But Barnhart reported that spring weighing 260 or 270 pounds. He was just a butterball. They did everything they could to get his weight down. They gave him steam baths, they exercised him and ran him and ran him and ran him. They got the weight off all right but the poor fellow was so weak he could hardly lift a bat."[28]

As a result, Lloyd got his chance and proceeded to register the third-highest average in the National League in 1927 (.355) while whacking out 223 hits, including a still-standing record of 198 singles. He would hit better than .309

in each of his 13 seasons as a regular. Lloyd was even a better contact hitter than Traynor, striking out only 173 times in 7,772 at-bats, and only 55 times in his last ten seasons. He missed much of 1930 with appendicitis, but came back strong the next year with a .322 average and 221 hits. Paul would make the Baseball Hall of Fame in 1952, Lloyd in 1967.

Traynor started his managing career with Glenn Wright as his shortstop, but Wright was now playing for Brooklyn and his replacement was a fiery competitor named Dick Bartell, who had trouble with Traynor. "Rowdy Richard" Bartell, who hit over .300 six times in an 18-year career (including .320 in 1930), had a short fuse and a long memory — at least where Traynor was concerned.

"He wasn't my idea of a great team player," Bartell mused, explaining that whenever Traynor fielded a ground ball, he liked to heave it over to first instantly, regardless of the first baseman's positioning. Bartell said Traynor was concerned that the longer he held on to the ball, the more erratic his throw would be. This forced the first baseman to play closer to the bag than he might otherwise. Bartell also complained that Traynor's great range sometimes caused the two of them problems. "A ball would be hit to me at short. As I came in to field it, Pie would cut across in front of me, trying to get it. Usually he would miss it, but as he crossed in front of me I'd lose sight of it. I was charged with plenty of errors that way.... Those were routine plays for me and most of the time he couldn't come close to making them." Bartell said he went to Traynor and told him to back off, but said Traynor snapped at him, "Don't you call me off! I'm going to take everything I can." Bartell kept his mouth shut after that. "I never called him off again."[29]

Two other solid hitters in the lineup were second baseman George Grantham, who came to Pittsburgh in a 1924 trade and had hit over .300 in each season since, and hard-hitting outfielder Adam Comorosky, a one-time coal miner (at the age of 12) who hit .315 in his first full year with the Pirates in 1929. Both would have Hall of Fame–type seasons in 1930 — Grantham hit .342 with 112 runs scored; Comorosky batted .315, led the league (and set a franchise record) with 20 triples, and tied Traynor for the team lead with 119 RBIs.

The Pirates were not ready for their first encounter with the Giants, losing 9–1 as Bill Walker hurled a tidy six-hitter and hit a grand slam. The next day, the Pirates let the Giants have their way through most of the game. The Giants built an 11–4 lead in the eighth inning on the strength of four home runs and Carl Hubbell's pitching. Then, as it would frequently on this road trip, the Giants' pitching faltered late in the game. Paul Waner singled and Comorosky walked to open the bottom of the eighth. Rookie first baseman Gus Suhr drove in two of his 107 runs for the season with a double, and he came around to score on a couple of outs. After Hubbell allowed two more singles, he was relieved by Joe Genewich, who allowed a run-scoring single, walked Grantham to load

A product of the nearby rugged coal mine country, Pittsburgh outfielder Adam Comorosky was only 25 in 1930 when he held his own in a Pirates lineup that hit .303 as a team and featured Hall of Famers Pie Traynor, Paul Waner and Lloyd Waner, He hit .313 with 119 RBIs that year but never attained such lofty numbers again.

the bases, and then walked Paul Waner to force in a run. He escaped further trouble and the Giants won, 11–9.

But the Pirates had given notice that they had found their hitting shoes again. The next day they let loose a torrent of 15 hits and scored six times in the first inning en route to a 16–8 victory. Suhr had three more hits and four

RBIs. With a pair of hits in the game, Paul Waner temporarily took over the league batting race with a .473 average (35-for-74).

The Giants sprinted to a 10–5 lead in the fourth game, with Travis Jackson hitting his sixth home run and Fred Lindstrom getting five hits and hitting for the cycle. The Pirates chipped away against Fred Fitzsimmons, scoring once in the sixth, twice in the seventh and once in the eighth to make it a 10–8 game. In the bottom of the ninth, Bill Walker, the hurling hero of the first game, struck out Traynor, allowed a Comorosky single, and then struck out Suhr. The last hope for Pittsburgh was Bartell, who swatted a game-tying two-run triple to deep center field. The Giants rebounded to score three in the tenth and win 13–10, giving them three of the four games and dropping the Bucs out of first place. But the Giants were not in the top spot, either. The red-hot Chicago Cubs had won seven straight and vaulted past both teams, and coincidently, Wrigley Field was where the Giants were headed next.

McGraw had no more luck solving his late-inning pitching problems in Chicago than he had in Pittsburgh and it cost him the opening game of the series. The Giants had reached Cubs starter Hal Carlson for 14 hits and took a 5–3 lead into the eighth inning. In the bottom of the eighth, with a runner on first and two outs, Gabby Hartnett and pinch-hitter Riggs Stephenson hit back-to-back doubles to tie the game. With Carlson due up next, McCarthy sent the still-hobbling Hornsby to the plate, then changed his mind and let Carlson hit for himself. The move paid off as Carlson singled home Stephenson with the decisive run in the Cubs' 6–5 victory.

Tragically, only two weeks after his heroics, the 38-year-old Carlson would be dead. On May 28, the veteran of World War I, who was gassed in France, complained of severe abdominal pains. Within two hours, he was dead of a stomach hemorrhage.

McGraw's men won the next two games, rapping out 16 hits (four by Bill Terry, including a home run) in a 9–4 victory, then 17 hits (three more by Terry) in a 9–7 triumph. The latter was another nail biter as Hubbell again faded late in the game and Fitzsimmons had to stave off a furious Cubs rally.

The final game of the series saw the Giants jump all over Cubs starter Sheriff Blake for six runs in the second and seven more in the third. By the fifth inning, with Mel Ott, Fred Leach and even starting pitcher Larry Benton hitting home runs, the Giants were ahead, 14–0. Even with his team's recent pitching woes, McGraw had to think this one was in the bag. It did not take long to change his mind. It began innocently enough when Benton gave up a solo home run to backup outfielder Cliff Healthcote, playing for Stephenson, who had injured his shoulder. The score was 14–1. In the sixth, Benton walked Hack Wilson and Hartnett before surrendering a three-run clout to utility infielder Clyde Beck, making it 14–4. Heathcote homered again to start the seventh (he would hit only seven homers the rest of the season), and after Kiki Cuyler grounded out, Wilson and Charlie Grimm hit back-to-back homers. Suddenly the score was 14–7. Hartnett batted next and struck out, but reached safely on a passed ball, bringing up Beck, who launched his second swat of the game (he would hit only five more all year), to make the score 14–9.

McGraw had finally seen enough, replacing Benton with Joe Heving, and temporarily, order was restored. But in the eighth, Cuyler singled in a run to make it 14–10. Then, in the last of the ninth, Les Bell singled and Hartnett doubled. Pinch-hitter Stephenson singled them both home and, incredibly, the Cubs were within two, 14–12. McGraw brought in Genewich, and he recorded the remaining outs, allowing the Giants to win a game in which they posted 15 hits and three home runs while surrendering 15 hits and six home runs. The nine home runs in the game came within one of the major league record, and the four homers hit by the Cubs in the seventh inning marked the first time a team had done that since Pittsburgh accomplished the feat in 1894. Only a week later, the Yankees and Athletics combined to hit ten home runs in a game at Shibe Park.

After this game, it was evident that McGraw has seen enough of the 1930 style of baseball.

"Nowadays, the game has become a case of burlesque slugging with most of the players trying to knock home runs and many of the pitchers becoming discouraged," he said. "Numerous games have been played this year that should not have been seen in the big leagues."[30]

The Giants left Chicago in first place with a 14–7 record and a 1½ game lead over the Cubs. To date on the road trip, they were 7–4, had scored 99 runs and allowed 90 (an average of nine scored and eight allowed per game). But the Giants were tired and their pitching frayed to its edge. They could not keep up the frenetic pace. They went into St. Louis and lost both games to the Cardinals, starting a precipitous collapse that saw them lose 15 of their remaining 18 games in May. Injuries to Ott, Lindstrom and Jackson did not help. By the end of the month, the Giants were in seventh place, seven and one-half games behind the Robins. And on May 21, McGraw traded Larry Benton, the pitcher tagged for the six Chicago home runs, to the Reds for Hughie Critz, who would hit .265 and become the team's regular second baseman for the rest of the season.

Joe McCarthy had problems similar to McGraw's. He had a high-octane offense in full gear, even with Hornsby limited to pinch-hitting duties, but his stalwart pitching staff of a year earlier was as shaky in 1930 as it had been dependable in 1929.

"There is a great disappointment about McCarthy's champions," reported the *Sporting News* on May 1. There seems to be an attitude of indifference or at least a tendency not to worry."[31]

Joe McCarthy probably never read or cared what the *Sporting News* or any other newspaper said. An intensely private man, he cared little for the press and when he consented to interviews, his answers were almost always guarded and restrained. As a result, he was seen as colorless, almost mechanical. That served as one of the reasons the press so readily labeled him a "push-button manager" when Jimmy Dykes (managing the White Sox at the time) used that phrase to describe McCarthy's job while managing the dominant Yankee teams of the late 1930s.

McCarthy never sought publicity for himself during or after his career, and he never penned a memoir, one of the reasons he does not have the share of mind among baseball fans that prominent managers like McGraw, Mack and Stengel enjoy.[32] Yet, McCarthy had a comprehensive knowledge of the game, an unceasing eye for detail, and an uncanny ability to make the right strategic moves, all of which helped him accumulate a major league record .615 winning percentage, and helped many of his players prosper, among them Hack Wilson, Joe DiMaggio and Ted Williams.

As to McCarthy's comprehensive knowledge of the game, Joe DiMaggio summed it up by saying, on more than one occasion, that "not a day went by that you didn't learn something from Joe McCarthy."[33]

As to McCarthy's strategic handling of a game, Paul Waner, who joined the Yankees at the end of his career, said, "his [McCarthy's] work has been a revelation to me. I got such a belt out of watching him operate." Called an "Einstein in flannels" by one writer, McCarthy's ability in the dugout can be simply summed up this way: in 20 years of managing, his teams never finished out of the first division, and he won nine pennants and came within a few games of ten more.[34]

When asked what made the Yankees such a great and dominate team for such a long period of time, Bill Dickey without hesitation pointed to McCarthy and said, "that man."[35]

Perhaps the most revealing testimony as to the respect (if not always the high personal regard) McCarthy commanded in the dugout came from Joe Page, a Yankee pitcher who had more run-ins and trouble with McCarthy than virtually any other Yankee player. "I hated his guts," Page said, "but there was never a better manager."[36]

Of all McCarthy's attributes as a manager, perhaps his strongest was his ability to handle players individually and motivate them.

Frank Crosetti played shortstop for McCarthy's Yankees during the 1930s. Before one game, McCarthy called Crosetti over and softly told him to pep up Lou Gehrig. McCarthy said the Yankee captain was dragging a little bit, so he urged Crosetti to gun the ball to him during warm-ups and talk it up. Many years later, at an Old Timers' Day celebration, Crosetti proudly recounted the story of how McCarthy had selected him to help revive the great Gehrig. McCarthy listened to Crosetti tell the story, then smiled and told Crosetti, "There was nothing wrong with Gehrig. You were the one who needed pepping up and that was my way of doing it."[37]

"He always managed to handle all 25 players on a team," said Yankee Hall of Fame shortstop Phil Rizzuto, who played under McCarthy from 1941 to 46. "I don't know how he did it."[38]

"He could handle anybody," agreed teammate Tommy Heinrich. "If he couldn't handle them, he'd trade them."[39]

McCarthy certainly understood how to handle Hack Wilson. He knew his Sherman tank of a slugger was gregarious, loved the night life, and often tried to pack 25 hours into a day. McCarthy never begrudged Wilson his drinking and carousing, as long as it did not interfere with his performance on the ball field. When he thought it did, McCarthy let Wilson know in no uncertain terms. Wilson respected McCarthy and thrived under him, winning four home run titles and two RBI crowns. He also appreciated McCarthy keeping faith in him after his difficult time in the 1929 World Series. Wilson lost two fly balls in the sun at Wrigley Field, which contributed mightily to Philadelphia's 10-run seventh inning, a backbreaking rally in the series' fourth game. McCarthy spent the off-season and spring training chiding sportswriters and Cubs fans who were giving Wilson grief over the Series, reminding them of the great season Wilson provided them (39 homers, 159 RBIs and a .345 average). In fact, the Cubs outfield of 1929 did something under McCarthy never done before or since — Wilson, Kiki Cuyler and Riggs Stephenson all drove in over 100 runs, becoming the only outfield trio to do that in the same season. The gentlemanly Cuyler, a Hall of Famer and lifetime .321 hitter, hit over .300 ten times; the bruising Stephenson was a former football player and a solid performer. Stephenson hit .336 lifetime, and would post his best mark — .367 — in 1930.

McCarthy's Cubs were a unique blend of brawn and brains. The next three Cub managers to succeed McCarthy were all playing for him in 1930 — Hornsby, first baseman Charlie Grimm and catcher Gabby Hartnett.

Grimm was a great fielding first baseman — he won nine fielding titles — while compiling a .290 average in 20 seasons. Grimm's personality was the opposite of his surname — he had a sunny disposition and optimistic outlook that earned him the nickname "Jolly Cholly."

Gabby Hartnett had been the Cubs' catcher since 1924, and like many players, 1930 would be his best season, hitting .339 with 37 home runs (second on the club to Wilson) and 122 RBIs. McCarthy, who managed Bill Dickey in New York and saw Mickey Cochran play frequently, called Hartnett the "perfect catcher."[40]

"Gabby was the greatest throwing catcher that ever gunned a ball down

Gabby Hartnett added a lot of sock to an already loaded Cubs lineup in 1930, hitting .339 with 37 home runs and 122 RBIs. Joe McCarthy, who saw or managed some of the greatest catchers, always called Hartnett the best he had seen.

to second base," said McCarthy. "He threw a ball that had the speed of lightning but was as light as a feather."[41] Hartnett was tapped for Cooperstown in 1955, and at the time was considered the best catcher in National League history.

Fresh on the heels of losing three of four to the Giants, the Cubs headed to Sportsman's Park for a quartet of games. The Cardinals were on their first roll of the season, having won eight straight, jumping from seventh to fourth place. They made it nine straight by whipping the Cubs, 9–8, in the first game, rapping out 21 hits, including ten by outfielder Taylor Douthit and shortstop Charlie Gelbert, both of whom went five-for-five.

The Cubs took their only win in the series, 9–6, in the first game of a doubleheader, with Hack Wilson hitting his tenth and 11th home runs. The Cards dominated the nightcap, 8–2, and the next day closed out the Cubs with a 16–3 win despite Wilson's 12th home run. The most noteworthy event of this game was Rogers Hornsby's return to the starting lineup. He managed two hits but his field work was severely limited by his bum heel. Hornsby's return lasted only two weeks. On May 30, with the Cubs playing a doubleheader against the Cards at Wrigley Field, Hornsby doubled home the only runs of a 2–0 win in the first game. After hitting the two-bagger, Hornsby tagged up on a fly ball and tried to advance to third, but he made an awkward half-slide and broke his ankle. He was carried off the field on a stretcher, effectively ending his season after 13 at-bats and six hits.

Whether the Cubs were inspired more by Hornsby's play or his absence is hard to know, but they took the nightcap, 9–8, and completed the sweep the next day, 6–5, by scoring three runs in the bottom of the ninth after two were out and nobody on base.

As for Hornsby, he would be on crutches for most of the rest of the season, which gave him ample opportunity to bend the ear of Cubs owner William Wrigley about McCarthy's performance as manager.

National League Notes for May

Hod Ford, Cincinnati's second baseman, collected three doubles and three triples in a 10–6 win over Boston on May 5.

Dave Bancroft, the Giants' backup shortstop and eventual Hall of Famer, played his last game on May 31. He finished the season with one hit in seventeen at-bats.

The Cardinals and Phillies tied a record set in 1883 by walloping 19 extra-base hits in their game of May 7, won by the Cards, 16–11 (the Phillies led 7–1 at one point). The Cardinals had five doubles, three triples and two home runs; the Phils had six doubles and three homers.

National League Standings on May 31, 1930

	W	L	Pct.	GB
Brooklyn	25	15	.625	–
St. Louis	23	17	.575	2
Chicago	23	19	.548	3
Pittsburgh	20	18	.526	4
Boston	18	18	.500	5
New York	17	22	.435	7.5
Cincinnati	16	23	.410	8.5
Philadelphia	12	22	.273	10

5

JUNE

On June 3, national newspapers carried the box score of a Class B Central League game in Fort Wayne, Indiana, showing the Springfield Blue Sox defeating the Ft. Wayne Chiefs, 38–18. The Blue Sox scored 16 runs in the top of the ninth inning to secure the victory; they hit eleven home runs in the game, and the first four hitters in their lineup had seven, six, five and five hits, respectively. The next day, Ft. Wayne's pitching staff "held" Springfield to 27 fewer runs and won, 12–11.

"At any moment," declared the *New York Times* about the state of baseball, "a ball game may explode in the face of a prospective winner. Any time a pitcher throws a ball now, he takes the chance of losing a ball game and an arm or a leg with it."[1]

John McGraw was quick to identify the culprit for the unprecedented onslaught of hits and runs. As reported by the *Sporting News*:

> John McGraw produced a ball used in 1916.... The seams or stitches were more prominent than those of the present ball. McGraw showed how the pitcher had a firmer grip, something that is impossible today. McGraw suggested reducing the pitching distance to 58 feet as a remedy for the ridiculous slugging and general discouragement of today's major league sharpshooters.[2]

"Our western trip and those nine home runs in our last game against the Cubs proved to me beyond a question of doubt that the ball is livelier than it ever was," McGraw said. "I never saw balls hit harder. The rabbit ball should be put out of business."[3]

McGraw also took a moment to pine for the good old days.

"I would like to see baseball go back to the game of tight pitching, sensational fielding, team play at the bat, base stealing and scientific methods. That's the kind of baseball I used to play and that delighted fans everywhere."[4]

Even Bill Klem, the prince of major league umpires at the time and a future Hall of Famer, weighed in on the makeup of the baseball during a conversation with the *Sporting News*. Klem bemusedly recalled when John McGraw would go home if his team had a six-run lead in the seventh inning, but he would be afraid to do so now because of the lively ball.⁵ "They made the cover of the ball a little thicker but instead of deadening the ball, we have the liveliest ball we have ever had...," Klem continued. "When you have 20 or 30 runs in a game, that is not baseball.... It is making the game ridiculous."⁶

The *Sporting News* was quick to refute McGraw and Klem. "John McGraw does not like the baseball which his team plays. He thinks it acts as an agency to destroy the delicate science of the game.... It's a shame Mr. Klem's spring has been spoiled. When has there been a limit on the number of runs to be made in a game? Who shall be the judge as to what the fan likes?"⁷

The American League

Entering June, the winningest pitcher in the American League did not pitch for a contending team. The honor went to a crafty left-hander who had managed to cobble together an 8–2 record for a miserable seventh-place team. He would go on to win 22 games in 1930, one of three times he achieved the 20-win plateau in a career shrouded in such obscurity that he may be the Baseball Hall of Fame's least-known player.

Ted Lyons made a career out of pitching well for bad teams. In his 21-year career — all with the Chicago White Sox — he won 53 percent of his games (260–230) while the Sox won only 46 percent of theirs. His teams finished in the first division only five times and never higher than third place.

"I never resented the fact that we usually finished down in the standings," Lyons said in Donald Honig's book *Baseball When the Grass Was Real*. "Sure you would have liked to finish higher; and if we could have won a pennant — just one to see what it was like, it would have been nice. But I never regretted being with Chicago. My ball club always hustled for me and I could never find fault with a ball club that put out."⁸

One hitter who ranked Lyons high for his ability to think as well as to throw was Ted Williams. "The Splendid Splinter," in his autobiography, *My Turn at Bat*, said:

> Lyons got tougher the more you faced him, because he'd learn about you and he'd usually outthink you. When the guys were telling me about Lyons, they'd say, "Well, he's not real fast, but he's *sneaky* fast," and "His curve is hittable, but he gets it in good spots," and "You've got to watch his change up," and "He's got a knuckleball and the one thing you *can't* do, you can't guess with the son of a gun."⁹

In 1931, arm problems almost ended Lyons' career, but he mastered the knuckleball and played for another decade. He became so popular in Chicago that, late in his career, he pitched only on Sunday afternoons to ensure a good crowd at Comisky Park. In his last four seasons (not counting his post-war 1946 comeback), he won 52 of 82 decisions and an ERA title.

Lyons also had the highest batting average of Chicago's non-starters in 1930, hitting .311 (38-for-122) and driving in 15 runs. Four of Chicago's regulars hit over .300, led by Carl Reynolds at .359 (22 home runs and 104 RBIs) and Smead Jolley at .313 (16 home runs and 114 RBIs). Yet despite these performances, the White Sox were never in contention. In fact, Chicago's Southside team had been out of the running for a decade, the grim fallout of the Black Sox scandal that fractured the franchise in 1920. Owner Charles Comisky hired the taut and dynamic Donie Bush to scrub away the last vestiges of the scandal and ignite a passion for winning into a team the *Chicago Tribune* suggested had a bad attitude.

"It is estimated that the minor leagues harbor at least 200 players more skilled and of better spirit than 80 percent of the present Sox."[10] Bush, a fundamentally sound shortstop who started his career as a teammate of Ty Cobb with the turn-of-the-century Tigers, was an uncompromising disciplinarian. He had managed the Pittsburgh Pirates to the 1927 World Series, but forever earned the enmity of Pirate fans when he benched the popular Kiki Cuyler for the entire World Series (which the Pirates lost in four straight to the Yankees) after Cuyler committed a late-season base running blunder and complained about his spot in the batting order.

Bush tried a variety of ploys in 1930, from reconstituted lineups to additional batting and fielding practice, but the White Sox sank like a stone. After a 6–4 start in April, they went 9–19 in May and an equally abysmal 9–17 in June, bottoming out on June 29 when they crashed into the American League cellar. They stayed there until the more inept Red Sox nudged them back into seventh place on July 7.

With editorial tongue firmly planted in cheek, the *Tribune* suggested that all Bush needed to turn the White Sox into contenders "is three big league catchers, two or three skilled and hustling infielders, three or four outfielders who can bat and catch flies and two or three calm, experienced and able pitchers."[11]

While the White Sox skimmed the depths of the league, the Athletics, Nationals and Yankees sat near its top and gave thanks to a generous schedule-maker. Each of them was slated to play only second-division teams for the entire month of June, with the exception of one home and one road series each against Cleveland. That made June a grueling and unforgiving month for the Indians. After starting with a four-game series against Boston, the schedule demanded the Tribe host Washington for two games, the Athletics for three games and the Yankees for three more. The Indians then had to get on a train and go to Philadelphia for four games, take the train back to Cleveland for one more game against the A's, and then head south to Washington for four games and north to New York for five games. Roger Peckinpaugh did not have to tell his men that this was the gauntlet they would have to run to survive the season. They started well enough, winning three of four from the Red Sox, the final two by counts of 17–7 and 9–4.

The real test began when Washington came to town the next day and Peckinpaugh handed the ball to Wes Ferrell despite the underlying tensions that existed between the two men, mostly caused by Ferrell's combustible nature. Over their time together in Cleveland, Peckinpaugh fined Ferrell on seven occasions and suspended him twice for his temper tantrums and related antics.[12]

Ferrell took issue with his reputation as a hot-head.

"I've got to laugh at that," he told Donald Honig in *Baseball When the Grass Was Real*. "I guess I have still the reputation but reputations aren't always justified. On the field I gave the impression I was mean. After all, this was my job, my livelihood. So I put an act on. I'd stomp and storm around out there like a bearcat, fight my way through a ball game, fight like the devil, do ANYTHING to win. And I got that reputation for being temperamental and mean and it stuck even with people who should have known better." As to his relationship with his manager, Ferrell could only shrug. "I couldn't get along with Peckinpaugh. The guy never spoke to me."[13]

"Wes was a marvelous character," recalled Bill Werber, a teammate of Ferrell's. "After being removed from a ball game, I've seen him hit himself in the jaws with both fists and nearly knock himself out, jump in the air and crunch the face out of an expensive watch and tear card deck after card deck to pieces because he wasn't getting good hands. He hated to lose, at anything. He was a very determined competitor, the kind you like to have on your side."[14]

Recalled Charlie Gehringer in Honig's book:

> He was one of your great competitors. One time he had us beat 6–0 in the fourth inning and he's going great guns. Then it starts to rain. The game was held up. After fifteen minutes the sun came out and before they could get the canvas off their field, there's Wes warming up. He was determined to get that one more inning to make it an official game. I happened to be the first man he faced after the delay and I hit a home run. That started it off. We began hitting and we didn't stop until we tied the score. The next inning we get two more runs and that finishes Wes. He went over to the bench, sat down, threw his glove disgustedly on the dugout floor, clamped down on it with his spikes, gritted his teeth and started pulling that glove to pieces, tearing the fingers and the webbing, the stuffing, the whole thing.[15]

Ferrell was at his competitive best against Washington on June 8, holding the Nationals to two runs and seven hits over eight innings while his counterpart, Adolf Liska, held Cleveland to the same totals. After Washington failed to break the tie in the top of the ninth, Earl Averill led off the bottom of the frame with a single and was sacrificed to second. Catcher Luke Sewell, the seventh batter in the order, dropped a short hit over the infield to move Averill to third. Knowing the pitcher was due up next, Walter Johnson ordered Liska to walk John Burnett, the number eight batter, to load the bases and set up a force at home or a double play. Peckinpaugh, knowing the volatile Ferrell's bat was as good as any left on his bench, allowed his pitcher to hit. Ferrell obliged Johnson's strategy by hitting a ground ball right to Joe Cronin, but the ball hit something and bounded away from the shortstop, allowing Cleveland to score and win the game, 3–2.

The next day, Cleveland trailed 4–3 going into the bottom of the eighth. Dick Porter drew a one-out walk for the Tribe against Nationals starter Fred Marberry. Then Johnny Hodapp and Earl Averill both singled, Porter scored to tie the game, and Hodapp went to third. Backup outfielder Bob Seeds batted next and hit a slow tap down the first base line. Washington catcher Roy Spencer jumped after the ball and threw Seeds out at first, but in doing so, left the plate uncovered. An alert Hodapp buzzed down the line and slid across with the decisive run. The Indians won another one-run decision, this time 5–4, moving them within a half-game of second-place Washington and three and one-half game of first-place Philadelphia (three behind in the loss column).

If anyone doubted the Indians were on a roll, the first game against the Athletics would convince the most stubborn of skeptics. The Tribe whacked Lefty Grove and a couple of relievers for 12 hits in a 6–2 victory. Cleveland was now only two games behind the A's in the loss column.

The next day Eddie Morgan hit two homers and backup catcher Glenn Myatt added a two-run dinger while Clint Brown whitewashed the A's, 4–0, on four hits. The Indians were only one game behind in the loss column.

The third game against Philadelphia was played on Friday the 13th before an overflow crowd at League Park. It proved to be anything but unlucky for Cleveland as they massacred the A's, 15–2, behind Porter's three-run homer and Hodapp's four hits and two RBIs. With this emphatic sweep, the Indians leapfrogged the A's and enjoyed a brief and shining moment at the top of the American League standings, albeit by .005 percentage points.

The celebration was short-lived.

Steamrolling into Cleveland behind the A's were the New York Yankees. After a number of fits and starts, they were playing their best ball of the season under Bob Shawkey, having won nine of their 11 June games, their offense pulverizing anything that even looked like a baseball. The Indians provided little resistance. When it was over, the Yankees had administered three merciless poundings by an aggregate score of 45–19, with Lou Gehrig acting as Chief Bludgeoner. In the first game, the "Iron Horse" recorded five hits, including a two-run homer and three-run double, as the Yanks won, 11–7. The next day,

After a strong 1929 campaign, Indian first baseman Eddie Morgan seemed ticketed for stardom when he hit 26 home runs and had 136 RBIs, a .349 average and 204 hits in 1930. Over the next two years, he lost his power stroke, hitting only a combined 15 home runs and was soon out of the game.

the Yanks rocketed 17 hits and won, 17–10, with Gehrig hitting two more home runs and Babe Ruth knocking his 21st. Starting pitcher Herb Pennock sailed to a complete-game victory despite allowing ten runs and 16 hits. Gehrig racked up homer number 18 in the series finale and drove in four runs as the Yanks spewed out 21 hits and pulverized the Tribe, 17–2.

With virtually no time to collect themselves, the Indians headed into Philadelphia and straight into the crosshairs of an Athletics team looking to avenge the Tribe's sweep of a week earlier. In the first game, Al Simmons, Jimmie Foxx, and Bing Miller hit consecutive fifth-inning home runs off a less-effective Wes Ferrell as the A's won, 7–2. The next day Simmons had two more RBIs to support Lefty Grove in a 4–2 win. Foxx smashed a three-run homer that backed George Earnshaw's five-hit shutout in an 8–0 third-game victory. Both Simmons and Foxx homered in the fourth game, a masterful four-hitter by Rube Walberg that the A's won, 7–1, to complete a sweep.

Only a week after looking like world beaters, Peckinpaugh's men retreated back to Cleveland in a seven-game tailspin in which they had been outscored 71–24. They earned a brief respite by downing the A's, 4–2, at League Park on July 22, but any glimmer of hope raised by that victory was snuffed out when they headed to Washington and lost all four games by an aggregate 32–12. The Indians then went into New York, where they lost four of five, surrendering 54 more runs to Yankee bats; Ruth hit three home runs in the series and Gehrig hit one, while Tony Lazzeri and the light-hitting Jimmy Reese each hit grand slams.

The Indians returned from their 1–8 road trip in fourth place, hovering at the .500 mark. In two weeks, they had gone from first place to fourth and from a few percentage points in the lead to a full 10 games out.

The Yankees took full advantage of their June schedule, going 20–8 and scoring 246 runs for the month (8.7 per game). On the last day of June, they claimed a slice of first place by tying the Athletics in the loss column (the A's were 46–25, the Yanks 42–25). The A's held their grip on the top spot with an able 19–11 month, needing only 161 runs because of their deeper and more consistent pitching. However, a third team had its fingers in the first-place pie. Walter Johnson's Nationals had the same record as the Yankees (42–25), no easy feat considering the cataclysmic shake-up they had endured in June.

The Nationals' train pulled into St. Louis late on Friday the 13th at the same time Cleveland was celebrating its advancement to the American League penthouse. The next day, Goose Goslin took advantage of some free time to take a morning walk through the streets of St. Louis. Though nothing like the fresh air and open farmlands of his native southern New Jersey, Goslin enjoyed the scenery nonetheless. He stopped at the St. Louis Zoo, one of his favorite places to visit. It helped him forget the fans' growing belligerence and his manager's increasing impatience with his performance.

No one can tell exactly when a slow start officially becomes a bad season, but the Goose was nearly at that point. A slow start in April had become an unproductive May, and now it appeared that June would be wasted as well. With the month half over, Goslin was hamstrung with an uncharacteristically low .278 average. He was not in the American League's top ten in extra-base hits. He had only seven home runs and 38 RBIs, number which seemed positively anemic compared to the league's most prominent sluggers—Babe Ruth had 22 home runs, Lou Gehrig 18, Jimmie Foxx 15 and Al Simmons 11 (the other American Leaguer in the double-figure club was Cleveland's Eddie Morgan with 12). In the RBI race, Gehrig already had 69, Ruth 61, Foxx 59 and Simmons 56 (Dale Alexander of Detroit had 52, the only other American Leaguer over the half-century mark).

It was not in Goslin's nature to fret about being benched. He had been the star in Washington for a decade and he felt his track record bought him time with Clark Griffith and Walter Johnson to work out his troubles. He had attacked the ball aggressively in Chicago and ripped one particular tough inside pitch for a solid single. That told him his swing was coming around and it would be just a few more days before he put an end to the whispers that his sore shoulder and lack of physical conditioning had pushed him over the hill. Sure, he had some trouble in the Chicago game the previous day, misplaying a looping fly ball into a triple, popping out while stranding a runner on third base with none out, and getting thrown out trying to stretch his single into a double. Despite all that, his team won, 6–2, and despite his troubled season, the team was a hair's width from first place. In fact, if the Nationals could win the four-game weekend series against the Browns, they might be back on top again. The thought of regaining first place was enough to get the Goose's competitive juices going, and he left the zoo with a spring in his step.

In *The Glory of Their Times*, Goslin explained what happened when he returned to the hotel:

> There's Sam Rice, my roommate, sitting in the lobby waiting for me.
> "Hey, you're in the wrong hotel," he says as soon as he sees me.
> I didn't get it.
> "I tell you, you're in the wrong hotel," he says again.
> "What are you talking about?"
> "Don't you know that they traded you to the St. Louis Browns?" he says.
> "No," I said. "Did they really?"[16]

They did, really. In a blockbuster deal, "the Wild Goose of the Potomac" suddenly became "the Wild Goose of the Mississippi." The Nationals traded Goslin to St. Louis for outfielder Heinie Manush, the Browns' best hitter and the man Goslin nosed out for the 1928 batting championship on the last day of the season. Ironically, Manush had won the 1926 crown on the last day of the season by going six-for-nine in a doubleheader and beating Babe Ruth, .378 to .372, denying Ruth a Triple Crown. This deal marked the first time batting champions had been traded for one another. The Nationals also copped right-handed starter Alvin "General" Crowder in the deal.

Leon "Goose" Goslin, the 1928 batting champion, was called "the Babe Ruth of the Potomac" for his RBI prowess in the 1920s. After an off-year in 1929 and a slow start in 1930, he wore out his welcome with Washington, prompting the biggest trade of the season.

"I don't think Goose is anywhere near through as a player," Walter Johnson said graciously in announcing the trade. "He simply got into a rut with us and he couldn't get out and I believe the trade will bring about a great improvement in his work."[17] Johnson's comments were more telling when he explained the rationale for the trade the next day.

"Here we are around the top of the league," said the Big Train, "even though we haven't had a hitter in the three hole [the third spot in the batting order] since the start of the season. If we had, we could be four or five games out in front now.[18]

"Of course I'm sorry to see the Goose go, but I believe he had outlived his usefulness with us and that Manush will give us the kick which Goslin has lacked this season."[19]

As for Manush, he was elated to escape the travail of playing for the Browns.

"I have never felt better in my life and I am tickled to death to get with a club which has a chance to cap the old rug," he said.[20]

Henry Emmit Manush started his career with the Detroit Tigers in 1923, becoming part of an all-batting champion outfield with Harry Heilmann (four batting titles) and Ty Cobb (twelve batting titles). Manush eventually replaced Cobb in center field, although Cobb remained his manager and hitting tutor. Manush learned well from the Georgia Peach, finishing with a .330 batting average over a 17-year career and making the Baseball Hall of Fame. The prevailing wisdom said the Nationals got the better end of the deal and that "the Old Fox," Clark Griffith, had lived up to his nickname and fleeced the Browns.[21]

"There are few who believe the Browns received ... the best of the transaction," editorialized the *Sporting News*, "unless they can become reconciled to that fact that [Browns manager Bill] Killefer was so desperate for someone he felt would produce a punch, that Goslin was cheap at any price."[22]

One look at the Browns' lineup was enough to illustrate why Killefer was looking for more power. Without Manush or Goslin, the Brown's most productive bat belonged to shortstop Ralph "Red" Kress, a .305 hitter with 107 RBIs in 1929. No one else had more than 71 RBIs and no one had more than Kress' nine home runs.

"The Browns have a hitting average so low, they have to send divers down every week to bring it up for the Sunday charts," quipped the *New York Times*' John Kieran.[23]

Traditionally the American League doormats, the Browns had not won a pennant to this point in their history and rarely contended for one. Their lack of competitiveness showed at the gate. They drew only 280,000 fans in 1929 and would draw only 152,088 in 1930, an average of less than 2,000 fans per game. "The fans don't dare boo us," one St. Louis Brown player quipped anonymously. "We outnumber them."

Heinie Manush, the 1926 batting champion, came to the Senators in the Goose Goslin trade and helped revitalize the Senators' struggling offense until an untimely injury hobbled him, and the team, in August.

Their last manager, Dan Howley (now with the Reds), stirred things up with a surprisingly strong third-place showing in 1928 but disputes with Browns management over player discipline sent "Howling Dan" packing and brought about the arrival of Killefer. Known as "Reindeer Bill" because he came from the rustic north country of Michigan, Killefer had been Grover Cleveland

Alexander's personal catcher during the hurler's heyday with Philadelphia. Killefer had a reputation for developing catchers and he had an apt pupil in the Browns' Rick Ferrell.

A good but not great hitter, Ferrell would have his best offensive years with St. Louis and later with the Boston Red Sox, to whom he would be traded in 1933. Defense was his stock in trade and he set an American League record by playing in 1,806 games (eventually broken by Carlton Fisk); in 1984, Ferrell was selected to the Hall of Fame. He was the brother of Cleveland's Wes Ferrell, although not at all like him.

"Wes was a prima donna and hotheaded," recalled long-time St. Louis sportswriter Bob Broeg. "Rick, though he lost his cool occasionally, was a soft-spoken team man."[24]

The siblings entered the record books when they became the first brothers to homer against each other in a game on July 19, 1933. In fact, Wes won life-time bragging rights by out-homering Rick 38 to 28 in their respective careers.

Killefer and Ferrell had little true talent on the Browns' pitching staff to mold, with the exception of Walter "Lefty" Stewart. Having almost died of a burst appendix in 1927, Stewart came back to post a career-best 20–12 record in 1930, proving to be a particular torment to Washington, whom he beat five times that year. In nine full seasons, he won 101 games.

The one other star in the Browns' 1930 firmament was shortstop Kress, who had two more seasons in which he hit over .300 and drove in more than 100 runs for the Browns. Curiously, he led the league in fielding in 1929, and in a complete reversal, led the league in errors in 1930. A trade to Chicago later derailed his career as he wound up playing behind Hall of Famer Luke Appling.

With the trade completed in the morning, the Nationals and Browns prepared to square off against each other in the afternoon, with Goslin and Manush each batting third for his new team.

"The trade broke my heart," Goslin recalled in *The Glory of Their Times*. "That afternoon [of the trade] I had to go to the other clubhouse and I played against all my old teammates, all my best friends."[25]

Goslin recorded his first hit as a Brown in his second at-bat, a single to left-center, but just as he did in Chicago the day before, he was thrown out trying to stretch it into a two-bagger. Manush got his Washington career off to a great start with a single in the first inning, which helped set up the Nationals' first run. The game seesawed back and forth, with Rick Ferrell's two-run home run providing St. Louis with a 5–4 margin after eight innings. The Nationals rallied in the top of the ninth with two outs when two singles and a walk loaded the bases, and as fate would have it, brought Manush to the plate. With a chance to deeply ingratiate himself with his new teammates, Manush unleashed one of his classic, perfectly level swings and drove a pitch to right field. He got under it, however, and the ball landed softly into the glove of right fielder Ted Gullic to end the game.

Afterward, Goslin vowed to make the fans of St. Louis love the trade that brought him to their town.

"The trade is likely to make a hero out of me for I sure can hit in the St. Louis park and I hope to start proving it right away," he said.[26]

The trade obviously rejuvenated his bat and he posted impressive numbers for the second half of the season, even if he did not lift the Browns out of the second division. Manush made his presence felt in Washington as well. The following statistics show how both players batted during the 1930 season.

	G	AB	R	H	2B	3B	HR	RBI	AVG
Goslin (Wash)	47	188	34	51	11	5	7	38	.271
Goslin (St.L)	101	396	81	129	25	7	30	100	.326
Goslin (Total 1930)	148	584	115	180	36	12	37	138	.308
Manush (St.L)	49	198	26	65	16	4	2	29	.328
Manush (Wash)	88	356	74	129	33	8	7	65	.362
Manush (Total 1930)	137	554	100	194	49	12	9	94	.350

The Browns took three of four games that weekend, but the Nationals recovered by sweeping four games from Cleveland and winning three out of four games against Detroit.

The three contenders could not have been much closer as June ended and the Fourth of July weekend — the traditional halfway point of the season — approached. The Athletics were still standing strong, the Yankees seemed to have regained their championship swagger, and Washington was hanging tough. The Nationals would need all the toughness they could muster. A more cataclysmic and far more tragic event awaited them in July.

American League Notes for June

Garland Braxton, a workhorse hurler, was traded by Washington the day after the Nationals swapped Goslin. In return, the Nationals received Art Shires, a third-year player loaded with talent and promise, all of which went unrealized because of his penchant for drinking in all-night speakeasies, boxing in the off-season and loudly promoting his own talent. The Nationals thought they could harness that talent (he hit .321 in 1929) while managing his wild side. They did not. Two years later he was out of the game.

Jack Quinn, a 46-year-old pitcher for the Athletics, connected for a home run against the Browns on June 27, making him at the time the oldest man ever to hit a home run in the major leagues.

Mickey Cochran led both leagues at the end of June with a .409 batting average, followed by Lou Gehrig (.397), Sam Rice (.393), Al Simmons (.391) and Bill Dickey (.390).

American League Standings on June 30, 1930

	W	L	PCT	GB
Philadelphia	46	25	.648	–
New York	42	25	.629	2
Washington	42	25	.629	2
Cleveland	35	34	.507	10
St. Louis	29	41	.414	16.5
Detroit	29	41	.414	16.5
Boston	26	42	.382	18.5
Chicago	24	40	.375	18.5

The National League

While the St. Louis Browns were trading Heinie Manush, their National League counterparts engineered a deal just prior to the June 15 trading deadline that did not generate as much attention but proved to have more effect on the 1930 pennant race.

The Cardinals sent veteran pitchers Bill Sherdel and Fred Frankhouse to the Boston Braves in exchange for grizzled old war horse Burleigh Grimes. The Cards were desperate to stabilize what had become a maddeningly inconsistent season. They had strung together winning streaks of nine and eight games, and at one point won 17 of 18. However, they also suffered through losing streaks of seven and five games and seemed stuck in the middle of the pack as a .500 team. Injuries were part of the reason. Frankie Frisch, the heart of the team, Chick Hafey, the team's best overall hitter, and Charlie Gelbert, the solid-as-a-rock sophomore shortstop, missed substantial time.

"Gabby Street must be singing the St Louis blues these days," conjectured John Kieran of the *New York Times* about the Redbird manager. "The St. Louis players hope the recent slump ... will be laid to the real cause — injuries and not to any mistakes in managing by Gabby Street."[27]

The 34-year-old Grimes brought a veteran's knowledge of how to win, a durable arm and a rough-hewn grittiness to the Cardinals' pitching staff — traits that seemingly abandoned him during his short and unpleasant stay in Boston. He was only 2–5 for the Braves with a 7.35 ERA in 11 games. It was not indicative of this eventual Hall of Famer's career or ability. During the 1920s, "Old Stubblebeard," as he was called for his practice of not shaving on days he was scheduled to pitch, won 20 or more games five times and led the National League twice in victories. He was a belligerent competitor, bordering on vicious.

"Old Stubblebeard" Burleigh Grimes came to the Cardinals in a June trade. The Hall of Famer and self-proclaimed "son-of-a-bitch" went 13–6 and brought a competitive fire and grittiness to steady a faltering pitching staff.

It was said by his contemporaries that his idea of an intentional walk was four pitches thrown at the batter's head.[28]

"I was a real bastard when I played," Grimes admitted after he retired.[29]

Grimes had just completed two solid seasons for the Pittsburgh Pirates, going 25–14 in 1928 and 17–7 in 1929. He expected his pay to be commensurate with his success, but the Pirates had a far lower view of his worth and dumped him on the Braves, getting virtually nothing in return.

Few expected he would reside in Boston for long. The Braves' owner, Emil Fuchs, ran a notorious penny-pinching operation. The New York attorney, nicknamed "Judge," bought the Braves in 1923 with a bevy of partners that included pitching immortal Christy Mathewson. Almost from the beginning, the team suffered debilitating financial problems that prevented Boston from attracting or holding good talent. Fuchs, who had obtained Rogers Hornsby from the Giants after "the Rajah" ran afoul of John McGraw, turned around and sold the superstar to the Cubs in 1928 for a much-needed infusion of cash. In 1929, he saved a salary by managing the team himself (they finished last with a 56–98 record). Despite his parsimonious penchant, Fuchs promised Braves fans Grimes would stay in Boston. He did — for two months.

Certainly one Boston Brave was happy with the trade. New manager Bill McKechnie was glad to obtain the services of two familiar veterans who had helped him win the 1928 pennant with the Cardinals.

McKechnie came to Boston after Fuchs decided to bite the financial bullet and hire an experienced manager for the 1930 season. The quiet and efficient McKechnie, nicknamed "Deacon Bill" for his frequent trips to his church where he was a regular voice in the choir, had a strong resume as a manager, leading the Cardinals to the 1928 flag, and the 1925 Pittsburgh Pirates to the world championship. Later, he would guide the Cincinnati Reds to a World Series, making him the only major league manager to win pennants with three different franchises. This accomplishment earned him a spot in the Hall of Fame. He had an encyclopedic knowledge of the game, prompting his former manager Frank Chance to say that "McKechnie knew more about the game than the rest of my team put together."[30]

"He knew how to hold on to a one- or two-run lead better than any manager," said Johnny Vander Meer, who played for McKechnie in Cincinnati.[31]

"McKechnie was the real fatherly type," said Frank McCormick, another of his Cincinnati alumni. "He was very understanding, very sympathetic. But I'll tell you one thing. When he put his hand across his chest and looked at you over his bifocals, he was mad. And as fine a gentleman as he was, he could be as rough as a corncob when he thought you hadn't done the right thing."[32]

Watching players not do the right thing was commonplace in Boston. The Braves were a moribund franchise caught in an endless rut of not just losing — but LOSING. The team had only seen the first division four times in the 20th century. From the years 1903 to 1912, they finished a mind-boggling 32, 51, 54, 66, 47, 36, 55, 50, 54 and 52 games behind the pennant-winner. In the previous four seasons prior to 1930, the Braves had finished seventh three times and last once.

Looking at his 1930 roster, "Deacon Bill" could have been excused if on one of his sojourns to church, he prayed for a repeat of the miracle that touched this franchise in 1914. That was the year the Braves came from nowhere and inexplicably went on a torrid second-half run to win the National League pennant and upset the heavily-favored Athletics in the World Series.

Rabbit Maranville, the sparkplug of the 1914 "Miracle Braves," was still the team's shortstop in 1930 at age 38. He hit a respectable .281 but had lost much of his range in the field. The first baseman was the great George Sisler, who was in the last year of a magnificent Hall-of-Fame career. Limited by eye problems, the 37-year-old Sisler batted .309 but could generate only three home runs and 63 RBIs. The one bright spot for the team was rookie outfielder Wally Berger, who finished his first season hitting .310, with 38 home runs and 119 RBIs (rookie records until Mark McGwire came along). Berger would post seven solid seasons for the Braves, his top performance being 1935 when he led the National League with 34 homers and 130 RBIs. A shoulder injury the next year started a slow, steady downfall that had him out of the game by 1940.

Boston Braves rookie outfielder Wally Berger exploded on the National League scene in 1930, setting a rookie record for home runs (38) and RBIs (119).

In early June, the Cardinals and Cubs were headed in the same direction geographically — to the East Coast for encounters with the Giants and Robins — but in opposite directions in the standings.

The Cardinals were some weeks away from feeling the positive effects of the Grimes trade. In the meantime, St. Louis looked like it could barely mount an argument, let alone a serious challenge for the league lead. The Cardinals won only 10 of 25 games in June, and were hanging in the race by their fingernails.

They opened the month by losing a doubleheader to Cincinnati and two of three to the lowly Phillies. When they arrived at the Polo Grounds for three games on June 6–8, the Cardinals had lost nine of their last ten and were facing the Giants at absolutely the worst time. The Giants were on the rebound and red-hot. They had lost 15 of 18 games in the second half of May, the kind of extended slump that might have sealed the fate of a team under the leadership of a lesser man, but John McGraw would not allow his boys to give up. The injury bug was partially to blame for the slump, as it bit such key players as Mel Ott, Fred Lindstrom and Travis Jackson. Not surprisingly, as each of them returned to action, the Giants started a winning streak. It began on June 1 with a doubleheader sweep of the Braves, 9–4 and 16–3 (highlighted by a 12-run third inning), and continued with a three-game sweep of the Reds.

The Giants had little trouble with the undermanned Cardinals. They won all three games (10–7, 9–7 and 4–1) to stretch their win streak to eight. Fred Leach had a single, triple and five RBIs in the first game; Ott was the star of the middle game, hitting a pair of three-run homers — one a tremendous upper-deck drive to right field and the second the kind of home run only possible at the Polo Grounds: a low liner to right that just cleared the wall at the foul pole, 257 feet from home plate; Bill Terry homered in the third game and Bill Walker limited St. Louis to two hits to complete the sweep. The Giants ran the win streak to nine with a 9–2 win over Pittsburgh before the Pirates' 10–7 win on June 12 ended the run.

The Redbirds fared slightly better in Brooklyn by winning one of three games, but they played only .500 ball against the Braves and Phillies for the rest of the month. By the time they returned to St. Louis, the Cardinals remained stuck in fourth place, eight games behind first-place Brooklyn and two behind third-place New York, with McGraw's men marching into Sportsman's Park for a month-ending five-game rematch.

If the Cardinals believed it was the time to play desperate, backs-to-the-wall baseball, they did not show it in the first game. The Giants pounded out 20 hits, four each by Howie Critz and Freddie Leach, and won easily, 12–4.

The outlook of the second game seemed considerably brighter for the Cards when Frankie Frisch clubbed a three-run first-inning home run. But in the fourth inning, Leach answered with a three-run clout of his own and the rout was on, the Giants roasting new Cardinal Burleigh Grimes, 9–4. With the pair of losses, the Cardinal season was now on life support with a 30–32 record, nine games behind Brooklyn and four behind the Giants.

In the third game, Carl Hubbell baffled the Cardinals, taking a no-hitter and a 1–0 lead into the bottom of the sixth inning. Jim Bottomley finally solved Hubbell's slants for a single and came around to tie the game on another single and a sacrifice fly. Outfield sub Ray Blades hit a seventh-inning homer to give the Cardinals their first lead of the game, and Frisch's two-run double capped a four-run rally that put the Cardinals out front to stay. They won, 6–2, a victory, which if nothing else, stopped the bleeding. But the win would not mean much if they failed to sweep the next day's doubleheader.

Leach got the doubleheader off to a good start for the Giants, hitting a triple and scoring in the fourth inning, but the Cards tied it in the seventh when Bottomley stroked a double down the right field line and Ott accidentally kicked the bouncing baseball into the crowd, which by 1930 rules made the hit a home run (the National League changed the rule after the 1930 season). Bottomley later singled home Frisch for a 2–1 Cardinal lead. The Cards took that lead into the ninth inning, but after getting two outs and two quick strikes on Leach, Cards pitcher Sylvester Johnson left a pitch too far over the plate and Leach hammered a long, game-tying home run to right field. The Cardinals responded quickly in the bottom of the ninth when speedy center fielder Taylor Douthit worked a walk, went to second on an infield out, and raced home to score the winning run on reserve outfielder George Fisher's hit.

In the nightcap, Fred Lindstrom's RBI single and Terry's sacrifice fly gave the Giants two first-inning runs, but Wild Bill Hallahan allowed only two more hits until the ninth inning, by which time the Cards had built a 5–2 lead (with Hallahan helping his own cause with two RBIs). The Giants rallied but came up short, the Cards winning, 5–4, and getting the sweep they needed.

They were not exactly back in the race, but they were out of intensive care.

While the Cardinals struggled, the Cubs soared. They ended May with four straight wins and continued their tear into June. Even with Rogers Hornsby on the disabled list, they were scoring runs at a prodigious rate.

Chicago opened the new month by crushing Pittsburgh, 16–4, with Hack Wilson upping his RBI total to 49 with the first of two five-RBI games he registered in June. The Cubs then stormed into Boston and demolished the Braves by scores of 15–2, 18–10 and 10–7. In these four games, Gabby Harnett hit three home runs, Wilson hit two, while Riggs Stephenson and Kiki Cuyler each contributed a five-hit game. The Cubs also had won eight straight.

"One of the highlights of this race is the ability of the Cubs to remain up there despite the loss of Hornsby and Carlson and the many strokes of bad luck suffered by McCarthy," marveled the *Sporting News*. "Joe's pitching has been in and out. His outfield has been spotty. But he has managed to get rallies when he needs them."[33]

With eight straight wins, the Cubs moved into second place, only two games behind the front-running Robins as they next invaded Ebbets Field on June 6–8.

For all their supposed daffiness, the Robins were playing seriously good baseball. They had their own spate of injuries, most notably an injured right ankle sustained by Glenn Wright, the team's all-star caliber shortstop, but Neal "Mickey" Finn, Jake Flowers and Gordon Slade picked up the infield slack. The Robins had not put together as much as a four-game winning streak since early May, but their offense, and especially their reliable pitching, had allowed them to win nine consecutive series.

There was nothing daffy about the Brooklyn lineup which boasted a major league–leading .328 team average, sparked by Babe Herman's almost-unconscious .420 average (to go with 13 home runs and 39 RBIs), first baseman Del Bissonette's .373, center fielder Johnny Frederick's .360, Jake Flowers' .359 and third baseman Wally Gilbert's .353.

The Cubs matched the Robins hitter for hitter — Stephenson .396, Cuyler .343, Wilson .342, Woody English .324, and Hartnett .323. It was easy to see why the McCarthyites were not missing Rogers Hornsby.

In the first of the three games, Brooklyn rolled out ace Dazzy Vance, and for the first three innings, he looked like the National League's most dominant pitcher, striking out seven of the first nine batters he faced. In the middle innings, Chicago hitters began measuring his fastball, and by the time the game was over, they had pummeled Vance and two relievers for 16 hits and a 13–0 win. The red-hot Harnett homered again (four in one week) as did Charlie Grimm, while Cub starter Charlie Root shut down the Robins' prodigious offense on two measly hits. The Cubs had now won nine straight, moved within a game of the Robins and, impressively, had scored 10 or more runs in five straight games (72 runs total).

A steady rain did little to slow the Cubs' offense the next day as they whacked four home runs (including Wilson's 18th) and scored nine runs. They had a 5–0 lead in the third inning, and led 7–3 in the fourth when Brooklyn rallied for five runs to take an 8–7 lead. The Cubs answered with two for a 9–8 lead in the top of the sixth. In the bottom of that frame, Finn and Al Lopez reached base, bringing up veteran relief pitcher Bill Clark — never much of a hitter. Wilbert Robinson decided to save his pinch-hitters for later in the game and let Clark hit for himself. The lefty hurler launched a tape-measure, three-run homer over the wall in right field, the only round-tripper of his 12-year career. The Robins scored once more and won the game, 12–9, ending the Cubs' win skein at nine.

The deciding game of the series was also played in the rain, but the Brooklyn fans probably did not mind getting wet. Their new darling, a 40-year-old master of the breaking ball named Dolf Luque, spun a masterful four-hit 6–0 shutout. With the win, the colorful Luque, who joined the Robins in spring training, improved his record to a National League–best 6–0.

Luque, "the Pride of Havana," came to the United States in 1912 and reached the segregated major leagues by virtue of a wicked breaking ball and his light skin tone and blue eyes. Playing a decade before Jackie Robinson broke baseball's racial barriers, the Cuban Luque endured racial taunts and insults regarding his Hispanic heritage, but unlike Robinson, the fiery and pugnacious Luque answered with a fist or a bean ball.

He pitched in Cincinnati for a dozen years, including in the 1919 World Series. In total, Luque pitched 20 major league seasons, retiring at age 44 with a 194–179 record. His best year was 1923 when he led the National League in wins (27) and ERA (1.93).

As for the Cubs, they left Brooklyn knowing that the ground they had gained during their nine-game winning streak had been negated by losing the last two games to the Robins. They started the streak four games out; now they were three out.

After splitting four games in Philadelphia, McCarthy led his men into the Polo Grounds, where the Giants were fresh off their own nine-game win streak.

The Cubs won the opener, 8–5, as two-run singles by Wilson and Stephenson negated a two-homer, four–RBI game by Fred Leach. In the second game it was the Cubs wasting a great hitting performance by Hartnett (four-for-four with a home run) as the Giants took a 7–4 decision behind catcher Shanty Hogan's three-run circuit clout in the seventh inning.

The third game saw the Cubs score two early runs, but the Giants answered with solo home runs by Bill Terry, Travis Jackson, reservist Ethan Allen and Leach over the first four innings. Carl Hubbell protected the 4–2 lead until the top of the eighth when Wilson walked, Stephenson singled and Charlie Grimm bunted his way on to load the bases. Hartnett, the league's hottest hitter, hit a long sacrifice fly to Leach in center, scoring Wilson and advancing Stephenson to third. McCarthy sent up pinch-hitter Chuck Tolson and he also lofted a fly to center. Leach made a running catch, and while on the fly, chucked the ball home to catcher Bob O'Farrell as Stephenson, a former college football star, came barreling in. The collision at home plate left O'Farrell sprawling on the ground, but still in possession of the ball. Stephenson was out and the Giants held the lead, 4–3.

In the ninth, the relentless Cubs produced two singles and a walk to load the bases with none out and bring up Wilson against Hubbell. Wilson took a tremendous slash at the first pitch but popped it up to the infield for the first out. Kiki Cuyler was up next and he took an equally vicious cut, but he also popped the ball straight up. With two outs, Hubbell faced Stephenson with the game on the line. Lunging at a plummeting screwball, the Cub outfielder hit a ground ball toward the middle of the field. Second baseman Howie Critz rushed over, but the ball bounced higher than he anticipated, and the best Critz could do was knock it down. The Cubs had tied the game and still had the sacks loaded with two outs. Charlie Grimm stepped in to hit next and he flailed helplessly at two Hubbell screwballs. When "King Carl" tried to sneak a fastball past the veteran first baseman, Grimm snapped his bat at the ball and hit a fly ball that carried into the lower tier of seats for a grand slam. In the bottom of the ninth, Hogan hit the Giants' fifth solo homer of the game, but that would be the end of the scoring, the Cubs prevailing, 8–5, in the game and in the series, 2–1.

While the Cubs rolled through their resurgence, the Philadelphia Phillies continued to play in one wild game after another. They met the fading Pittsburgh Pirates in a June 14 doubleheader, losing the first game, 19–12, before winning, 5–4. The next day, they blew a 12–2 lead, but hung on for an 18–14 win in a game that featured 38 hits.

A week later, the Phils were at Wrigley Field on June 23–25 for three equally wild games, losing 21–8, 6–1 and 12–11. In the first game, Hack Wilson hit for the cycle and added a fifth hit — a single — and enjoyed his second five–RBI game of the month.

The next day, the Phils dropped into last place, where they would stay for the rest of the season. While most last-place teams are shrouded in ignominy and forgotten quickly, the 1930 Phillies are an exception. They have gained a cult status with baseball fans and historians for finishing last (52–102), 40 games out, despite hitting .315 as a team, scoring 944 runs, and featuring two of the game's greatest hitters performing in their prime — Chuck Klein and Lefty O'Doul.

The well-liked and respected Klein had one of the most prolific first six seasons in baseball history — five 200-hit seasons, a batting title, four home run titles and two RBI crowns, plus a Triple Crown in 1933. He set the short-lived NL record for home runs in 1929 with 43, and near the end of his career would become one of the few players to hit four home runs in one game. Unfortunately for Klein, his performance was mostly wasted on bad teams — his Phillies teams had a collective .364 winning percentage and finished a cumulative 614 games out of first place. There was no doubt the lefty swinging Klein's numbers were aided by the very friendly dimensions in Baker Bowl's right field. After he was traded to the Cubs over a salary dispute, he never put up numbers close to those he posted in Philadelphia. However, for his career, he hit .320 with an even 300 home runs (which at the time of his retirement ranked as the second

The Napoleonic John McGraw (left) and the studious Burt Shotton. Shotton would earn a dubious place in baseball history as the manager of the 1930 Phillies — a team that hit .315 but finished in last place with 102 losses, 40 games out of first place.

highest in National League history to Mel Ott), good enough for the Veterans Committee to elect him to the Baseball Hall of Fame in 1980.

Francis Joseph "Lefty" O'Doul started out as a pitcher with the Yankees and Red Sox (1919–23), but a sore arm turned him into an outfielder. He tried out with the Cubs in 1926, only to be rejected by Joe McCarthy — a move that would come back to haunt the Cubs' skipper in September. As a result, O'Doul was late to the major leagues as an offensive force, but he made his mark fast and forever once he arrived. He debuted as an outfielder with the Giants in 1928 at the age of 30. He was traded to the Phils, where he had an all-time season in 1929, winning the batting title with a .398 average, posting a then-record 254 hits, 32 home runs, 122 RBIs and 152 runs scored. He contributed a .383 mark in 1930, with 22 homers and 97 RBIs. For his career, as brief as it was (four years as a pitcher, seven as an outfielder), his lifetime average was .349, a mark topped only by Ty Cobb, Rogers Hornsby and Shoeless Joe Jackson.

While Klein and O'Doul were a nightmare for opposing pitchers, the Phillies' pitching staff was a dream for National League hitters. The 14 hurlers that made up the Phillies' staff in 1930 combined to allow an all-time record 1,199 runs, a league-worst 1,993 hits and 543 walks. They registered an astronomical team ERA of 6.71 (Pittsburgh's was next worse at 5.24).

The best ERA on the staff (minimum 10 games) was starter Phil Collins at 4.78. Collins actually managed a 16–11 record, which means the rest of the staff was a combined 55 games under .500. The only other pitcher who reached double figures in wins was starter Ray Benge at 11–15. At the other end of the spectrum, Les Sweetland was 7–15 with a 7.71 ERA and Claude Willoughby was 4–17 with a 7.59 ERA.

By sweeping the Phillies and pounding the hapless Boston Braves, the Cubs kept the pressure on the Robins. By the time Brooklyn came to Wrigley for a highly anticipated five-game face-off at the end of the month, only one game separated the two teams.

Before sending his minions out to do battle with the Cubs on June 26, Uncle Robbie called his troops together for a rare team meeting. He urged his men to get the jump on the Cubs, reminding his boys that the Philadelphia Athletics had beaten the Cubs in the 1929 World Series by doing exactly that.

Heeding their manager's advice, the Robins reached Charlie Root for five second-inning runs in the first game and Dazzy Vance, remembering the rude treatment he received at the hands of the Cubs in Brooklyn, earned a measure of revenge by scattering nine hits and winning, 7–1. Brooklyn again led by two games.

More than 45,000 fans were shoehorned into Wrigley Field for the second game, causing a portion of the outfield to be cordoned off for the overflow crowd and forcing a ground rule to be added which awarded a batter a double for any fly ball hit into the overflow section. The Robins scored early again in this one, getting single runs in the first, second and fourth innings, the last one on Babe Herman's homer. The Cubs scored three to tie the game in their half of the fourth inning, and they took the lead in the fifth when Riggs Stephenson doubled into the overflow section to score Hack Wilson. In the sixth, a Kiki

Cuyler sacrifice fly upped Chicago's lead to 5–3. In the seventh, Brooklyn took advantage of the overflow crowd to tie the score. Neal Finn lined a double into the crowd and scored on Al Lopez's single. With pitcher Ray Moss batting next, Uncle Robbie eschewed the sacrifice bunt and Moss rewarded his manager's judgment with a fly ball of his own into the overflow section for a game-tying double. The score remained 5–5 until two out in the bottom of the tenth when Cuyler smashed a two-run, walk-off home run, moving the Cubs within a game of first place.

The Cubs picked up that game the next day as Pat Malone kept the Brooklyn hitters at bay and the Cubs won, 4–2. The Cubs were now 41–26 (.612), while the Robins were .007 points better at 39–24 (.619).

The fourth game of the series turned out to be the finale (inclement weather washed out the fifth game). Played on June 29, which happened to be Wilbert Robinson's 66th birthday, it was not a happy day for Uncle Robbie. Avenging his loss in the series opener, Charlie Root shackled the Robins on seven hits and the Cubs jumped past the Robins with a 5–1 win.

For good measure, the Cubs spanked the Giants, 10–3, at Wrigley on June 30, scoring eight first-inning runs and getting another Gabby Hartnett home run to add a half-game to their margin over idle Brooklyn.

The next day, Kiki Cuyler homered twice and Hack Wilson also connected, but Travis Jackson's two-run homer and Bill Terry's clutch three hits helped the Giants win 7–5. In the finale of the series, the Cubs scored five in the first inning, the Giants countered with six in the fourth, and the Cubs plated one in the fourth to make it 6–6. The game stayed knotted until the ninth when a Terry single, a throwing error and a wild pitch gave New York three runs and a 9–6 lead. Never ones to go quietly, the Cubs rallied in the bottom of the ninth, but veteran Joe Genewich, who allowed the eight first-inning runs in the series opener, snuffed the rally and saved the game for New York.

Ironically, as McGraw's maneuvering helped his team sweep the last two games from the Cubs, it enabled his long-time Brooklyn nemesis Wilbert Robinson to regain a share of first place as the Robins split a pair of games in St. Louis.

National League Notes for June

Brooklyn still occasionally lapsed into daffiness. On June 4 the Robins committed eight errors in one game, losing to Pittsburgh, 12–6.

Riggs Stephenson of the Cubs led an impressive array of batting averages atop the National League on June 8. The Cub outfielder was hitting .420, followed by Babe Herman of the Robins at .414, Chuck Klein of the Phillies at .401, Harry Heilmann of the Reds at .400 and Bill Terry of the Giants at .399.

The order had changed a bit by the end of June, with Philadelphia teammates Lefty O'Doul (.401) and Chuck Klein (.399) at the top of the heap, followed by Paul Waner (.392) and Riggs Stephenson and Bill Terry (.387).

National League Standings on June 30, 1930

	W	L	Pct.	GB
Chicago	43	26	.623	–
Brooklyn	39	25	.609	1.5
New York	34	32	.515	7.5
St. Louis	33	32	.508	8
Boston	30	33	.476	10
Pittsburgh	30	34	.469	10.5
Cincinnati	27	40	.403	15
Philadelphia	24	38	.387	15.5

6

July

All 16 major league baseball teams played doubleheaders on the Fourth of July. Meanwhile, Americans found many other ways to celebrate their country's 154th birthday:

- Over a million people packed Coney Island in New York City and the area's other beaches to worship the sun.
- Herbert Hoover signed into law a bill allocating three million dollars to raise the pay of 45,000 Federal Government workers.
- Calvin Coolidge, Hoover's predecessor and the only president to share his birthday with the Declaration of Independence, went to his modest Vermont office, where he was greeted by a mountain of cards and letters wishing him a happy 58th birthday.
- Mayor Harry Mackey of Philadelphia spoke before a crowd of 7,000 at Independence Hall and called for an end to Prohibition, labeling the law "unenforceable."
- The house of famous poet Joyce Kilmer ("I think that I shall never see, a poem as lovely as a tree") was dedicated as a national landmark in New Brunswick, New Jersey. Kilmer was killed in action during World War I.
- Thousands in downtown Washington, D.C., watched a torchlight parade in honor of America's founding, then stayed to admire the fireworks show that used the Washington Monument as a backdrop.
- Outside of Rapid City, South Dakota, a huge American flag adorning the side of an otherwise inconspicuous mountain was removed, unveiling the 700-foot face of George Washington on what would soon be known as the Mount Rushmore National Monument. Sculptor Gutzon Borglum promised the gathered crowd of 2,000 that the faces of Thomas Jefferson, Abraham Lincoln and Teddy Roosevelt would soon accompany the first president.

- In Rocky River Ohio, west of Cleveland along the shores of Lake Erie, George M. Steinbrenner was born to Henry and Rita Steinbrenner at 9:00 P.M.

The American League

"One way of sizing up the American League race," said John Kieran of the *New York Times*, "is to say that the Athletics have the punch, the Senators have the pitching and the Yankees have Babe Ruth."[1]

More so than anything else, it was Ruth's incomparable slugging that kept the Yankees in the race. He was first to the 30-home run plateau in 1930, knocking one on the last day of June as the Yanks closed out the month with a 15–4 drubbing of the White Sox at Yankee Stadium. After a rainout the next day, he whacked his 31st of the season in the opening game of a July 2 doubleheader, leading the Yanks to a 5–1 win. But Ruth's slugging could only do so much to hide the Yankees' flaws.

New York lost the second game of the doubleheader to Chicago, 15–4, as White Sox outfielder Carl Reynolds, known as a solid hitter (six .300 seasons and a lifetime .302 average) with little power (80 home runs for his career), did his best Babe Ruth imitation. In the first inning, Reynolds drove a long shot to the cavernous swatches of Yankee Stadium's power alley and circled the bases for an inside-the-park home run. In the next inning, with two aboard, he drove one over the fence in right field, and in the third inning, he shot another laser beam to the furthest reaches of the outfield and legged out a second inside-the-park homer.

Reynolds, who also had two singles and eight RBIs in the game, became only the second hitter to ever hit three home runs in three consecutive innings, matching the feat turned in by George "Highpockets" Kelly of the New York Giants in 1923. Ironically, only a week later, Kelly would be released by the Cincinnati Reds, for whom he had played the previous two seasons. The 34-year-old future Hall of Famer latched on with the Chicago Cubs for the remainder of 1930, where he would post a hefty .331 mark in 39 games.

On July 3, the Yankees squared off against the Philadelphia Athletics. Ruth again tried to lift his team, drawing two walks and hitting a sacrifice fly to help build an early 3–0 lead. But as it did so many times in this season, Yankee pitching betrayed the advantage. Jimmie Foxx hit a two-run, bases-loaded single in the fifth, and then after an intense thunderstorm stopped play for 30 minutes, two Yank errors, an Al Simmons double and a single by Bing Miller plated three runs to give the defending champions their final margin of victory, 5–4. The Yankees' tenuous hold on contender status was beginning to slip, and over the next few days in Washington, it would unravel completely.

The Fourth of July found the Yankees in the nation's capital for two games. Ruth provided his share of the fireworks, connecting for his 32nd home run, but the Nationals prevailed in both games. The first win was 8–0 as Heinie Manush went four-for-five, getting as many hits as the entire Yankee lineup managed against Sad Sam Jones. Buddy Myer's three-run homer was decisive in the second game, a 7–3 Washington triumph.

With New York's season now teetering, the Yankees gave it all they had a day later with veteran Herb Pennock pitching perhaps his best game of the season. The score was tied 2–2 in the bottom of the ninth when the Nationals' Dave Harris opened the inning with a shot to center field. Harry Rice ill-advisedly stretched out in a full dive in an attempt to catch it. He missed and the ball got behind him, permitting Harris to scamper all the way to third base. Pennock intentionally walked the next two batters to set up a force play, but he then surrendered a full-count single up the middle to Ray Spencer, and Washington had its third straight win.

The teams were tied again 2–2 the next day behind Roy Sherrid's best outing of the season, and things looked more promising for the Yanks when in the top of the tenth, Rice doubled and scored on a single by Ben Chapman. In the bottom of the tenth, Joe Judge opened with a single, and Sherrid began to weaken as he walked the next two hitters. Bob Shawkey brought in Henry Johnson to try and save the one-run lead, but pinch-hitter Art Shires' ground ball found enough room up the middle to sneak through for a two-run game-winning single. The Yankees staggered out of town having lost six straight, a season-shattering slump that suddenly dropped them 6½ games off the pace. With New York's inconsistent and thin pitching, the damage was irreversible. The Yankees could manage only a 17–18 record through the month and faded from view.

"The trouble with the Yankees is that they have broken down defensively," said John Kieran of the *New York Times*. "A poor defense makes the pitching look bad."[2]

That left only the Nationals and the Athletics standing in the American League arena. Washington was flying high in early July, its four-game sweep of the Yankees during the middle portion of a ten-game winning streak put them back in first place — although only by a half-game as Philadelphia was playing well, too. After watching the Nationals sweep his Red Sox, Heinie Wagner was impressed with Walter Johnson's aggregate, calling them "the best team in the league," rating their infield the best, and their pitchers "without a doubt the best in the league as Johnson has at least five men who should turn out a victory every time they go to the hill." Wagner closed his comments by saying that "the acquisition of Manush just about guarantees the Nats the pennant."[3]

For the Athletics, the growing cacophony of admiration for Washington among the pundits, players and managers no doubt angered and motivated the world champions (Heinie Wagner was the third American League manager to publicly rate Washington better than Philadelphia — Roger Peckinpaugh of Cleveland and Bucky Harris of the Tigers had recently done the same).[4] They responded by shifting into high gear and staying there for the rest of the season. They would win 23 of 32 games in July. One day after Washington's ten-game win streak ended, the A's started an eight-game win streak of their own from July 10 to the 18th, during which they scored 97 runs. They started it with a 9–1 pasting of the fading Yankees. They destroyed the Browns in four straight, 15–7, 12–1, 9–7 and 11–6, and then turned their thunder on the White Sox by scores of 14–7, 12–8 and 15–1. Showing the depth of their lineup, the A's had either a three- or four-hit game from seven different players during the win streak. Miller and Simmons did it twice and Foxx accomplished the feat three times. Foxx also hit three homers during the streak, two of them in the last win when he also drove in six runs. With the eight straight wins, the Athletics regained first place and opened a 3½-game gap between themselves and the Nationals.

The Athletics were able to open this gap because the Nationals literally ran into a significant problem. Heinie Manush had been hitting at a .407 clip since joining Washington and had infused the lineup with both the enthusiasm and the punch that Walter Johnson had hoped for and expected. But in the second game of a July 9 doubleheader, he injured his leg running out a ground ball. At first, the injury was diagnosed as a groin muscle pull and thought to be severe enough that the team sent the outfielder home for weeks of rest. Two days later, however, another doctor examined the outfielder and declared Manush had only aggravated an old injury and that a couple of days of rest and ice packs would be enough to get him back on the field. While Walter Johnson was overjoyed at the newer, more positive prognosis, team trainer Mike Martin, who had spent his life recognizing and treating sports injuries, publicly scoffed at the doctor's opinion. He believed and said publicly that Manush suffered the muscle pull as originally diagnosed and that the player would be out for a considerable amount of time. Unfortunately for Washington, Martin proved to be right.

When Manush limped off the field in Boston on July 9, only one-half game separated Washington and Philadelphia. He missed the next 15 games, and the Nationals went 6–9, falling four games behind. Johnson was not pleased, and he publicly questioned his team's character.

"I expect us to be beaten at times," he told the *Washington Post*, "and I have no kick coming if we go down fighting. We are talking about winning a pennant but we are not playing that kind of ball."[5]

The heart of the Philadelphia Athletics' batting order in 1930, Jimmie Foxx (left), Mickey Cochran (center) and Al Simmons, combined for 408 RBIs. Left Gomez once observed that with men on base, "Foxx was a pain but Simmons was a plague."

The losing began to ebb the Nationals' energy, and by the time they arrived in Chicago for a quartet of games beginning July 23, their morale was as low as it had been all season.

"We seem to be getting our slump now," Johnson sighed before his team took on the White Sox, "while the Mackmen keep on winning. I'm not worried particularly much, however, for I know the Athletics will have one [a slump] too, for all teams do. What I'm trying to do is get us out of our slump so that when Philadelphia experiences its letdown, we will be able to regain the ground we lost."[6]

In the week preceding the Chicago series, it had become a daily ritual for the Washington sportswriters to speculate and report that Manush was close to returning to the lineup. As the Chicago series began, one dissenting voice was Frank Young, a *Washington Post* sportswriter who suggested the Nationals continue to rest Manush.

"The Nats have beaten Chicago seven of eleven games this season and should have little trouble taking three of four," he reasoned. "The great rush to get Manush back in the lineup at this time is not apparent except to bolster the team mentally."[7]

Not heeding Frank Young's advice, Walter Johnson put Manush back in the lineup for the Chicago series. Manush responded grandly, going three-for-four in each of the first two games and one-for-four with three RBIs in the fourth game. However, his heroics did not inspire his teammates, who may have been guilty of taking the Sox as lightly as did Frank Young, and for this they paid dearly. The Sox ambushed the Nats in the first three games of the series, winning 10–4, 6–5 and 4–1. The Nationals salvaged the final game, 10–1.

At the same time, Philadelphia manhandled a dispirited Cleveland club, taking three of four to increase its league lead to six games. Emblematic of the Athletics' aggressive style of play was the second game of the series. Although Miller, Simmons and Max Bishop all smashed home runs to ignite a 14–1 victory, it was the A's base running that made the headlines. In one of baseball's rarest feats, the Athletics pulled off a triple steal — not once, but twice in the game. In the first inning, Simmons barreled home to score while Miller swiped third base and Dib Williams second base. To rub Cleveland's nose in it, they repeated the triple theft in the fourth inning, this time with Mickey Cochran scoring, Simmons taking third and Jimmie Foxx second.

It was a cocky group of Athletics that boarded the train after the fourth game in Cleveland. They headed down to Washington for a pair of contests against their only remaining challengers and they were confident a sweep would all but bury the Nationals as contenders. Many who had watched the A's elevate their game in the previous few weeks agreed that Connie Mack's boys had reason to be confident. "The way they are playing," marveled John Kiernan of the *New York Times*, "nothing can halt the Mackmen but a train wreck."[8]

The A's were firing on all cylinders, the team smacking the ball at a .297 clip, their 621 runs scored second to New York's 669 but well ahead of any other team. The defense was solid, having committed only 96 errors — the only AL club under 100 at this point in the season. Foxx (.349, 27 home runs, 104 RBIs) and Simmons (.393, 22 homers, 99 RBIs) were doing the damage expected of them against opposing pitchers, and Cochran (.375) was guiding and cajoling a pitching staff boasting the league's top two winners in George Earnshaw at 16–6 and Lefty Grove with a 15–4 record.

The Nationals were in a darker mood on their train trip home. To a man they knew they had dug themselves a deep hole by blowing the Chicago series and now they faced a pair of must-win games against Philadelphia. For Walter Johnson, the Chicago series was an unpleasant reminder of the problems of 1929 when the Nationals consistently failed to play up to their potential and too frequently lost to inferior teams. Despite his own exhaustion, he was determined to figure a way to recapture the determination and energy that his team displayed early in the season. A very tired Johnson believed that getting home, seeing his family and sleeping in his own bed would rejuvenate him.

All of Johnson's worries about the Athletics, the pennant race and his team's inconsistencies vaporized the moment he got off the train in Union Station. He was told that only hours earlier, his wife, to whom he had been devoutly married since 1914, had been taken to the hospital suffering from heat exhaustion — a condition brought on by an unmerciful heat wave that had baked the eastern half of the country for the past few weeks.

Hazel Lee Rogers Johnson was a vibrant 36-year-old woman and a one-time Washington socialite. She was the daughter of Edwin Roberts, who was Nevada's lone congressman when he introduced Johnson to his daughter 17 years earlier. Walter and Hazel went through a proper courtship and a quiet wedding, building a happy marriage around four children and their unquestioned love and fidelity. She was going through the usual challenges of a mother with four young children and had been particularly drained during the hour-to-hour care she provided for her 15-year-old son as he recovered from the traffic accident that broke both his legs. While Walter and the Nationals were on their most recent road trip, Hazel had packed the kids in the car and driven to Kansas to visit relatives. She drove all the way back home in the worst of the heat wave, which transformed their unventilated car into a blast furnace on wheels.

Johnson immediately headed to Georgetown Hospital where he spent the entire night at her bedside. By morning, the doctors and Hazel reassured Johnson that rest and relaxation was all she needed to restore her vigor. He felt confident enough in their diagnosis that he made it to Griffith Stadium in time for the game against the A's.

President Herbert Hoover was also on hand for the first time since Opening Day and announced to Johnson and Clark Griffith that he was there to lead the Nationals out of their slump — no small task considering Lefty Grove was on the mound for the Athletics.

While Grove mastered the Nationals' lineup through the early innings, Philadelphia scored in the second inning on singles by Foxx, Williams and

Mr. and Mrs. Walter Johnson. Her unexpected death in August of 1930 devastated the Washington manager. He was never the same again — on or off the field.

Jimmy Dykes, and then added two more in the third when Cochran tripled, Simmons walked, Foxx lifted a sacrifice fly to score Cochran, and Simmons came all the way around on two throwing errors. Manush (double) and Joe Cronin (single) combined to get Washington on the board in the fourth to make the score 3–1. In the fifth, Dykes slammed a two-run triple and scored when Grove tripled. Grove scored on a Bishop single, and the A's had a 7–1 advantage. The Nationals seemed as dead as the heavy Washington air.

The Nationals stirred a slight breeze in the sixth inning when Judge and Cronin singled, and both scored on an Ossie Bluege double. Bluege came home on utility man Jackie Hayes' single to make it 7–4. The winds of a comeback began to blow more seriously in the eighth inning when Cronin and Hayes both singled off Grove with two out and pinch-hitter Dave Harris walked to load the bases for Buddy Myer, a gritty and pesky hitter who had been mired in a two-week slump. With the crowd screaming for a clutch hit, Grove offered and Myer let loose, but his drive to center field was too high and Miller was able to catch up to it for the third out. Grove allowed a Judge double in the ninth but left him stranded, giving the A's the victory and a seven-game lead.

"At least we put up a battle," manager Johnson said afterwards. "We had Grove on the verge of being yanked twice. I see signs of us coming out of our slump and I wouldn't be surprised if we started off by winning tomorrow."[9]

A spirited and feisty Johnson arrived at Griffith Stadium the next day convinced his team would end its slump and turn the season around with this game. He was shouting encouragement to get his players in the same frame of mind when he was told he had a phone call in the clubhouse. When he emerged, an ashen and shaken Johnson asked Joe Judge, his best friend on the team, to take over the manager's duties as he was headed immediately back to the hospital. To the doctors' surprise and chagrin, Hazel had taken a turn for the worse.

By game time, most of the players had surmised why Johnson had left, and without anyone saying so out loud, they all vowed to do whatever was necessary to win this game for their manager.[10]

The crowd was also unaware of the dramatic events involving Johnson as they watched starters Bump Hadley and George Earnshaw throw five scoreless innings at each other before the Mackmen opened the scoring in the sixth. Eric McNair slapped a double, becoming the first Philadelphia player in the game to reach second base, and he moved to third when Doc Cramer beat out a bunt. Cochran walked to load the bases, bringing up Simmons, who, as he usually did in big situations, delivered. He ripped a shot to right field for extra bases. Both McNair and Cramer scored easily and Cochran came chugging around third as Rice heaved a desperation throw towards the plate. It went right into the glove of catcher Spencer, and he tagged out his Philadelphia counterpart to the raucous delight of the crowd. They had little time to savor the play, however, as Miller rapped a two-bagger to score Simmons with the third run. In the top of the ninth, Dykes singled in an insurance tally, making it 4–0. The Nationals' bats had been silent all day against Earnshaw and now only three outs stood between the A's and an eight-game lead.

Sam West was first up and he grounded a ball through the left side for a

Connie Mack (right) holds his ever-present scorecard in one hand and greets fellow manager Walter Johnson before the A's and Senators waged one of their titanic 1930 battles.

single. Bluege followed and beat out a swinging bunt to the delight of the crowd. At this point Judge, making his first key decision as manager, sent rookie Joe Kuehl up to hit for Hayes. Kuehl had just joined the club the day before, and in his inaugural big league at-bat, worked the count full against the veteran Earnshaw. The crowd stood transfixed as Earnshaw delivered the payoff pitch. It missed the strike zone and Kuehl did not offer. The rookie trotted down to first and the bases were loaded with none out. Dave Harris, another pinch-hitter, stepped in against the suddenly shaky Earnshaw. To the deafening roar of the grandstand, Harris clobbered a pitch to right field where Cramer, subbing for the injured Mule Haas, could not catch up to it. The ball banged against the right field wall while West and Bluege scored, Kuehl went to third base and Harris, limping on a recently injured ankle, turned first and headed for second. Cramer, making a fast recovery, delivered a true throw to Bishop as Harris began his slide. The second baseman caught the ball and quickly brought it down for a slap tag, but not before Harris' foot reached the base; the crowd went into a delirium when he was called safe. With the score 4–2, the tying run was at second with none out. Never one to baby his pitchers when the season's stakes were at their highest, Connie Mack calmly signaled to his bullpen and summoned his best. Lefty Grove, despite having pitched a complete-game victory the day before, answered the call.

To counter this move, Judge sent up his third straight pinch-hitter, a seldom-used first baseman and former catcher named Patsy Gharrity. At this point in his career, Gharrity was 38 years old. He had been one of Walter Johnson's favorite catchers when Johnson was in his prime. Gharrity, a career .262 hitter with little power, stopped playing regularly in 1923 and had become one of Johnson's coaches in Washington. He was activated for a few games in 1929 and again in 1930. This appearance against Grove would be his only at-bat of the season. Not surprisingly, he was overmatched, and all he could do was pop up one of Grove's fastballs to Dykes at third base for the first out.

Rice, still hitting a blistering .350 for the season, stepped in next. He swung hard and rapped a ground ball at shortstop Williams, who fielded it cleanly, allowed Kuehl to score and Harris to go to third while he threw Rice out at first base. Now with two out, it was up to the day's player-manager, no slouch with a season average at .330, to be the hero. Judge stood ready in the batters' box as Grove fired another heater. Much like Gharrity, Judge got under the ball and lifted a fly straight up, which Williams snagged for the final out. Grove had snuffed out the Washington rally and with the 4–3 win, the A's boarded their train for home with the Nationals now eight games in their rearview mirror.

If that was not bad enough for Washington, the Yankees had put together a mini-spurt in the last week of July, winning four of five, including three straight against Boston by scores of 8–2, 10–1 and 14–13. While it did not put

New York back into contention, the streak did move the Yankees with one and one-half games of second place.

After the game, word of the Johnson family plight began to spread through the city and suddenly no one cared a lick how far Washington was behind Philadelphia or ahead of New York. All attention focused on the Intensive Care Unit at Georgetown Hospital.

American League Notes for July

Lou Gehrig led the Yankees' end-of-July spurt. In the Yanks' last four games of the month, he had ten hits in 18 at-bats, vaulting him ahead of Al Simmons in the batting race, .392 to Simmons' .383. Three of his teammates were in the top ten as well—Babe Ruth at .363 (and leading baseball with 39 home runs), Bill Dickey at .362 and Earle Combs at .349.

Gehrig smashed four home runs in the four games (one a grand slam), giving him 33 for the year; he also collected 18 RBIs, giving him 135 and thrusting him considerably ahead of Jimmie Foxx (110), Al Simmons (109) and Babe Ruth (105).

The Yankees were hitting .315; Cleveland (.307) was the only other American League club over .300, while Washington was at .299.

Lefty Grove was the winning pitcher on July 25 against Cleveland, a win which started a mind-boggling stretch of excellence. Grove would win 46 of his next 50 decisions through September 24, 1931.

American League Standings on July 31, 1930

	W	L	Pct.	GB
Philadelphia	69	34	.700	–
Washington	59	40	.596	8
New York	59	43	.578	9.5
Cleveland	53	50	.515	16
Detroit	48	56	.462	21.5
Chicago	43	58	.426	25
St. Louis	42	62	.404	27.5
Boston	35	65	.350	32.5

The National League

Rube Marquard came to the New York Giants in 1908 and after a few nondescript seasons, burst into stardom with a 24–7 record in 1911, followed by records of 26–11 and 23–10 in his next two seasons. In 1914, he slipped to 12–22. Convinced Marquard had lost his stuff, John McGraw decided to jettison the 28-year-old southpaw. He sold him to his Brooklyn rival, Wilbert Robinson.

Uncle Robbie did not use Marquard for the first few weeks he was on the roster, saving him for when the Giants came to Ebbets Field. That day Robinson told Marquard to secretly warm up out of sight, and when the game got underway, Uncle Robbie sprang Marquard as a surprise starter and the hurler responded with a ten inning, 1–0 win.

"Robbie was always looking to put something over on McGraw," Marquard remembered. "I still remember how he grabbed his left cuff with his right hand and laughed up his sleeve right in front of McGraw."[11]

Wilbert Robinson was still laughing and John McGraw was still scowling 16 years later. As their teams prepared for a Fourth of July doubleheader at the Polo Grounds, Robinson playfully held court in the Brooklyn dugout, complaining to all who would listen about the cost of feeding his six dogs and wondering what kind of gasoline was best for his car.

In the other dugout, the humorless McGraw was not in a celebratory Fourth of July mood. Bad enough his team was in third place, but Wilbert Robinson's team was in first. McGraw was well aware of the long-standing baseball maxim that the team in first place on Independence Day usually won the pennant. McGraw, however, could take solace in two things. First, the Robins' lead over the second-place Cubs was only a few percentage points. Second, if his Giants swept this three-game series, his boys would pull within two and one-half games of his former friend and business partner.

No doubt Robinson had a few guffaws in the early innings of the first game as his team jumped out to a 4–0 lead, two of the runs coming on Babe Herman's 19th home run. McGraw would have the last laugh, however. The Little Napoleon brought in Hub Pruett and then Fred Fitzsimmons in relief and they combined for five innings of no-hit relief while the Giants' offense shifted into gear. Shanty Hogan started the comeback with a two-run homer in the seventh off Dazzy Vance, and Bill Terry brought his team within one with an eighth-inning sacrifice fly. Vance recorded one out in the bottom of the ninth before Hogan doubled, and with two out, outfielder Wally Roettger ripped a two-strike single to center field to tie the game. Vance got the third out to force extra innings. In the bottom of the eleventh, Bob O'Farrell worked Vance for a walk and then Travis Jackson doubled him to third. Roettger, batting in the eighth spot, was intentionally walked to allow Vance to get at opposing pitcher Fitzsimmons. The hurler swung and bounced one toward the middle, but Neal Finn grabbed the ball and threw home to nip O'Farrell on the force play. Next up was the leadoff hitter, Howie Critz. He got a Vance pitch to his liking and dropped a liner into center field for a game-winning single.

In the second game, the Robins broke out to a 4–0 lead again, only this time they prevailed, 5–2, as starting pitcher Bill Clark allowed only six hits.

The Giants made the third game of the series anticlimactic when they sent

By 1930, the long-raging feud between John McGraw (left) and Wilbert Robinson prevented them from shaking hands during traditional pre-game photograph opportunities.

14 men to the plate in the fifth inning and scored nine runs en route to an 11–3 victory. This loss dropped the Robins out of first place, an extra-added measure of satisfaction for McGraw. The two teams were scheduled to meet at the Polo Grounds for a single game in one week, but before that, the Robins would meet Boston for five games and the Giants would play Philadelphia six times.

The last-place Phillies arrival to the Polo Grounds on July 6 brought together two of the best hitting teams in the game — the Giants' team average was .313 to Philadelphia's .326.

"The Phillies are leading the league in club batting," observed an unimpressed John Kiernan of the *New York Times*, "which proves nothing except that pitching is very important, especially if you haven't got it."[12]

The Giants swept the doubleheader in New York, 10–8 and 6–2, with Terry, Jackson, Fred Lindstrom and Fred Leach each hitting home runs on the day. The teams moved to the Baker Bowl for the next four games and the Giants jumped on top in the initial game with four first-inning runs. Chuck Klein responded with a two-run homer in the fourth (his 24th to tie Hack Wilson for the league lead), and Lefty O'Doul hit a three-run shot as part of a five-run fifth as the Phils took control, 10–7. Two hits and three Philly errors helped the Giants tie the score, 10–10, in the top of the sixth, but the Phils bunched together three singles in the bottom of the inning to regain a one-run lead. Each team scored once in the eighth to give the Phillies a 12–11 lead going to the ninth. It was no shock to anyone that the Phils could not hold the lead in the ninth. The Giants loaded the bases with two out and Lindstrom singled to right-center on a two-strike pitch to put New York ahead, 13–12. It was equally unsurprising that the Phils' offense rallied in the bottom of the ninth. They loaded the bases with two out, and with Klein due up, John McGraw brought in Carl Hubbell to save the game. Hubbell won this duel of future Hall of Famers by striking out Klein.

After the Phils won two relatively tame affairs, the Giants took the getaway game, 19–8, pounding out 26 hits, five of them by Lindstrom, whom McGraw pulled from the game in the sixth inning to rest his still-bothersome leg. Klein knocked his league-leading 25th home run, but the Phils were already training 17–0 when he connected.

While the Giants won four of six from the Phillies, Brooklyn bullied the Boston Braves, taking four of five games. At least one Robin had three hits in each of the five games—Babe Herman did it three times, including hitting home runs 20 and 21; Wally Gilbert, Johnny Frederick, Neal Finn and newcomer Ike Boone also managed the three-hit trick. In the meantime, the Cubs dropped four straight to the lowly Cincinnati Reds, jumping Brooklyn back into first place when the Robins returned to New York for their single-game return match with the Giants on July 12. If seeing the Robins back in first place put John McGraw in a bad mood, he was positively sour at the end of the day after watching his team commit five errors and lose, 10–4.

Joe McCarthy's Cubs split their July 4 doubleheader with the Pirates at Forbes Field. They won the first game behind a rookie southpaw named Bud Teachout, who threw zeros at the Pirates until the ninth inning, but in the nightcap they were tamed, 5–1, by Ray Kremer, Pittsburgh's best pitcher. The Cubbies easily won the rubber game of their series the next day, 12–3, as Hack Wilson drove home three runs, giving him 80 RBIs for the season — an impressive number but not one that suggested the explosive, record-shattering performance still lurking in his bat. In fact, his 80 RBIs at this point of the season only equaled teammate Kiki Cuyler's total, and trailed Chuck Klein's 91. At this juncture, he also lagged behind all four premier American League sluggers Ruth, Gehrig, Foxx and Simmons.

The Cubs left Pittsburgh for Cincinnati, where a seventh-place Reds team was lying in wait.

Howling Dan Howley had a lightly talented team at Crosley Field but that was the only kind of squad Howley knew. He had just come off a three-year stint managing the St. Louis Browns, where he made a name for himself by bringing in a roster of no-names to a surprisingly strong third-place finish in 1928. When new ownership took over the Reds in 1930, they were determined to revive their lagging franchise and began by hiring the inspirational Howley. They then sought to acquire veteran players, which they did. Unfortunately for Cincinnati, these veterans were past their prime and did nothing for the roster but age it. The Reds were the only team in the major leagues with an average age over 30.

Their biggest name was outfielder Harry Heilmann. He first came to the major leagues with the Detroit Tigers in 1914, where under the tutelage of manager Ty Cobb he became one of the greatest right-handed hitters in American League history. Because he mostly played for second-division teams during an era of glorified sluggers, the quiet and gentlemanly Heilmann and his hitting exploits are largely forgotten. A four-time American League batting champion, he is one of eight players in the 20th century to hit over .400 in a season — .403 in 1923. In his three other batting championship seasons, he missed hitting .400 by only a few hits—1921 (.394), 1925 (.393) and 1927 (.398). He was also a productive power hitter, registering eight seasons of at least 100 RBIs. His career .342 batting average ranks 13th in baseball history. The 35-year-old Heilmann would challenge the .400 mark as late as June in 1930, and he finished the season at .333 with 91 RBIs.

Another veteran acquisition was left fielder Bob Meusel, a staple of the Yankee championship teams of the 1920s. Managers and teammates suggested the sullen and moody outfielder never fully achieved his potential because of an indifferent attitude that followed him throughout his career.[13] Nevertheless, he led the American League in home runs and RBIs in 1925, and, in his prime, he was considered among the top defensive outfielders in the game. He also had very good speed, leading the Yanks in stolen bases five times, and twice stealing home in the World Series. By 1930, the 33-year-old outfielder's skills had eroded considerably and in this, his last season, he would contribute only a .289 average, ten home runs, 62 RBIs and nine stolen bases.

Horace "Hod" Ford was a 32-year-old second baseman who broke into the major leagues as a shortstop in 1919. Always considered among the league's best fielders, he was never much of a hitter, even in this season of inflated averages when he posted a .231 mark. The highest he ever hit in his 15 seasons was .279 (twice).

Leo Durocher was the team's young shortstop. He would spend five decades in the game thanks as much to his shrewd self-promotion as his skills as a player or manager. He hit .247 in a 16-year career, during which he gained a reputation as a hard-nosed hustler with an abrasive manner. He hit .243 for the Reds in 1930, and three years later was traded to St. Louis where he had his best playing years and forged his long-term relationship with Branch Rickey. Rickey gave Durocher his start as a manager in Brooklyn, and in over 20 years of managing, Durocher would win 2,010 games piloting the Dodgers, Giants, Cubs and Astros.

Eppa Rixey was the elder statesman of the Reds' pitching staff and today remains another Hall of Famer largely forgotten because he toiled for less-successful teams. Rixey was a lanky 6-foot 5-inch gentleman Virginian who rode an unconventionally twisted windup and excellent control to a 21-year career in the National League. He started with eight on-and-off years for the Phillies, and then blossomed in Cincinnati where he won 20 games four times and won in double figures ten straight seasons. When he retired in 1933, his 266 victories made him the winningest left-handed pitcher in National League history, a distinction he eventually yielded to Warren Spahn. His career record is tinged by the fact he lost 251 games, still a record for southpaws. In 1930, he was pushing 40 years of age and would amass a brutal 9–13 record and 5.10 ERA. He managed to hang on for three more seasons and two years hence, at age 42, would compile an impressive streak of 27 consecutive scoreless innings.

This uneven Reds team toiled in the second division all season, but the Cubs caught them just as they were hitting a hot streak. The Reds swept four games, beginning with a July 6 doubleheader. They won the opening game, 5–4, with three runs in the bottom of the ninth — a rally which featured three consecutive hits by three consecutive pinch-hitters against Sheriff Blake. In the second game, the Cubs rallied from a 7–1 deficit to even the score, only to lose when the Reds scratched across a run in the bottom of the eighth. Both Hack Wilson and Gabby Hartnett wasted home runs during the afternoon. The next day, the Reds scored a 4–2 win, and then completed the sweep with a 5–4 triumph on July 9 when Durocher successfully squeezed home the winning run in the bottom of the tenth.

"A play almost extinct in present day baseball," said the *Chicago Tribune*, "the venerable squeeze play was employed in the tenth inning and when the end came [for the Cubs] their feet were almost as flat as their spirits."[14]

The Reds would go on to win three more in a row from Philadelphia to run their win streak to seven before it was stopped by the Giants on July 13.

The Cubs moved on to Boston where they split four games and then headed to New York, arriving at the same time as the St. Louis Cardinals. Both midwestern teams were in Gotham for what amounted to a round-robin tournament among the four contending clubs—first the Cubs would visit Brooklyn for five games while the Cards played four at the Polo Grounds. Then the Cards would move to Brooklyn and the Cubs to the Polo Grounds, each for a five-game set.

The matchup between the Cubs and Robins got ugly early. They played a doubleheader on July 16, which was watched by a capacity crowd whose collective mood became more tense and angry as the day wore on. The Cubs disappointed the Flatbush faithful with three early runs and were controlling the game, 5–2, with two out in the eighth inning when Robins first baseman Del Bissonette drove an extra-base hit deep to center field. The hit scored a run, and Bissonette, not satisfied with a triple, turned and headed for home at full speed. The relay throw to catcher Hartnett beat Bissonette to the plate and the ensuing collision sent both men reeling into an angry cloud of dust. Hartnett emerged, holding the ball. He had successfully blocked the plate and denied the run. Bissonette was out—literally. He had to be carried off the field and did not appear in the second game. The crowd, already frustrated with the way the Cubs were handily controlling the game and fired up after witnessing Joe McCarthy get tossed for vehemently arguing a call, poured down their wrath on Hartnett as he headed back to the Cubs' dugout. They jeered him fiercely and pelted him with anything they could find to throw. A pair of bottles just missed his head. Nothing the fans did changed the outcome—the Cubs won, 6–4.

In the third inning of the second game, umpire Bill Klem called Glenn Wright out on a close play at second base, reigniting the jeers and the bottle throwers. A few innings later, Brooklyn starter Dolf Luque was hit by a Charlie Root pitch and angrily charged the mound. Both pitchers were separated before blows could be exchanged. Luque got sweet revenge, chucking six shutout innings and riding Wright's fourth home run in three days to a 5–3 victory.

The next day, July 17, Brooklyn rallied from a 3–0 deficit to tie the game in the eighth inning and force extra frames. Babe Herman, constantly maligned for his lack of defensive prowess, made two sparkling outfield plays to save Brooklyn. In the tenth, he played the carom of a Guy Bush ringer off the right field wall perfectly and gunned a strike to Wright at second base to nail the over-aggressive pitcher, who was trying for a double. In the 12th inning, Herman raced back on a Hartnett blast and with his back to the plate snared the ball at full gallop by the wall. The Cubs got smart in the 13th inning and stayed away from Herman and right field, with Clarence "Footsie" Blair, Woody

English, Kiki Cuyler and Riggs Stevenson all poking hits to the left field side, bringing home three runs and a 6–3 Cubs win.

Bissonette was back in the lineup on July 18 and he whacked a two-run home run for Brooklyn. His inspirational moment, however, was easily negated by long balls from Wilson, English and Clyde Beck as the Cubs won again, 6–2. Wilson's shot was his 25th of the year, but Chuck Klein hit two during a 13–6 loss to Cincinnati to give him 27.

Wilson hit another home run the next day as the Cubs made it four of five against their hosts, winning 5–4. The Robins wasted Babe Herman's 22nd home run.

Over at the Polo Grounds, no one was quite sure what to make of the Cardinals. Every time it seemed the National League race was slimming down to the Robins, Giants and Cubs, the Redbirds would surge. They swept a Fourth of July doubleheader from the Reds in Cincinnati, 15–4 and 6–2, and then completed the series sweep the next day, 6–4. Starters Flint Rhem, Syl Johnson and Hi Bell all pitched complete games. On July 6, the Cards took another doubleheader, this time from the Pirates, 2–1 and 12–4. This moved them within four games of first place and within a half-game of the third-place Giants. Then, as they had been doing all season, the Cards tripped over themselves, losing four of their next five to the Pirates and stumbling to seven and one-half games back.

The first two Cardinal-Giant games were thrilling. In the first one, the Redbirds got 20 hits to the Giants' 15 and the Cards committed four errors to the Giants' five. New York built a 9–2 lead through five innings, the highlight being Bill Terry's three-run upper-deck homer to the opposite field. The teams traded middle-inning runs, bringing the Cardinals to bat in the ninth inning, trailing 12–5. They scored on a single, a couple of outs and a wild pitch. Terry made an error on what should have been the last out of the game, and with the additional life, outfielder George Watkins hit one of his 17 home runs on the season to make it 12–8. Two walks and a single loaded the bases and Ernie Orsatti slapped a base hit to make the score, 12–9. McGraw brought on Carl Hubbell, who saved the day by getting catcher Jim Wilson on a ground ball.

In the next day's game, Terry and Mel Ott drove in first-inning runs with singles and a Fred Lindstrom homer in the third gave the Giants a 3–0 lead. Frankie Frisch took over at this point for St. Louis, walloping a three-run homer in the third and a two-run shot in the eighth while teammate Watkins had two RBI hits to give St. Louis a 7–3 lead going to the bottom of the ninth. Travis Jackson and Wally Roettger opened the last frame with singles. After Bob O'Farrell struck out, Howie Critz singled home Jackson and then Ethan Allen walked. Burleigh Grimes came on in relief, but Lindstrom singled home Roettger and Terry singled home Critz and Allen to tie the game. Grimes walked Ott and fanned Shanty Hogan for the second out, leaving it up to Jackson. In his second at-bat of the inning, the shortstop drove a single to left field to score Terry to win the game 8–7.

Knowing they could not afford to lose any more ground or games to the Giants, the Cardinals' survival instinct kicked into gear the next day. They came out and took a doubleheader from the Giants, 4–1 and 8–4. Jess Haines made quick work of the Giants in the first game with a seven-hitter, and in the nightcap a three-run homer by Gus Mancuso and a solo shot by Chick Hafey was the difference.

The Cards moved to Brooklyn on July 20 for four games and it was very much the Frankie Frisch show for St. Louis. In the first game, he smashed his third home run in two games and added a double while driving in six runs as the Cardinals won, 15–6.

The teams split a crazy doubleheader on July 21 with the fans being treated to 44 runs, 54 hits, seven home runs—four by pinch-hitters—three triples, eight doubles and 11 errors. In the opener, Frisch and Jim Bottomley homered as did pinch-hitters Mancuso and George Puccinelli as the Cards built an 8–6 lead heading into the ninth inning. However, in the bottom of the ninth, pinch-hitter Harvey Hendrick swatted a two-out, two-strike, three-run homer to make the Robins 9–8 winners. In the second game, Brooklyn's Hal Lee came off the bench to slug his first major-league home run, becoming the fourth pinch-hitter on the day to hit one over the fence. Lee's blast was not enough as the Cards racked up 18 hits, with three by Frisch (including another home run), and they prevailed, 17–10.

The Robins' pitchers took control, holding the Cardinals to one run in the remaining two games. Hollis Thurston tossed a three-hit 1–0 shutout on July 22 and Dolf Luque did the honors on July 23, winning 4–1.

Over at the Polo Grounds, the Giants and Cubs did some slugging of their own. Hack Wilson hit his 27th home run in the opening game to help the Cubs build a 4–0 lead, but the Giants pounded out 17 hits and overcame Chicago, 13–5. Fred Leach had four hits, including a home run.

Wilson hit two the next day (numbers 28 and 29) and Pat Malone pitched one of his best games of the season, clamping down the Giants on eight hits in a 6–0 win.

A doubleheader on July 22 saw the teams split—the Cubs won the opener, 6–3, and the Giants the nightcap, 6–1. To win the first game, the Cubs broke a 3–3 tie in the ninth inning on hits by Kiki Cuyler, Wilson, Zack Taylor and Charlie Grimm. The Giants rode a grand slam by Ethan Allen to the second-game victory. The McGrawmen won the fifth and deciding game of the series, 8–6, scoring four decisive runs in the fifth inning aided by five walks—two with the bases loaded.

Chicago and St. Louis left town with little decided. Brooklyn had fared the worst in the round-robin dates, going 4–6 and seeing its league lead shaved from three games to one game by the Cubs.

Brooklyn would recover to go 7–3 for the rest of July by beating up on Cincinnati and Philadelphia. They finished the month with a 21–14 record. The Giants kept pace with a 7–2 mark at the end of the month, earning them a 21–12 record, the best mark among National League teams in July. St. Louis, long past the early-month surge that had pushed them into contention, had a disastrous last week of July, going 3–6 against Pittsburgh and Philadelphia. Having closed to within four games of first place after the Fourth of July, the Cardinals ended the month 11 games behind and one game under .500.

On July 23, the day the round-robin series concluded in New York, the Phillies lost a doubleheader to Pittsburgh, 2–1 and 16–15. Pie Traynor hit home runs to decide both games—a solo shot in the ninth inning of the first game and a three-run blast in the 13th inning of the nightcap. The second game saw the teams combine for 50 hits, including three each for Lefty O'Doul and Chuck Klein, giving them both .405 averages. These losses started an 11-game losing streak for Philadelphia, even though they scored 68 runs or 6.1 runs per game in the 11 games. In reporting that more and more minor league teams were experimenting with night baseball, and at the same time pointing out that the Phillies had just recently scored 30 runs in two games and lost them both, *New York Times* columnist John Kiernan wrote, "The Phillies' pitchers are said to be in favor of night baseball with no lights turned on at all. That would give them an even chance with the batters."[15]

Two of the notable games during the Phils' skein came against Chicago. On July 24, the Cubs outscored the Phils, 19–15, in a game that featured 34 hits, 29 of them singles (the other five were doubles). Chicago leadoff batter "Footsie" Blair had three at-bats in the first two innings as the Cubs scored 13 times. The Phils went into the bottom of the eighth inning trailing, 18–8, and scored seven runs and had two men on base when umpire Lou Jorda called Klein out on strikes. The normally mild-mannered Klein exploded, and after a violent argument, he was tossed from the game, causing him to miss the ninth inning. It was the only inning he missed all season.

A few days later, on July 27, the Cubs enjoyed a 16–2 feast, with Hack Wilson clubbing three homers and driving in five runs. He finished the month with 33 home runs and 104 RBIs (he would get 45 percent of his record-setting RBI total in August and September).

The Cubs were only 15–15 in July but closed the month in second place, only two behind Brooklyn. Many considered it a masterful piece of managing by Joe McCarthy, considering his veteran pitchers were mostly delivering subpar performances, and the team had to deal with the death of popular pitcher

Hal Carlson as well as significant injuries to Riggs Stevenson, Charlie Grimm, infielder Les Bell (who was supposed to be the team's starting third baseman), and Rogers Hornsby.

"The Cubs, with all their injuries, have needed a pilot more than any team in the league," said revered *Chicago Tribune* sportswriter Arch Ward. "They have players of various mental abilities and personality traits and it has been no mean task to weld them into an efficient and concerted machine. It has taken strength of human nature as well as a baseball mind to take a last place team like the Cubs and build them up to title contenders and eventual league champions. And it has been even harder to hold that level."[16]

"McCarthy once more is proving to the baseball world that he is one of the greatest managers of modern times," agreed George Barton of the *Minneapolis Tribune*. "Along with being a strategist, he is a natural leader of men."[17]

Not everyone shared that sentiment. Rogers Hornsby had become restless and began making noise about rushing back to the lineup as soon as his cast was removed. McCarthy doubted it would be a wise move.

"Hornsby's broken ankle may have mended," said the skipper, "but even if it has, I doubt he could get into a game for two or three weeks. If he isn't in top shape I wouldn't dare take a chance on crippling him again."[18]

The egocentric Hornsby did not appreciate McCarthy's cautious view. He had convinced himself that he would be a better manager for the Cubs and that McCarthy's statement was a ploy to keep him out of the lineup. Hornsby was sure McCarthy saw him as a threat to his job security.[19] Hornsby's ensuing actions made his perception self-fulfilling. Hornsby began studying games and bending the ear of Cubs owner William Wrigley with less-than-stellar appraisals of McCarthy's managerial ability.... According to Hornsby, McCarthy was not handling the pitchers correctly ... he was playing Cuyler too much and wearing him out ... he was too lenient with the carousing Hack Wilson. Wrigley, still devastated at the way the Cubs lost the 1929 World Series, began to listen.[20]

National League Notes for July

Cy Williams, a 42-year-old outfielder, replaced Chuck Klein after the slugger was thrown out of the July 24 game with the Cubs. It was the last appearance for Williams, in what was his 19th season. He was the first National League player to reach 200 career home runs, won four National League home runs crowns (1916, 1920, 1923, 1927), and his 251 career home runs had been the league's all-time high until surpassed by Hornsby in 1929.

Fred Lindstrom had his third five-hit game of the season against the Phillies on July 10.

Chuck Klein and Lefty O'Doul remained an amazing tandem; Klein was hitting .411 at the end of July, O'Doul .402. The Phils were hitting .327 as a team. George Fisher of St. Louis, playing in only about half his team's games, was hitting .410. Babe Herman was at .397 and Bill Terry .396.

Chuck Klein ended the month with 113 RBIs. Hack Wilson had 104.

Ray Kremer of Pittsburgh led the league in wins at the end of July with 13.

National League Standings on July 31, 1930

	W	L	Pct.	GB
Brooklyn	60	39	.606	–
Chicago	58	41	.586	2
New York	55	44	.556	5
Pittsburgh	48	49	.495	11
St. Louis	48	49	.495	11
Boston	45	53	.459	14.5
Cincinnati	44	52	.458	14.5
Philadelphia	32	63	.337	26

7

August

Under a stark and relentless August sun, Jack Quinn retired the Boston Red Sox in the top of the seventh inning. His uniform shirt soaked through with sweat, the ageless pitcher, now 46, flipped his glove behind the Shibe Park pitching mound and started toward the Athletics' dugout. The brutal heat had drained him, and Quinn had to push his rubbery legs forward, first into a slow gallop and then with a burst of energy into a sprint as he reached the Athletics' dugout. After all, a 46-year-old pitcher cannot afford to hint at weariness or exhaustion — not with a battalion of young lions chomping at the bit for a chance to pitch in the major leagues.

The dugout provided no relief from the equatorial playing conditions. The sun was beating on the low roof, there was no air circulation, and players were cramped together shoulder-to-shoulder on the bench. Quinn decided not to take a seat, standing instead on the steps in the faint hope of catching a breeze of relief. He was due to bat in the inning, but he first grabbed the ladle floating on top of a large water bucket and took a few sips. The water was too warm to provide much relief, so he pulled off his cap made heavy with sweat, closed his eyes, and poured the remaining water over his head. As it trickled down his face, he heard the familiar and refined voice of his manager.

"That's enough for today, John," Connie Mack said softly. The patrician Mack, still the old-world gentleman, referred to almost all his players by their formal names. Dressed in his signature Victorian-style dark suit, Mack stood cool and statuesque among the sweating gaggle of players he managed, his only visible concession to the heat being the removal of his jacket and fanning himself with his ever-present scorecard. "It's too hot for you out there today." Quinn's immediate instinct was to protest, as it always was when someone suggested he was too old or too tired to play. Then, recalling the searing conditions he had been dealing with and the fact that his team was well on its way to a doubleheader sweep of the last-place Red Sox, he decided not to say a thing. Suddenly, the manager did something Quinn had never seen. Mack's normally taciturn and expressionless face broke out into a broad, almost impish grin. "We'll let the youngsters relieve you for the rest of the day," he said, returning to the bench without explaining the reason for his amusement. Quinn caught on a moment later when he caught sight of the man Mack had sent up to pinch-hit for him. It was the 43-year-old Eddie Collins — the oldest active player in baseball after Quinn.

Few truly appreciated the astounding amount of baseball history both Jack Quinn and Eddie Collins had witnessed and of which they had been part. The two men shared a special distinction at this point in their lives. They were the only remaining active players who began their careers in the first decade of the century — Quinn in 1909 with the Yankees and Collins in 1906 with Philadelphia.

Both men competed against 19th century immortals such as Cy Young, Wee Willie Keeler and Nap Lajoie, as well as 20th century superstars like Ty Cobb, Tris Speaker and Walter Johnson. Because they bridged the dead ball and modern eras of the game, they witnessed the emergence of the men responsible for that change — players like Babe Ruth, Lou Gehrig, Jimmie Foxx, Al Simmons and Charlie Gehringer.

They began playing when their deeds were reported only by newspapers and word of mouth, then by teletypes, and now by the burgeoning popularity of radio.

Both men pre-dated every major league ballpark in use in 1930 other than Sportsman's Park in St. Louis and the Baker Bowl in Philadelphia. They watched first hand as ball parks grew from turn-of-the-century, single-tiered wooden structures to the multi-tiered concrete-and-steel stadiums popping up throughout the country. The builders of these facilities were installing public address systems and electric lights while paving parking lots for the growing number of cars being driven to each game.

John Quinn Pincus had been a Pennsylvania coal miner before his talent to throw a baseball was discovered. Despite a healthy size, he was a control pitcher rather than a power pitcher. He was 25 when he came to the major leagues, and wound up pitching for 23 years, winning 247 games, throwing 27 complete games in 1914 (at the age of 30) and completing 18 games 14 years later (at the age of 44). Over the course of his career, Quinn would share the same dugout with a remarkable 31 Hall-of-Fame teammates and share the pitching mound with such stars as Jack Chesbro and Waite Hoyt in New York, Herb Pennock and Red Ruffing in Boston, and Eddie Cicotte in Chicago (in 1918, the year before the Black Sox scandal). He pitched with Chief Bender in the Federal League in 1915 and later with Lefty Grove in Philadelphia, two pitchers who started and ended their careers 38 years apart. Quinn would pitch until 1933, appearing in his last game at the age of 50.

Eddie Collins was finishing his career where it started. He arrived in Philadelphia in 1906 and quickly became one of the game's great hitters and a member of baseball's best infield—a superstar quartet known as Connie Mack's "$100,000 infield," reflecting the combined salaries of Collins, first baseman Stuffy McInnis, shortstop Jack Barry and third baseman Frank "Home Run" Baker. These Athletics won a world championship in 1910, giving Collins the chance to play against the Cubs' equally immortal infield of Tinkers, Evers and Chance in the World Series. The A's also won world championships in 1911 and 1913, with Collins playing against John McGraw's Giants and batting against the likes of Christy Mathewson. Collins also had a front-row dugout seat as the Miracle Braves upset his heavily favored A's in the 1914 World Series.

After nine years with Philadelphia, Connie Mack sold Collins to Chicago, where he played the next 13 years with the White Sox alongside Shoeless Joe Jackson and Hall of Famers Harry Hooper and Ted Lyons. He captained Chicago's legitimate 1917 world championship team and was one of the honest players on the infamous 1919 Black Sox. He returned to the A's in time to be part of the Athletics' historic 1928 roster, a team that just missed the pennant but boasted eight Hall of Famers (Quinn was on that team, too).

His confident and intellectual approach to the game and an intuitive understanding of its strategy earned him the nickname "Cocky." He was an excellent fielder, bunter and base runner, and finished his career with a .333 batting average and more than 3,000 hits. While he rarely led the American League in significant offensive categories (three times in runs scored and four times in stolen bases), he was always among the league leaders. Although he never won a batting title, he hit over .300 in 17 seasons. And while he only had one 200-hit season, he had ten in which he surpassed 180 hits. It was left for Bill James, the noted baseball historian who revolutionized statistical analysis of the game, to conclude that Collins was the greatest second baseman in history.

"Collins sustained a remarkable level of performance for a remarkably long time," James said. "His was the most valuable career any second baseman ever had."[1] Collins was elected to the Baseball Hall of Fame with Lajoie and Keeler in 1939.

As much as baseball is a game that reveres its history, it is also a game of the moment, and in this moment on August 3, 1930, Collins stepped in against Boston's Danny MacFayden. These days Collins was more of a coach and part-time manager for Connie Mack than he was a player. Although he was on the active roster, he only batted seven times in 1929, and this was only his second at-bat in 1930. Nonetheless, the basic talent and skill was still there, and when he saw a pitch from MacFayden that he liked, Collins slapped it through the infield for a single. It was his 3,315th career hit in what was his 9,949th at-bat. It turned out to be the last hit and the last at-bat in his incredible career.

Eddie Collins (right) confers with Connie Mack. The Hall of Fame second baseman was already more coach than active player in 1930, batting only twice all season, getting his 3,315th and final career hit in August.

The American League

By the time Walter Johnson reached Georgetown Hospital on the afternoon of July 31, his wife's condition had taken a severe downturn. Her condition was complicated by a case of pleurisy and she was weakening by the hour. The doctors told Johnson they would do all they could, but that he should prepare for the worst. He remained stoic and immovable from his wife's bedside as July gave way to August and Hazel's life gave way to the infection. The end came for Hazel Johnson in the early-morning hours of August 1. To describe Johnson as grief-stricken was as inadequate as describing him as a mere sports legend in Washington, D.C. He left the hospital and sequestered himself at his home with his five children in Alta Vista, Maryland, where he received condolences by the thousands from fans, Washington politicians, sports luminaries and even the president of the United States.

"Walter Johnson was kneeling at his wife's bedside when she died," wrote Roger Pippen of the *Baltimore News*. "He was born with a wonderful pitching arm, probably the greatest the game has ever known. And the Giver of that prized possession saw fit to guide the Big Swede over a road of trouble and disappointment and sorrow."[2]

While August 1 was a day off for the Nationals, they were obliged to travel north to New York for an August 2 doubleheader, and then head back to Washington for an August 3 twin bill against the Red Sox. They were then scheduled to head north to New York again for a game on August 4, but Mrs. Johnson's funeral was set for that day. The game was postponed and made part of another doubleheader on August 5.

It was a very different Washington Nationals team that Joe Judge was leading into New York. The players endured a sullen train ride to New York, vowing to sweep the upcoming week of critical games (four with New York, two with Boston and two in Philadelphia) so that whenever their manager rejoined them, they would be back in the middle of the pennant hunt. There were no smiles during the cab rides to the ball park, no light-hearted banter during batting practice and very little bench jockeying during the game. Their steely determination paid off with a sweep of New York, 9–3 and 9–5. Heinie Manush had one of his best days as a National, hitting three home runs and three singles in the two games and driving in five runs. The Nationals dominated both games, with the Yanks' only stir coming in the bottom of the ninth in the nightcap when Bill Dickey hit a towering foul to the right field seats that just missed being a game-tying grand slam home run. Dickey then grounded out harmlessly to end the game. With the two wins, Washington opened up a three-game lead on the Yanks for second place. The Bombers had no one to blame but themselves, having lost 11 of the 13 games on the season to Washington.

Walter Johnson (left) with his close friend Joe Judge, who managed the team while Johnson tried to cope with the death of his wife. Despite his stature (5 feet, 8 inches), Judge was one of the best fielding first basemen in the game.

The Nationals returned to Washington the next day to face a hapless Red Sox team that had not won since July 24 (ten straight losses). The all-business attitude won Washington the first game, 11–2, with Manush again the big gun, going four-for-four while rookie Joe Kuhel added two hits and three RBIs. However, their attitude could not solve the slants of Red Sox veteran Jack Russell in the second game. He limited the Nats to five hits and Boston snapped its losing streak, 7–1.

Baseball took a back seat the next morning as the Washington Nationals family gathered at Bethesda Episcopal Church. All of Walter Johnson's players were there and acted as honorary pallbearers while Clark Griffith and trainer Mike Martin led the active pallbearers. After a short, dignified ceremony, Mrs. Johnson was laid to rest in the Rockville Union Cemetery. The weather that day was oppressively hot, and it served as a haunting reminder to Johnson about the extreme weather conditions that had claimed his wife. Thermostats on Pennsylvania Avenue that day topped out at 104 degrees. It was a record eighth time that the city had endured a 100+ degree day in the same season. In Kansas, where Mrs. Johnson began her ill-fated car trip a week earlier, the temperature reached as high as 114.

Walter Johnson had little to say to anyone at the ceremony, and afterward he headed directly home, having been told by Clark Griffith to take as much time as he needed to recover, even if it meant the entire season.[3] Johnson biographer Jack Kavanagh said the tragedy of Hazel's death would "haunt him forever," and that it changed Johnson personally and as a manager.

"He managed more, left less to the judgment of the players, began to call pitches from the bench, and displayed a coldness toward the failure of others which replaced the forgiving shrug that had characterized his playing years," said Kavanagh. "The missing element in his life was his wife. Hazel had been the balance wheel."[4]

While Johnson grieved at home, his players parted from the church and headed directly to the train station for what had to seem an interminable train ride. They arrived in New York for another doubleheader on August 5 and continued their mastery over the Yankees with a 6–4 win in the first game. Acting Manager Judge hit a big home run to negate one hit by Babe Ruth. However, like the second game against Boston a few days earlier, Washington ran into a dominant starting pitcher in the nightcap — this time Red Ruffing — and lost, 7–1. Ruffing pitched a complete game and hit a home run to boot.

The Nationals left New York physically and emotionally spent. It was hardly the way to head into Philadelphia for a pair of critical games against the Athletics.

The Athletics team waiting for them enjoyed a seven and one-half game lead (six in the loss column). They opened their month with a 9–3 loss to the

Yankees, victimized by Babe Ruth's 40th home run, and then returned home to slash the Boston Red Sox in three of four games. Al Simmons drove in eight runs in the series, including hitting home runs 26 and 27.

There was some added drama in the first of the two games between Washington and Philadelphia on August 6 when Judge selected Sad Sam Jones to pitch. Jones had always been a competent major league pitcher, but some of the Athletics, most vocally Mickey Cochran, questioned his fortitude, pointing out that Jones' spot in the rotation never seemed to come up when Washington played the A's. Jones replied to Cochran's barbs by twirling a nifty five-hitter and winning the game, 5–1. The win nudged the Nationals to within six and one-half games of Philadelphia (five back in the loss column).

To make the win count for something, Washington had to win the next day as well. They got off on the right foot when Joe Cronin singled in the sixth inning, stole second and scored on Sam West's base hit. But this time the one-run lead was not enough. Mule Haas rapped a two-out triple in the bottom of the sixth for the A's, and after Cochran coaxed a walk, Simmons drove a game-tying single to left field. Next up was Jimmie Foxx, and he settled matters for the day with a prodigious clout to the roof in left field, giving the A's a 4–1 win and a split of the series.

Despite their stated determination, the Nationals only managed a 5–3 record in the crucial eight-game stretch while Johnson was gone, gaining them virtually no ground in the standings. They were tired and drained as they returned to Washington for a five-game series against the Indians and a reunion with their manager.

On August 10, the Detroit Tigers defeated the Boston Red Sox, 4–2, a result only the most die-hard Tigers fans cared much about. Tiger pitcher Earl Whitehill, a dependable middle-of-the-rotation starter who would win 218 games over 17 years and retire with the highest ERA (4.36) for any 200-game winner, won his ninth consecutive decision on this day while Tiger outfielder John Stone had his 27-game hitting streak snapped. Stone was making a name for himself in 1930 — he had the just-concluded hitting streak, stroked six extra-base hits in one doubleheader (May 3), and owned a .311 average for the season. He would hit over .300 for Detroit for the next three years, with his high-water mark coming in 1932 when he drove in 108 runs. He was traded to Washington where he continued to hit .300 for a few more years, but his continually diminishing run production eventually caused him to lose his starting job.

The win on August 10 pushed the Tigers' record to 56–57, just one game away from the .500 mark. It was the culmination of a long, difficult climb out of a hole the Tigers dug for themselves at the start of the season when they lost 19 of their first 28 games, virtually destroying any hope they had of being a factor in the pennant race.

The fact the team continued to play hard was a tribute to its professionalism and the leadership of manager Bucky Harris. They went 19–14 in July, opened August with six wins in a row, and Whitehill's win over Boston made it eight out of nine. They were finally playing like the team many experts in spring training thought could challenge the Yankees for second place. They certainly had talent.

To begin with, they had Charlie Gehringer at second base, one of the great all-around players in the history of the game. Gehringer's consistent level of excellence earned him the nickname "the Mechanical Man" from teammate Doc Cramer because, as he said, "you wind him up on opening day and forget about him."[5] Starting in 1926, Gehringer anchored Detroit's infield and was a feared slugger for 19 years. He became a full-time player in his third season, hitting .277. After that he hit over .300 in 13 of the next 14 seasons, exceeding .320 nine times. He also managed to accomplish a feat only one other player had ever done. Gehringer and Rogers Hornsby are the only two hitters to improve their home run/RBI/batting average numbers each year for five straight seasons. All told, Gehringer hit .321, had 2,839 hits, collected seven 200-hit seasons, and seven 100+ RBI seasons.

Detroit's Hall of Fame second baseman Charlie Gehringer hit .330 in 1930. He made such a habit of batting over .300 every season, he was dubbed "the Mechanical Man."

Wes Ferrell, in the book *Baseball When the Grass Was Real*, gave the pitcher's perspective on Gehringer: "He was the toughest hitter I ever faced. He'd never offer to hit the first pitch. You could just lob it in there, throw it right down the middle of the plate and he'd just stand there and follow it into the catcher's mitt. Sometimes he'd spot you two strikes. And you'd say to yourself, as good a pitcher as I am, I'm gonna get him out; but you couldn't do it. He'd hit that ball and he'd beat you in ball games."[6]

This was Gehringer's perspective as a hitter, taken from the same book: "I had the reputation for taking the first pitch and I guess I did that a lot. I thought I was a better hitter with a strike or two on me. Too many times you go up there with the attitude of 'well, this is the first pitch, I'll take a swing at it.' You're apt to be a bit careless, try to go for distance and the next thing you know, you've popped up. But with one strike or even two strikes, you're not going to be careless. You really knuckle down."[7]

In 1969, during the game's centennial celebration, Gehringer was named the game's greatest second baseman of all time.

First baseman Dale Alexander was a true "what might have been" story for Detroit. He exploded into the Tigers' lineup in 1929 with a .343 average, 25 home runs and 137 RBIs as a rookie. The next year, his numbers were equally impressive at .326–20–135. However, in 1931, something went wrong. While he managed to hit a robust .325, he hit only three home runs. When he showed no improvement in his power stroke, the Tigers traded him to the Red Sox, where a year later he suffered a career-ending knee injury. His doctors tried a new heat therapy on his injured leg that led to third-degree burns and a case of gangrene, almost forcing Alexander to have his leg amputated.

After climbing within one game of .500, the Tigers never did make it to the mountaintop. They fell to the Red Sox the next day, 5–1, proceeded to lose seven of their next ten games, cementing their status as a sub-.500 also-ran.

To the warm applause of the crowd and greetings from his players, Walter Johnson returned to the Nationals' dugout on Friday, August 8. Eager to get busy, he pitched all of batting practice and immediately put his stamp of authority back on the team when he told reporters he was not going to grant Sam Rice's wish for a day off. The 40-year-old outfielder, complaining of exhaustion, had publicly said he thought he needed a rest. Johnson would not hear of it. It was time for everybody on the team to put their best foot forward, Johnson declared, saying the pennant race was far from over.[8] The Big Train's return to the dugout no doubt inspired the Nationals' 5–4 win over Cleveland that day, but the afterglow did not last long. A flat Washington club lost two to the Tribe the next afternoon (August 9), 13–7 and 4–2, while Philadelphia was having its way with two wins against the White Sox. The Nationals were suddenly a whopping ten games out.

Still, Johnson refused to throw in the towel.

"I have been in the game a good many years and I know the conditions can change fast and that the Mackmen's lead with the season still more than a month to go isn't big enough to permit the Athletics to do any loafing," he said. He also pointed out that his team had five more games left with Philadelphia, three of them commencing two weeks hence.[9]

To Johnson's credit, his team responded with an 18–6 pummeling of the Indians the next day, which featured a chaotic 11-run bottom of the eighth inning in which 15 Nationals batted. The Indians made two errors, committed two wild pitches and gave up a bases-loaded walk and seven hits. The victory sparked a six-game winning streak that shaved Philadelphia's lead to eight.

The Athletic's sweep of the White Sox on August 9 was the second straight day they had taken two from Chicago. On August 8, the verdicts were 5–1 and 4–1, with Al Simmons acting as the catalyst. He drove a three-run homer in the first game and collected three hits and two RBIs in the second. On August 9, it was Jimmie Foxx's turn to be the hero. He had three hits in a 9–3 first-game win, and his mammoth three-run homer (his 32nd) turned out to be the only runs in a 3–0 nightcap whitewash.

Philadelphia next took three out of four from Cleveland, with Simmons getting six RBIs in the three Athletic's wins. With his recent tear, Simmons had pulled within a hair of Lou Gehrig in the batting race, .383 to .3829.

"If you saw them [Gehrig and Simmons] sitting together ... the resemblance would be striking," reported Harold Burr of the *Brooklyn Eagle* newspaper. "But at bat you would never mistake Gehrig for Simmons. Gehrig ... combs the ball great distances with ease and horsepower. Half the time, Simmons is off balance and reaching far across the plate for the pitch with those strong arms."[10]

Cleveland managed to win the last game of the series in a performance reminiscent of its better times in May. They pounded the A's, 15–0, allowing Wes Ferrell to become the first 20-game winner (20–9) of the season. It was also his ninth win in a row, and his mark against Philadelphia improved to 5–1.

The A's had a lot more difficulty in their next series with St. Louis. They needed late-game rallies to win both of the first two games. The first game was a 2–2 duel until the bottom of the seventh when Mule Haas singled with two out, Eric McNair doubled and Mickey Cochran singled them both home for a 4–2 victory. The win was Lefty Grove's ticket to the 20-win club. The next day, the A's trailed by two in the bottom of the eighth when Cochran started the winning rally with a leadoff home run (he, too, was on a tremendous hitting tear and had raised his average to .375, putting him third in the league). Simmons and Foxx followed with back-to-back doubles, Bing Miller singled and winning pitcher George Earnshaw doubled. In a flash, the A's had four runs, a

6–4 win, and Earnshaw was a 19-game winner. The Browns finally prevailed in the third game, 7–0, as George Blaeholder tossed a five-hitter and Goose Goslin helped his old Washington chums by hitting three home runs in the game to seal Philadelphia's fate.

The A's then took three of four from Detroit before heading into Griffith Stadium for what was their penultimate showdown of the season with the Nationals. The lead was eight and one-half games and both teams knew the Nationals needed a three-game sweep to keep alive a realistic chance of winning the pennant.

The intensity of the first game exploded in the eighth inning, and not surprisingly, Al Simmons was the lightning rod for the controversy. The A's had scored early, but Joe Judge's RBI single and Sam West's two-run triple put Washington on top, 4–2, going into the top of the eighth. Mickey Cochran opened with a double and Simmons singled to make the score 4–3. Then the trouble started. Jimmie Foxx rapped a ground ball to second, which Buddy Myer fielded cleanly and flipped to Joe Cronin for the force on Simmons, but the hard-charging outfielder stayed on his feet and slammed into Cronin before the shortstop could complete the relay for the double play. The crowd was livid when the umpires failed to call Simmons for interference and rule it a double play. The jeers and taunts were followed by some bottle throwing. One bottle just missed on-deck hitter Jimmy Dykes, and a bunch were directed at Simmons when he took his position for the bottom of the inning. Order was finally restored and the Nationals posted three more runs and won the game, 7–3. For the Nationals, it was one win down, two to go.

The venue changed to Philadelphia for the next two games and it was Cronin's time to put on a show. He hit a two-run homer in the fourth inning and broke a 2–2 tie in the eighth with a clutch run-scoring hit. The Nationals took their 3–2 lead into the bottom of the ninth when Connie Mack made a curious decision. With two outs and the tying run on first base, Mack allowed Lefty Grove—not among the upper tier of hitting pitchers—to bat for himself. The superstar hurler struck out on three pitches. For Washington it was two wins down and one to go; the A's lead was reduced to six and one-half games (five in the loss column).

Clearly riding the momentum they had built with two straight wins, the Nationals came out in game three and blew the doors off Shibe Park with a five-run first inning. Cronin singled in one run, another scored on a ground out, Roy Spencer singled in two, and pitcher Bump Hadley even got in on the act with a run-scoring single. But the A's had some door-busters of their own. Against Hadley in the bottom of the first frame, Max Bishop and Cochran singled and both scored on Simmons' triple. Simmons came home on Foxx's sacrifice fly to make it 5–3. Cronin countered in the second inning with a home

Clark Griffith (left) with Joe Cronin, whose .346 average in 1930 made him the league's premier shortstop. Cronin would marry Griffith's neice in 1934, but business interests trumped Griffith's family loyalty and he sold his niece's husband to the Red Sox a year later.

run to increase Washington's lead to 6–3. Cochran replied with a sacrifice fly in the third to make the score 6–4. Washington stretched the lead in the fifth when Ossie Bluege and Spencer both singled and then pulled off a double steal. Ad Liska (in relief of Hadley), Myer and Rice each took turns rapping RBI singles to give Washington a hefty 9–4 lead.

Walter Johnson asked Liska to hold that lead for the last half of the game. He faltered a bit in the sixth inning when he surrendered a two-run triple to Foxx, making it 9–6. He made it through the seventh unscathed, but in the bottom of the eighth, the A's went on more of a rampage than a rally. Little-used outfielder Homer Summa singled and Cochran drove one over the wall to make it 9–8. Before Liska could collect himself, Simmons sent one to another zip code, tying the game 9–9. Foxx then walked and Bing Miller drove a bad-hop single past Ossie Bluege. Dykes sacrificed, and Eric McNair scored Foxx with a sacrifice fly. The A's combined power and small ball into a four-run inning and a 10–9 lead. which Lefty Grove preserved in the ninth with one inning of lights-out relief. It was probably the Nationals' toughest loss of the season.

Roger Pippen of the *Baltimore News* later reported that before the A's batted in the bottom of the eighth inning, "Mickey Cochran roused the sleeping champs. He called the players of the A's together on the bench. It held the game up for a few minutes. Washington players got nervous and began yelling for action. Cochran went to the plate carting one of Jimmie Foxx's heavy clubs for luck. He swung it as it was intended to be swung and lifted the ball out of the

Catcher Mickey Cochran demonstrates the all-out competitiveness that made him the undisputed on-field leader of Connie Mack's Athletics.

park for a homer. Al Simmons picked up the same bat also for luck and again the charm worked for another homer."[11]

"We were naturally disappointed that we couldn't make it three in a row but we have not given up hope," said Johnson after the game, putting on a brave front. "We will be out there battling to the finish. Of course we can't win the pennant without help for some of the other teams have to beat them [the A's] while we are winning ourselves. I'm playing the percentages that they will have a slump before the finish, for all teams do. If we can gain three or four games on them in the course of regular play and the showdown is to be decided between the two of us, then Washington fans might just as well get in their bids for World Series seats for we will surely take the Athletics in our remaining two games with them."[12]

Johnson's bravado was admirable, but the Nationals had to be kicking themselves. They went 3–2 against Philadelphia in their five August meetings, but in both losses, they led halfway through the game. Had they been able to hold on to those leads, they would have gone 5–0; instead of sitting seven and one-half games behind the A's, they would have closed to within three and one-half games.

American League Notes for August

Lou Gehrig held off Al Simmons' charge and maintained his lead in the batting race with a .393 mark to Simmons' .385. Mickey Cochran slipped ahead of Babe Ruth, .363 to .360, for third place.

Babe Ruth was still comfortably ahead in the league's home run race with 44 to Lou Gehrig's 37. Jimmie Foxx and Al Simmons each had 32 and a rejuvenated Goose Goslin 31.

Charlie Gehringer had four hits and six RBIs on August 4, his 12th inning grand slam the difference in a win over Chicago.

Boston's Red Sox earned the ignominious designation as first out — they dropped a doubleheader to Cleveland, 9–2 and 2–0, on August 17, mathematically eliminating them from the pennant race. The remaining second-division teams, Chicago, St. Louis and Detroit, would all be eliminated by month's end.

American League Standings on August 31, 1930

	W	L	Pct.	GB
Philadelphia	88	44	.667	–
Washington	80	49	.620	6.5
New York	73	55	.570	13
Cleveland	69	63	.523	19
Detroit	62	70	.470	26
St. Louis	53	78	.405	34.5
Chicago	51	78	.395	35.5
Boston	44	83	.346	41.5

The National League

Rogers Hornsby returned to active duty on August 19 and expected to be back in the Cubs' starting lineup right away. Joe McCarthy, true to what he said in July, preferred to work his superstar back into the lineup slowly. As a result, the Rajah did little through August but pinch-hit and sit on the bench while the lightly-regarded Clarence "Footsie" Blair continued to be the starting second baseman. Was McCarthy truly looking out for Hornsby's health and best interests, or was he punishing Hornsby for his backbiting and his surreptitious conversations with William Wrigley? It was difficult to know because McCarthy never said anything about it or indicated any knowledge of Hornsby's behind-the-scenes activities (although it is hard to believe he did not have a notion of it). As each day of inactivity passed, Hornsby's festering resentment of McCarthy

Two of the National League's greatest hitters co-existed uncomfortably in 1930. Temperamental slugger Hack Wilson (left) loved his beer and late night parties; the brilliant but brusque Rogers Hornsby had no respect for players less obsessively dedicated to the game than he was. Hornsby's desire to manage the Cubs made life especially difficult for Joe McCarthy.

intensified, and he became convinced the Cub manager was vindictively trying to bury him.[13]

If McCarthy was having trouble making one of his superstars happy, his fatherly, "tough-love" approach with his other standout was paying huge dividends. Hack Wilson was locked in and about to have an amazing August. He would hit 13 home runs for the month and drive in a staggering 53 runs (compared to the 61 RBIs he would have for all of 1931). He drove in at least one run in 21 of the Cubs' 29 games in August, with the breakdown as follows: one game with six RBIs, three games with four, five games with three, eight games with two, and four games with one. After he clobbered his 34th home run of the season on August 2, he felt confident enough to predict to the press that he would break Chuck Klein's National League home run record of 43, which had been set the year prior. Citing the fact he was averaging a homer every eleven at-bats, Wilson did some simple math to arrive at his conclusion—he had a little more than 200 at-bats left in the season, which meant 19 more home runs.

"Any schoolboy knows that 34 and 19 equals 53 which will make me beat Chuck Klein's record by 10 homers," the slugger told Chicago reporters. "I hardly believe it myself but the figures don't lie and that's the reason I have no reluctance in coming out with this announcement."[14] He moved a step closer to fulfilling his prediction the next day when he victimized Pittsburgh for number 35.

"They are calling the Cubs the Rah-Rah Boys," reported Murray Tynan of the *New York Herald Tribune* on the Cubs' very visible and vociferous demonstrations of enthusiasm when they played. "It seems the Cubs have too much of it to suit some of the other lifeless clubs.... The opposing boys are not keen on the way the Cubs go about their work."[15]

The Cubs lost two of the three to the Pirates (the only series they would lose in August), and then visited Sportsman's Park where the Cardinals were barely lurking on the peripheral of the pennant race. The first two games were a microcosm of St. Louis' season to date—they lost a game they should have won and then won a game they should have lost. In the first instance, Cardinal pitching blew a 3–0 lead and lost, 5–4, as Wilson hit number 36 and Chicago scored three in the top of the ninth. In the second game they fashioned a ninth-inning miracle finish. The Cubs were leading by one run and St. Louis had a runner on first with one out when George Watkins hit a hard but catchable ball to center field. Wilson took one step and, in a moment eerily reminiscent of his 1929 World Series nightmare, froze. He lost the ball in the sun's glare and it sailed over his head, allowing Watkins to scamper around the bases for a two-run, game-winning inside-the-park-home run. The Cubs eased their pain the next day with a 6–5 win to even their August record at 3–3, good enough to keep pace with the first-place Robins as they prepared to next host the Boston Braves on the weekend of August 8–11.

The Robins opened the month with a four-game dance against the New York Giants that produced the kind of intensity and drama normally involved when these two teams got together.

The Giants took the lead three times in the first game and three times the Robins came back to tie the score in the sixth, the eighth and the tenth innings. Rube Bressler was a hero for Brooklyn. In the top of the eighth, he robbed Fred Lindstrom of a home run and later in the inning threw out a Giants' runner at home plate. In the eighth, he hit a game-tying triple, and in the tenth he singled and scored the tying run. The game went to extra innings tied 4–4, and both teams scored in the tenth. But the Giants' relentless offense finally put the game away, 8–6, with three runs in the 11th while Brooklyn could only counter with a single tally.

The next day, August 3, Carl Hubbell and Dazzy Vance hooked up in a pitching duel worthy of Hall of Famers. Brooklyn scored the game's only run, a controversial winning run, in the bottom of the ninth. Babe Herman started the rally by dropping a pop fly double to left field. Wilbert Robinson decided to pinch-hit for the hard-hitting Del Bissonette with Eddie Moore, one of his best bunters. Moore rewarded his manager's strategy with a perfectly executed sacrifice, moving Herman to third. McGraw countered by ordering Hubbell to walk Glenn Wright and Bressler to load the bases with Jake Flowers coming up. Flowers worked the count full against Hubbell and flinched at the payoff pitch but did not swing. Umpire Lou Jorda called it a ball to the howls of the Giant bench. Brooklyn had a run and the win, and Jorda had a bevy of livid Giants to escort him off the field.

The next day, Giant hurler Fred Fitzsimmons returned the shutout favor, limiting Brooklyn to six hits while Bill Terry, Fred Lindstrom and Ethan Allen all homered in a 4–0 win.

That set the stage for one final barnburner on August 5. The Robins built a 6–1 lead through eight innings, but the Giants scored five in the ninth to tie it, the last three on Terry's two-out, two-strike, three-run homer. Lindstrom doubled home two runs in the tenth to give the Giants the lead, 8–6. In the bottom of the 10th things looked bleak for Brooklyn when Wright opened the inning by grounding out to Terry and Bissonette hit a fly ball to center. But Fred Leach misjudged the ball and it fell out of his reach for a double. Al Lopez then singled to put runners at the corners. Bressler whacked a hard hopper to the left side of the infield that Lindstrom moved quickly to his left to snag, but it deflected off his glove and rolled into the outfield, allowing Bissonette to score and Lopez to gain third base. The next batter was Flowers, the man who drew the bases-loaded walk to defeat McGraw's strategy two days earlier. McGraw, never reticent to gamble, ordered his infield to play in to cut off the tying run at the plate. Flowers short-circuited the strategy again when he lifted a line drive to shallow center field for a game-tying single, which also sent Bressler to third with the winning run. He scored on Moore's sacrifice fly, and as he did, Lindstrom ripped off the glove that had betrayed him on Bressler's grounder and threw it into the stands in anger.

The Robins then won two relatively easy affairs against the Pittsburgh Pirates to maintain their lead over the second-place Cubs. They headed into St. Louis for five big games on the weekend of August 8–10 while the Cubs visited Boston for four games. The results of the weekend's games would radically alter the pennant race.

The Robins began the series against the Cardinals showing no indications that they were in trouble. In fact, it was the Cardinals that looked to be fading from the race. St. Louis was stuck in fourth place, 11 games behind Brooklyn. The deficit quickly became 12 games when the Robins took the opener, 11–5, behind Babe Herman's two home runs (giving him 26). Meanwhile, Chicago put a 6–1 hurting on the Braves to stay three and one-half games behind.

On August 9, Herman earned a defensive gold star for Brooklyn in the fourth inning when he made an incredible leaping grab of a long drive off the bat of George Watkins. The Cardinals had two base runners at the time — Jim Bottomley on second and Chick Hafey on first — and they both took off with the crack of the bat, assuming the ball was an easy extra-base hit. After making the snag, Herman gunned a perfect throw to Jake Flowers at second base. Flowers tagged the base to retire Bottomley, who was already past third base, and he tagged a shocked Chick Hafey standing on second to complete a triple play. That was not enough for the Robins, however, as the Cardinals broke a tie game in the bottom of the ninth when Jim Bottomley singled, Chick Hafey doubled and George Watkins hit a sacrifice fly. The Cubs did not play and so they gained one-half game to trail by three.

The Robins were awful on August 10 as the Cardinals won a doubleheader, 8–2 and 4–0. Third baseman Earl "Sparky" Adams drove the Robins crazy by getting three hits in both games, including a double, triple and three RBIs in the first game and two triples and an RBI in the nightcap. The Cubs were as good as the Robins were bad, chopping up the Braves in a twin bill, 6–0 and 11–1. They were now only one game behind Brooklyn.

On August 11, the Robins snapped out of their funk and played well enough to take a 6–4 lead heading into the bottom of the ninth. But the Cardinals rallied again on a pair of singles, Del Bissonette's two-run throwing error, and a game-winning single by Frankie Frisch. Meanwhile, the Cubs had their way with the Braves again, closing out the sweep with a 4–2 victory. Hack Wilson slammed three home runs (giving him 39) and drove in seven runs (giving him 121 RBIs) during the series. In the span of three days, the Robins had lost the entirety of their lead in the standings and were limping into Chicago for four games against the team with which they were now tied for first place.

The Chicago press was calling the Robins-Cubs match-up "the Little World Series" and it began at Wrigley Field on August 12. In the opening game, Babe Herman showed why he was both an asset and a liability to Brooklyn. He ripped four hits in the game, including a double and triple. But after smacking his triple in the eighth inning, Herman was caught off third base on an ensuing ground ball and tagged out. His mistake was amplified when Bissonette hit the next pitch for a single. Bissonette advanced to second and tried to score on Lopez's single, but Kiki Cuyler uncorked a laser beam of a throw home to deny him. The Robins frittered away chances to score in both the ninth and tenth innings. Chicago, meanwhile, took advantage of its opportunity in the bottom of the eleventh when Woody English and Cuyler pumped singles through the infield, and after a walk to Hack Wilson, Riggs Stephenson bounced one off the hard infield and over Wally Gilbert's head at third base for a game-winning hit. The Cubs were on top of the National League by a game, and had the Robins' misadventures on the bases to thank.

"In discussing the National League's chances of winning in the World Series," quipped John Kieran of the *New York Times*, "...why overlook the strong point of the Robins? They might bewilder the Mackmen with their base running."[16]

The next day, the Robins rebounded and reclaimed their share of first place by pounding the Cubs, 15–5, surviving Wilson's 40th home run. The Cubs answered with solid pitching in the final two games, winning 5–1 and 4–3, and pulled out to a two-game lead.

In the span of eight days, the Robins lost four of five to the Cardinals and three of four to the Cubs, slipping to second place. The worst was not yet over. Beginning August 18, they would endure a seven-game losing streak and lose eight of twelve for the rest of the month. None of Wilbert Robinson's best efforts, kind words or homespun humor could prevent the Daffiness Boys from losing their grip on second place to the Giants.

"There hasn't been anything so tragic ... since the wreck of the Hesperus," moaned *New York Times* columnist John Kieran in speaking for all of Flatbush. "The Robins rose from nowhere to be monarchs of all they surveyed. ... Battered and baffled..., they crashed and crumpled as thoroughly as the storm-tossed Hesperus went to pieces on the reef of Norman's woe."[17]

Having dispatched the Robins, the Cubs entertained Chuck Klein and the Phillies for five games, billing it as a duel between the National League's top two sluggers. Hack Wilson had moved far ahead of Klein in the home run race, 40 to 30, but Klein was still ahead in the RBI count, 129 to 126, when the series started. Wilson had one significant advantage over Klein — he got to hit against

Babe Ruth (right) and Brooklyn's "Other Babe"— Babe Herman — who was given to defensive miscues and base running boners that earned him the leadership mantle for "the Daffiness Boys." Herman's bat was no joke. He posted a .393 average in 1930, smacked 241 hits and drove in 130 runs.

Philadelphia pitching for 22 games while Klein had to bat against Chicago's more talented staff. The advantage was never clearer than in this series. The Cubs scored 57 runs, winning four of five with one game ending twice in a tie (an August 16 game ended in a 10-inning deadlock, and when it was replayed on August 19, it ended as a 16-inning tie). Wilson drove in 12 runs in the series to claim the RBI leadership from Klein and also clobbered three home runs, the third of which came on August 19 off Les Sweetland to tie Klein's National League home run mark of 43. As Wilson ran out his milestone home run, Klein tossed him a gracious congratulatory wave, which must have been tough for the Philadelphia outfielder, considering how bad things were going for him. His chances for a Triple Crown, so vibrant only a month earlier, were in a shambles. Wilson had built up a lead of 13 home runs and now had snatched the RBI leadership. Klein had started the month with a .411 batting average but was currently mired in a 21-for-75 skid, a still-solid .280 clip, but in this super-heated offensive campaign, it allowed both Bill Terry and Babe Herman to pass and stay ahead of him in the batting race for the rest of the season. The "slump" dropped Klein's season average below .400; he was never able to reach that high again.

The Cubs had little chance to enjoy their devastation of the Phillies or to celebrate Wilson's achievement. Their next challengers for dominion over the league were already on their way to Wrigley Field. For the second time in as many weeks, Chicago was about to host a New York team with first place at stake.

The Giants were bearing down on Chicago, having won nine of 12 games on a long western road trip. They took three of four from the Pirates and then pillaged the Reds for four straight, climbing within three games of the Cubs for first place and one-half game of Brooklyn for second place. They split four games in St. Louis, the worst moment of the trip coming on August 20, when New York blew a two-run lead in the bottom of the ninth inning to lose, 5–4. Still, the Giants left St. Louis and headed for Chicago only three behind the Cubs with four games upcoming.

John McGraw was missing all the fun. He opted out of the road trip to stay home and nurse a severe case of sinusitis. He charged one of his all-time favorite players, the recently retired Dave "Beauty" Bancroft, with managerial responsibilities for the trip. Bancroft earned his nickname from constantly yelling "beauty" after watching one of his pitchers bend off an effective pitch. He played his first five years with the Phillies prior to being traded to the Giants to lynchpin McGraw's three straight pennant winners (1921–23). A decent hitter, his quickness and defensive prowess allowed him to set a litany of fielding records, prompting sportswriter Frank Graham to call him "the greatest shortstop the Giants ever had and one of the greatest who ever lived."[18] He was considered a walking encyclopedia of hitters' tendencies and one of the best sign-stealers in the business. After coming over from Philadelphia, a Giants' coach offered to show Bancroft the team's signs. "Why?" Bancroft smiled wryly. "Have they changed?"[19]

The excitement and anticipation of the Giant series surpassed that of the recently concluded Brooklyn series. Ticket demand at Wrigley Field was unprecedented; the series set an attendance record with 178,000 people attending the four games, 155,000 of them paid (the freebies were mostly due to a Ladies Day promotion). In each game, overflow spectators rimmed the entire crescent of the outfield. Even Manager McCarthy did something rare — he acknowledged in advance how important the series was and delivered a message to his pitchers through the news media.

"We need good hurling right now," McCarthy was quoted in the *Chicago Tribune*, "because the Giants and Robins are getting it. Our great opportunity lies ahead. If we can take three of four from the Giants, we will be well along the championship trail."[20] The overflow crowd at Wrigley Field was hardly settled into their seats for the first game of the series when the Giants clubbed the Cubs into submission, helped considerably by the hosts' defense. Howie Critz and Fred Leach, the first two batters, reached when their ground balls were flubbed for errors. After Fred Lindstrom walked, Bill Terry drove home a run on a force out at second base, Mel Ott walked to load the bases and Travis Jackson singled in another run. Wally Roettger effectively ended the competition for the day with a grand slam on the next pitch. The Giants had a 6–0 lead and the Cubs had not been to bat yet. The home team did get as close as 8–5 in the latter innings, but the Giants cashed in six singles and an error in the eighth inning for five runs and a 13–6 victory.

The Cubs used a similar playbook to turn the tables on the Giants the next day. This time Chicago produced the grand slam, scored big in the first inning, and after the Giants got close, scored late to put the game away. Their first-inning mayhem came courtesy of singles by Footsie Blair, Woody English, Kiki Cuyler and Hack Wilson. George Kelly, the former New York Giants star recently acquired by the Cubs to replace an injured Charlie Grimm, drew a walk, as did Gabby Hartnett. Les Bell, who had a great series, capped the five-run inning with a two-run single. When the Giants closed to within 7–4, Hartnett put a period on the day's affairs with an eighth-inning grand slam and the Cubs won, 12–4.

The next day, August 23, Cuyler gift-wrapped the Giants' first two runs when he chased a long drive off the bat of Jackson and caught up to it on the warning track, only to have the ball pop high out of his glove and go into the stands for a home run. The Cubs eventually tied the game on sacrifice flies by Dan Taylor in the fourth inning and Wilson in the sixth. The Giants made a serious bid to regain the lead in the fifth when they loaded the bases with two out. Bob O'Farrell hit a scorching shot that Kelly dove for and caught in the instant before it was past him and down the right field line for what could have been a bases-clearing hit. O'Farrell was later robbed of another bases-loaded hit in the seventh when Blair made a great play behind second base on his ground ball. In the bottom of the eighth, with each team having scored twice,

English singled and Cuyler doubled him to third. Bancroft decided not to walk Wilson with first base open and he paid for the decision when Wilson slapped a two-run single to right, giving the Cubs the 4–2 victory. The three RBIs in the game gave Wilson 144 for the year.

The series concluded the next day with a scintillating finale. The Giants trailed 2–1 in the ninth when Terry opened with a single and moved to third when Lindstrom also singled. Poor O'Farrell, victimized twice two days earlier, hit into a double play that scored Terry with the tying run. In the bottom of the ninth, the speedy Danny Taylor lined a two-out triple. With the winning run ninety feet away, acting manager Bancroft decided to force Joe McCarthy's hand. He knew McCarthy's pitching staff was tired after the two extra-inning games against the Phillies a few days earlier, so he ordered his pitcher, Joe Heving, to walk the next two batters and load the bases. That brought up the pitcher's spot in the Cubs' batting order, which in this case was Guy Bush, who was tossing an extremely effective game. McCarthy, not trusting his worn bullpen, decided to keep Bush in the game and let him bat. By doing so, McCarthy bypassed Rogers Hornsby as a pinch-hitter, another decision that must have stuck in Hornsby's craw. Bush stood at the plate against Heving and looked at strike one on a fastball and strike two on a curveball. Heving went into his delivery for the next pitch, and at that moment, Taylor lit out for home. Heving's pitch was a high, slow breaking ball and by the time O'Farrell grabbed it, Taylor was hook-sliding across the plate with the winning run. All of Chicago went wild on Taylor's steal of home. The Cubs had won three of four from the Giants and had built their lead to a season-high five games.

"It is possible, even probable, that McCarthy's decision to send Taylor home won the 1930 league championship for the Cubs," crowed Arch Ward of the *Chicago Tribune*. "The Cubs know now they can lick the two teams challenging them for the 1930 flag."[21]

It was true that the Cubs had managed to beat the two teams most prominently challenging them. But in the excitement of the Cubs' conquests over the Robins and Giants, no one in Chicago, or anywhere in baseball for that matter, noticed the tempest brewing lower in the standings.

Until the middle of August, it was difficult to know whether or not to categorize the St. Louis Cardinals as contenders given their extreme winning and losing streaks and maddening inconsistencies that shackled them to the middle of the National League pack. They began August in fourth place, 11 games out, and fell as far out as 12 games on August 8 (when they lost the one game to Brooklyn). By the middle of the month, they had cut four games off the deficit, but like an infantry charging in mud, they were back to ten games out by August 18.

Gabby Street had spent his first few months as manager getting acclimated to the situation, dealing with mediocre pitching performances and helping his team fight through injuries to such key players as Chick Hafey and Frankie Frisch. But after a string of frustrating one-run losses in late July, he had tolerated enough and began to firmly assert himself.

"I'm tired of having persons tell me we have the best team in the National League and then watch it lose games which should be won," he said after assessing a series of fines to veteran players he thought were guilty of lackadaisical play and conduct detrimental to the team. "...I am tired of continually seeing throws to the wrong base and rallies snuffed out by dumb plays made on the sacks."[22]

Street's fines were a culture shock to the St. Louis team. Up to this point, fines and disciplinary actions originated in the Cardinals' front office, where the heavy presences of Breadon and Rickey dwarfed the manager. Street's actions brought a new measure of respect from the front office—on August 7 he was re-signed to manage the team for 1931—and from the players who suddenly turned it on.[23] It began with the four straight wins over the Robins and continued when they completed a stirring 5–4 comeback victory against the Giants on August 20. That particular victory was the springboard for a nine game winning streak.

The win streak came at a good time for Manager Street because his boss, team owner and president Sam Breadon, was a notoriously impatient man. He had run through five managers in the previous five years and no one had managed the team for two successive years since 1923–24. Breadon was a shrewd and hard-driving businessman who had made his money in the automobile business. Sportswriter John Drebinger spoke for many in reciting an exchange he had with an observer on the beach one day as the two watched Breadon, an avid and excellent swimmer, go far out into the ocean. The observer told Drebinger he was concerned that Breadon was taking a chance while swimming out by the sharks. "What about the poor sharks?" Drebinger asked.[24]

Breadon became majority owner of the Cardinals in the early 1920s and brought in Branch Rickey, spurring the Cardinals to a decade of dominance that included appearances in two of the previous four World Series. Breadon was not amenable to the players' exorbitant salary demands, which explained Rogers Hornsby's departure from St. Louis despite six straight batting titles, a .397 average during that span and a world championship as player-manager in 1926. When Hornsby demanded a stratospheric salary following the 1926 success, he was traded to the Giants for Frankie Frisch in one of the most celebrated trades of the era.

Frankie Frisch was now the heart and soul of the Cardinals. Known as "the Fordham Flash" for his affiliation with the New York City College of that name,

Charles "Gabby" Street (left) signs to become manager of the St. Louis Cardinals under the eye of impetuous owner Sam Breadon. Despite two World Series appearances in the previous four years, Breadon had chewed through seven managers in five years.

he came to the Giants and won John McGraw's respect and the designation as the team's captain with his fearless and ultra-aggressive style of play. The two had a falling out after McGraw publicly blamed and berated Frisch for the Giant's poor showing in 1926, the year Hornsby was leading the Cardinals to the Promised Land. When the Cardinals proposed swapping the league's two most prominent second basemen, McGraw jumped, and Frisch did not speak to him for years. St. Louis fans were angered initially that Frisch replaced their beloved Rajah, but they eventually took to the colorful Flash and he rewarded their support with the on-field leadership that resulted in four pennants.

"Frisch didn't make them forget the Rajah," St. Louis sportswriter Bob Broeg once wrote, "but he made them remember the Flash."[25] Frisch would bat over .300 on 13 occasions and post a .316 average with 2,880 hits, a record for switch-hitters until the mark was broken by Pete Rose. He was elected to the Baseball Hall of Fame in 1947.

Frisch's teammates included bespectacled outfielder Chick Hafey, who

Wearing his signature spectacles, Cardinal outfielder Chick Hafey hit .336 in 1930. Contemporaries said no one hit the ball harder. His vision problems and injuries limited his playing time each season and shortened his career, making his selection to the Hall of Fame by the Veterans Committee a controversial one.

brought a solid bat to the lineup and strong arm to the outfield. Hafey overcame severe sinus problems, weak eyesight and several beanings to play 13 seasons and hit over .300 in nine of them.[26] In 1929, he had 10 consecutive hits over three games, and in six straight years, hit better than .329. His lifetime average was .317, and in 1930 he was the midst of three consecutive 100+ RBI seasons. His hitting talent prompted both John McGraw and Branch Rickey to say that had it not been for his vision problems, he might have become the greatest right-handed hitter in history.[27] The quiet and reserved Hafey was elected to the Baseball Hall of Fame by the Veterans Committee, one of its more controversial selections in that Hafey's health problems severely limited the length of his career and his playing time during it. He appeared in more than 100 games in only seven of his 13 seasons and had only 1,466 hits.

Jim Bottomley was known as one of the National League's top run producers, beginning with his sophomore year (1924) when he parlayed a grand slam, a second home run, a double and two singles into 12 RBIs, still a record for a single major league game. He had six straight 100+ RBI seasons through 1929 and led the National League in home runs in 1928 and in RBIs in 1926 and 1928. "Sunny Jim," as he was called for his consistently positive demeanor, hit over .300 nine times, finishing with a career .310 mark. The 1930 season was the first hint that the 30-year-old first sacker was slowing down. He hit only 15 home runs and drove in 97 runs. The next year, he slipped to nine homers and 75 RBIs. He was traded to Cincinnati and later closed out his career with the Browns.

The Cardinals also had two players whose overall careers were relatively short, but both of whom were in their primes in 1930. Shortstop Charlie Gelbert contributed four solid seasons to St. Louis (hitting .304 in 1930), but an off-season hunting accident in 1932 shattered bones in one of his legs and he was never the same player again. Taylor Douthit was a wide-ranging center fielder and primarily a singles hitter who put together five good major league seasons, with 1930 being the last of them. During this time, he amassed 889 hits, twice topping 200, and three times bested the .300 mark.

With the first eight wins of their nine-game streak under their belt, the Cardinals had moved within percentage points of the Robins and Giants and within six and one-half games of the Cubs.

Some were not convinced the Cardinals were for real. The *Sporting News* gave them the same chance as "a drowning man who has gone down for the third time."[28]

That opinion notwithstanding, the Cardinals swooped into Chicago to challenge the Cubs' supremacy. For the third time in as many weeks, Wrigley Field hosted a four-game series with significant pennant implications. In fact, the first two games of this series would be among the most important and influential games of the entire season.

Just before the Cardinals hit town, Hack Wilson made good on his home run promise. On August 26, he delighted the hometown fans by connecting for his record-smashing 44th home run against Larry French of Pittsburgh. He also drove in four runs in the game, giving him 148 for the year.

"Hack tied Babe Ruth with his 44th home run," noted the *Chicago Tribune* the next day. "Ruth gets $80,000 for hitting home runs. Hack gets something less than 25 percent of that amount."[29]

The huge crowd treated to the August 28 series opener between the Cardinals and Cubs called it one of the most thrilling games ever. The Cards broke out to a 5–0 lead behind the hitting of Bottomley, who homered and had a sacrifice fly. The Cubs tied it with three in the seventh and a pair in the eighth. Then both teams settled in, their pitchers holding hitters at bay and their defenses snagging hard-hit balls at opportune times to keep the game scoreless for the next six innings. No play was more important than in the bottom of the 15th, and it involved Bottomley again. In the top of the 15th, the Cards had grabbed the lead, scoring two to go ahead, 7–5, on a single by pitcher Sylvester Johnson. In the bottom of the inning Dan Taylor and Gabby Hartnett hit one-out doubles for a run, and then Les Bell singled to tie the game again. Bell moved to second on a ground out, bringing up Woody English. He hit a shot that looked like it was headed through the right side of the infield for a game-winning hit, but a diving Bottomley knocked it down. When the ball squirted away, Bell turned third and came barreling for the plate. Bottomley recovered and, from his knees, threw the ball to catcher John Wilson, who had to reach up and to his right to snare the throw. He caught it and crashed down on Bell with a tag just an instant before the diving Bell would have wiped his hand across the plate for the winning run.

The game continued scoreless for four more innings. Finally, in the top of the 20th inning, Taylor Douthit singled, moved to second on a ground out and scored on a single by utility infielder Andy High. High was thrown out at second base just after Douthit crossed the plate with what turned out to be the deciding run. The Cubs ran out of miracles in the bottom of the 20th, and the Cardinals had their ninth win in a row, 8–7. They were now in a virtual three-way tie for second place and within five and one-half games of the Cubs.

Players, reporters and fans had barely absorbed this great game when they were presented with an equally thrilling affair the next day. Again the Cardinals broke out to a 5–0 lead and again the Cubs rallied to tie, only this time they did it in one fell swoop — scoring five times in the bottom of the ninth inning on two-run singles by Hartnett and English and a bases-loaded walk. George Kelly made a bid to win the game for his new team with a two-out bloop hit to right field, but George Watkins made a great diving catch to save the tie. Tension mounted as neither team could dent home plate in the next two innings. Finally, it was Bottomley, in the midst of playing a great series, who tilted the scales to St. Louis in the 12th inning with a three-run homer. But incredibly, in the bottom of the inning, Riggs Stephenson and Kiki Cuyler opened with singles, Dan Taylor doubled home one run, Kelly's ground out scored another, and Les Bell's clutch two-out single tied the game yet again. All of Wrigley Field exploded when Stevenson opened the bottom of the 13th with a triple and Bell won the game, 9–8, with a single. Ironically, for all his prodigious run production during the month, Wilson did not drive in a run in either of these marathons.

The remaining two games of the series were somewhat anticlimactic. On August 30, the Cubs' hitters spoke loudly and clearly that they had no interest in playing another exhausting extra-inning game, ringing up Cardinal pitching for a 16–4 win. Wilson made up for his lack of production in the two marathon games by smashing three hits, two home runs and six RBIs, running his season total to 157. On August 31, Bill Hallahan struck out 12 to lead the Cards to an 8–3 win and a split in the series. More importantly, the victory launched another significant winning streak for St. Louis as they headed into September.

On the surface, the split seemed to be a good thing for the Cubs. They successfully defended the high ground against St. Louis while the Robins and Giants were bashing each other to a pulp at the Polo Grounds. The two teams split four games that the *New York Times*' John Drebinger called "a thoroughly unprofitable division of the spoils" since the split prevented either New York team from gaining on Chicago.[30]

Below the surface, however, things were not so rosy for the Cubs. The two marathon games against the Cardinals cost them dearly. McCarthy had to use his entire pitching staff in the 33 innings, and his pitchers' exhaustion began to manifest itself in injuries, most prominently Charlie Root, who hurt his arm, and Sheriff Blake, who suffered a serious back injury. Looking back in future years on the two games against St. Louis, McCarthy mused that his team would have been better off losing both games in the regulation nine innings than going 33 innings to earn a split.[31]

However, for the moment McCarthy had led his team to a 19–10 record in August. They started the month in second place, two behind Brooklyn. By August 15, they had regained first place and survived critical tests against the Robins, Giants and Cardinals. By the end of the month, they had built themselves a season-high five-game lead. Hack Wilson was going great guns and the team was on a roll. Even Rogers Hornsby could not complain ... for the moment.

National League Notes for August

Fred Lindstrom could not have enjoyed the series in Chicago—not only did his team lose three of four, the Giant third baseman had a 24-game hitting streak stopped on August 24 — the game Dan Taylor won for Chicago when he stole home in the bottom of the ninth.

Mel Ott became the fourth major league hitter to hit three consecutive home runs and the third to do it in 1930 when he connected in the second game of an August 31 doubleheader against the Braves. He also whacked a double and drove in six runs, but the Giants lost, 14–10, as rookie Wally Berger hit two homers and the veteran George Sisler hit one.

Bill Terry of the Giants ended August with 210 hits and a .405 batting average to lead both leagues. His average was a key reason the Giants sported an unbelievable team average of .320 at the end of August. The other teams hitting over .300 were Philadelphia at .317, Chicago .314, St. Louis .312, Pittsburgh .306 and Brooklyn .302.

The Phillies on August 10 gave the National League a chilling view of how good they might have been with some decent pitching. They swept a doubleheader in Cincinnati, 18–0 and 4–3, with Klein and O'Doul each getting six hits on the afternoon.

Chick Hafey hit for the cycle in the Cardinals' August 21 win over Philadelphia, 16–6.

Ray Kremer of Pittsburgh was the league's highest winner at 19–9, with Chicago's Pat Malone at 16–6 the runner-up.

National League Standings on August 31, 1930

	W	L	Pct.	GB
Chicago	77	51	.602	–
New York	71	55	.563	5
Brooklyn	72	58	.554	6
St. Louis	71	58	.550	6.5
Pittsburgh	68	61	.527	9.5
Boston	58	70	.453	19
Cincinnati	53	73	.421	23
Philadelphia	42	86	.328	35

8

SEPTEMBER

During the summer of 1930, newspapers around the country diligently compared the home run pace set by American League leader Babe Ruth and National League leader Hack Wilson to the day-by-day pace Ruth had set in 1927 when he hit his vaunted total of 60 home runs. For much of the summer Wilson and Ruth stayed comfortably ahead of that pace and it seemed the home run record would likely fall. However, the comparison failed to take one important element into account — Ruth had an incredibly torrid September in 1927, hitting 18 of his 60 home runs. As August melted into September, Ruth could not maintain the frenetic pace he had set three Septembers earlier; Wilson managed to hang on a little longer, but he eventually fell by the wayside as well. There was, however, one slugger who managed to not only keep pace with, but surpass Ruth's 1927 threshold.

Measuring in at a very average 5 feet 10 inches and 175 pounds, Joe Hauser played for the Baltimore Orioles of the International League. He did not look like a slugger until he stood at the plate, unleashed his short compact swing and sent the ball on a long hanging arc over the fences of the various International League parks. Hauser kept up with and ultimately bested Ruth's 1927 pace, finishing the year with a then-professional baseball record of 63 home runs.

Hauser started a promising major league career in 1922 when he hit .323 for Connie Mack's Athletics. Two years later, he slugged 27 home runs (second to Babe Ruth) and knocked in 115 runs. A frightening kneecap fracture abruptly ended his big league career in spring training of 1925, and after an unsuccessful comeback attempt the next year, he managed to give the A's decent productivity in 1928 with 16 home runs in about half the season. Unfortunately, Hauser was a first baseman, and that year Jimmie Foxx joined the Athletics, pushing Hauser to the bench and eventually off the team. After an abortive attempt to play for the Indians the next year, Hauser was relegated to the minor leagues for the rest of his career, where he made his home run mark in Baltimore in 1930 and then bested it three years later when he hit 69 home runs for the Minneapolis Millers of the American Association. He holds the distinction of being the first player to hit 60 or more home runs in two professional seasons.

Home run were flying out of minor league parks as frequently as major league parks, one of the reasons attendance remained healthy in most parts of the country despite the growing economic jitteriness. Another trend drawing fans to minor league parks was night baseball. More and more teams were installing lights and more and more fans were coming to games after the end of the traditional workday. Even the New York Giants played an exhibition game under the lights in Connecticut in August, observers and many were predicting night baseball was the wave of the future for the major leagues.

The president of the National League was not one of them.

John Heydler had been a sportswriter and an umpire and later became an assistant to National League president Harry Pulliam. He succeeded Pulliam in 1918.

"None of our teams would be allowed to engage in a championship game after sundown under the [league] constitution," said Heydler, "and ... I find that there is no demand in the Major Leagues to get away from baseball ... and get it into show business which is all night baseball is or can be."[1]

As tradition-bound as Heydler sounded in his attitude toward baseball under the stars, he did devise or support a number of innovations to the game, including the establishment of the Commissioners' Office and the Baseball Hall of Fame. In 1928, he went so far as to propose that baseball adopt the designated hitter, an idea that had the avid support of John McGraw.

"Baseball fans are tired of watching weak-hitting pitchers come to bat," he claimed. Ironically, his proposal was rejected because the American League was against it.[2]

The American League

September meant shorter days and longer odds for the Washington Nationals. They trailed Philadelphia by six and one-half games (five in the loss column); if the A's merely split their remaining 22 games, Washington would need to win 20 of its remaining 25 contests to win the pennant — a tough task made tougher by the fact they only had four home games all month. To make matters worse, the Nationals had only two games remaining against Philadelphia, so they would have to rely on help from other teams — an unlikely proposition considering most of the A's remaining games were against second-division clubs. Finally, the Athletics had a relatively gentle September schedule with a two-day break and a three-day break, meaning Connie Mack would have ample time to rest his regulars.

Walter Johnson did not care about the odds or the numbers. He was looking for something his boys could rally around. He thought he found it when the Nationals swept a September 1 doubleheader from Boston while the Mackmen only managed to split a pair against the Yankees. The Nationals had pulled within five and one-half games, and within four in the loss column. Johnson told his men that all it took was for Philadelphia to have one bad series to change the complexion of the race, and he reminded them that in 1925, the Nationals trailed Philadelphia by four games in September and rallied past them to win the pennant.[3]

Johnson led his minions into New York for four games, hoping to continue their season-long dominance of New York, but this time the Yankees did not cooperate. The Bombers won two games in the series—the first one, 10–7, as Bill Dickey had a home run, two triples and six RBIs; and the last one, 3–2, with Lou Gehrig smashing a home run after almost sitting out the game because of a badly dislocated finger. The Nats managed to win the middle two games of the series, 3–2 and 14–5.

The Athletics did not cooperate, either. While the Nationals were splitting four with New York, the Athletics swept a four-game series against Boston, a team inexorably marching to a 100-loss season. Jimmie Foxx hit his 33rd home run as the A's won the first game, 11–4. The second game went into extra innings, tied 4–4. Both teams scored once in the tenth and twice in the 14th (the two Philadelphia runs coming courtesy of an Al Simmons home run), and the A's finally won it in the 15th on Simmons' single. Simmons connected for another home run the next day as the A's won easily, 5–1. They finished the sweep when Mickey Cochran hit a two-out, two-run game-winning home run in the tenth inning of game four. Lefty Grove started one game in the series and pitched in both of the extra-inning contests, winning all three times. He now had 25 wins for the season.

With their sweep, the Athletics increased their lead over Washington to seven and one-half games as they headed into the nation's capital for a single contest. The size of Philadelphia's lead took some starch out of the matchup but Walter Johnson insisted his team would ignore the standings and fight hard to the very end. No one who watched his team play that day could doubt it.

Sad Sam Jones took the mound hoping to repeat the gem he hurled at the A's in August, but he got rapped for five second-inning runs; after three innings, he was losing, 6–1. Fred Marberry relieved Jones and shut down the A's for the rest of the game. In the fourth, Muddy Ruel banged a two-run single to cut the deficit to 6–3, and two innings later, Washington moved within a run as Joe Cronin singled, Dave Harris tripled him home and Ossie Bluege skied a sacrifice fly. In the seventh inning, Simmons stepped into the batters' box and ignited another controversy. Marberry chucked a high hard one that Simmons jackknifed to avoid. Hard words ensued and Marberry and Simmons had to be restrained by teammates. Having stirred the passions of the Washington fans as he did a month earlier with his football-like block on Joe Cronin, Simmons was the target of Washington's wrath — boos and curses rained down on him for the rest of the at-bat, and after he grounded out, bottles joined the rain of invectives. Simmons made it safely back to the dugout where he continued to jaw at Marberry. The Washington pitcher made a beeline for the A's dugout but was restrained by Ruel and Bluege. Things finally calmed down and the next two innings proceeded uneventfully.

When the Nationals came to bat in the bottom of the ninth against George Earnshaw, they still trailed, 6–5. Bluege bunted his way on and Ruel moved him to third with a single to right field. Suddenly, Mother Nature opened the heavens for a half-hour rain delay that may have cooled the field, but not Washington's passion to win. When the game resumed, Earnshaw returned to the mound and walked pinch-hitter Art Shires to load the bases. Jack Hayes tied the game when he lifted a sacrifice fly, and then Sam Rice slapped a ground ball up the middle that ticked off Earnshaw's glove and bounced into center field, scoring Ruel. The crowd erupted and celebrated with the Nationals as though they had just won the pennant. With this victory, Washington fans would forever be convinced theirs was the better team despite the fact they trailed by six and one-half games with only 18 left to play (Philadelphia had only 15 left to play).

The *Sporting News* observed that nothing short of "a cataclysm or train wreck can knock the Philadelphia birds off their perch."[4]

As both teams left after the game for their final western road trips of the season, the *Washington Post* provided an apt epitaph for the home team: "Using common sense instead of hope, it must be admitted that the Nats' chance of copping the flag are mighty slim but they must be given credit for not giving up and the fact they apparently have second place sewn up places them among the 'wonder teams' of recent years, for they were generally regarded as a seventh place club in the preseason dope."[5]

Cleveland and Chicago got together on September 6 for one of the last intriguing matchups of the season. White Sox ace Ted Lyons, looking for his 20th victory, was matched against Cleveland ace Wes Ferrell, already a 24-game winner. Ferrell had not lost a game since the Fourth of July, winning 13 in a row, only three short of the all-time consecutive win record held jointly by Walter Johnson and Joe Bush in 1912. Lyons specifically recalled this game in *Baseball When the Grass Was Real* and how he played a little mind game on Ferrell beforehand.

"Wes was superstitious about having his picture taken on the day he was going to pitch. We had this photographer on the bench and I told him he should get a picture of us shaking hands. So Ferrell comes out and I come over. 'How about letting me get a little shot?' Ferrell said all right. While we were shaking hands, I said to Wes, 'He's taking a picture of us shaking hands and wishing each other bad luck.' He laughed but gave me a funny look. I'm sure that was on his mind the whole game."[6]

Lyons' ploy worked. In a rare (for 1930) pitcher's duel, the White Sox won, 2–1. Lyons contributed to his 20th win with a key fifth-inning triple and a run scored.

"There was a big potbellied stove in the clubhouse and [Ferrell] went in and pretty near tore the whole thing up," said Lyons, recalling Ferrell's reaction to the loss.[7]

The Athletics arrived in Detroit and split a pair of games, then went to Cleveland and swept two, tightening the noose on Washington's neck. On September 16, they took a doubleheader from the White Sox, and when they clobbered the Chisox again the next day, they moved within a game of mathematically ending the race.

Washington did what it could to keep up with Philadelphia, winning four of six from St. Louis and Chicago, but the schedule was running out of games. They pulled into Cleveland knowing they were one loss (or one Philadelphia win) away from elimination.

On September 18, they ran into an ornery Wes Ferrell, no doubt still steaming over his loss to the White Sox a few days earlier. Ferrell surrendered two early runs then clamped the lid on the Washington offense for the rest of the day. Sam Jones gave back one run in the sixth and the tying run in the seventh. In the bottom of the ninth inning, Charlie Jamieson reached Jones for a single. He stole second and came around to score on Dick Porter's double. As Jamieson's foot touched the plate, Washington's pennant chase officially came to an end and Wes Ferrell earned his 25th win.

About 400 miles to the west, the Athletics left no doubt by laying waste to the White Sox, 14–10. Philadelphia banged out 20 hits, with every position player in the lineup except leadoff batter Max Bishop getting either two hits or three hits. Fittingly, Simmons and Foxx led the onslaught—both homered, with Simmons scoring four times and Foxx driving in five runs. Grove picked up another win in relief.

The American League pennant race was over. Philadelphia clinched the pennant with a 99–48 record, eight and one-half games better than Washington's 90–56 mark. The A's did very little celebrating after the last out, departing the field in a workmanlike manner and leaving their manager on the field to collect the kudos. Connie Mack was going back to the World Series for the eighth time.

"I am very happy about winning again," Mack said. "While we won by a comfortable margin, it was a battle all the way. Washington kept us busy. If it hadn't been for their slump in mid-season, they would still be in the race. I appreciate the efforts of my players in battling their way to a second straight league championship."[8]

Connie Mack was perhaps the most revered and respected man in the game during the first half of the 20th century. He was respected for his stately demeanor and his knowledge of the game. He was almost always described as unfailingly polite and a model of self-control. These same qualities made him a distant man to most—few knew him in a friendly or familiar enough way to address him by his first name. Even his players, whether they were wide-eyed rookies or grizzled veterans, almost always referred to their manager respectfully as "Mr. Mack."

But if Mr. Mack was the game's most revered personality, he perhaps was also its most contradictory. The same Connie Mack who was courtly and gentlemanly was also known to possess a particularly salty vocabulary that he did not hesitate to use with his players when he thought it necessary.

"He'd never bawl you out for a mistake until the next day," said Doc Cramer, who played under Mack for seven years. "Then you'd go up to his little office up there and he'd be waiting for you. Boy, he could tell it to you when he had to!"[9]

Red Smith, one of the game's most revered sportswriters, once described him as "tough as rawhide or as gentle as a mother, reasonable and obstinate beyond reason, and courtly and benevolent and fierce. He was kindhearted and tight fisted, drove a close bargain and was suckered in a hundred deals. He was generous and thoughtful and autocratic and shy and independent and altogether loveable."

John Drebinger of the *New York Times* had a similar take, writing of Mack that he could be "domineering and austere as the mightiest of rulers. Then again he can become extremely unobtrusive as often happens during the early days of training when he prefers to keep himself in the background and leave his lieutenants to break in the rookies...."[10]

Mack's contradictory nature may have been born in the dual role he filled for the Athletics. On one hand, he was the team manager, burning with a fervent desire to win and with an obligation to put the best and most competitive team he possibly could on the field. On the other hand, he was an uncompromising, bottom-line businessman whose top priority was to maintain the profitability of the business. Too frequently, Connie Mack the businessman cancelled out Connie Mack the manager.

Mack once confided that, to him, a dream season was one in which his team contended strongly in the first half, and then faded weakly and finished fourth. The strong first half of the season meant increased attendance and ensured all the bills would be paid. The weak second half meant he would not have to worry about giving raises to his players.[11]

Players were constantly fighting with Mack for more money. Although Al Simmons was the publicized holdout before the start of the 1930 season, Mack had difficulty over the years coming to terms with a number of his stars. Jimmy Dykes made the same $7,000 in 1930 that he made in 1929. Foxx, just coming into his own as a feared slugger, signed a three-year $50,000 deal that pushed his annual salary to about $17,000. Grove and Cochran both pulled down about $20,000 in 1930. Yet, despite his penurious dealings with his players, virtually all of them liked and respected him.

"I got along fine with him," said Grove in *Baseball When the Grass Was Real*. "He was just like a father to everyone. He knew how to treat each man."[12]

He was nicknamed "the Tall Tactician" for his encyclopedic knowledge of his opponents and their tendencies.

"You had what amounted to a fourth outfielder on the bench," recalled Cochran. "He knew hitters' weaknesses and their strength. And while he might have ordered a pitcher to pitch to a slugger's weakness, he also played his defensive alignment to a man's strength." Mack would move his defensive players around by waving his scorecard at them.[13] This became such a signature move that when Mack was honored by the city of Philadelphia in 1944, President Franklin Roosevelt sent a congratulatory telegram that said "long may your scorecard wave."[14]

Ty Cobb, who finished out his career in Philadelphia, recalled one time in 1928 when Mack waved his scorecard to get Cobb's attention and reposition him in right field. This was something Cobb, with 22 years of experience, did not appreciate until that batter scorched a line drive which, had he not moved, Cobb would not have been able to catch. Cobb claimed this happened on more than one occasion.

"I always heard about that scorecard of Mack's. Now I'm starting to believe in it," Cobb said.[15]

Arch Ward of the *Chicago Tribune* said of Mack that "he is a curious combination of the manly elements. Writers of baseball tell us that he is the perfect general; his success remarkable because he has made his men come around to his way of doing things. He has had his prima donnas and his duffers. But he ultimately turns them into a perfect machine."[16]

The pennant clinching on August 18 surely elated Connie Mack the manager, but it probably troubled Connie Mack the businessman. He knew it would not be long before the elements of his latest "perfect machine" would be at his office doorstep looking for salary increases commiserate with their success. And, in an age before there were juicy television contracts, lucrative stadium-naming rights and big-time souvenir businesses to augment a club's revenue, a team like the Athletics lived or died on gate receipts, and at the moment, they were closer to dying. Despite a second straight championship season, attendance at Shibe Park in 1930 was down severely—from 839,176 in 1929 to 721,663, a precipitous drop of over 117,000, or 14 percent. Davis Walsh, sports editor of the International News Service, speculated that Philadelphians had become apathetic to the A's success. They were bored by the A's dominance and their lopsided wins, and he said the A's were "experiencing something of the same situation that confronted them in 1914 [during their last dynastic run] when everybody stayed away from the ballpark very resolutely."[17]

Equally to blame was the fact Philadelphia was hit early by the Great Depression. By the start of the 1930 baseball season, unemployment in the city reached 15 percent, and in the neighborhoods around Shibe Park, it reached as high as 30 percent.[18] By 1933, despite the success of Connie Mack the manager—three straight pennants (1929–31), a second-place team (1932) and a third-place team (1933)—attendance had skidded to a paltry 297,138.

Those grim numbers forced Connie Mack the businessman to do what inevitably he did with all of his championship clubs—he sold the players to keep the franchise financially afloat. In the mid 1930s, Mack sold off Grove and Foxx to the Red Sox, Simmons to the White Sox and Cochran to the Detroit Tigers, getting cash in return but no talent. The A's plummeted in the standings and Mack never again finished higher than fifth place after 1933.

By the time he relinquished the leadership of the A's at the age of 88 in 1950, Mack was a walking anachronism, still calling people by their formal names, still wearing his funereal dark suits in the dugout. He left the game deservedly saluted as one of its greatest personalities and pioneers, but the same game he pioneered had long ago passed him by. He left behind a moribund, perennial second-division team unable to draw more than a smattering of fans to a crumbling stadium in an increasingly decrepit neighborhood. Connie Mack died in 1956, having won 3,776 games as a manager, by far the most in the game's history. His 4,025 losses are also far ahead of anyone else.

"Connie entered the game when it was a game for roughnecks," said Red Smith in tribute. "He saw it become respectable, he lived to be a symbol of its integrity, and he enjoyed every minute of it."[19]

While many saluted Walter Johnson for the job he did in leading a perceived second-division club to a strong runner-up finish, the Big Train felt little satisfaction and an intense, gnawing frustration as he reviewed the few missteps that cost his team the pennant: there were the two games in August when the Nats blew leads to the A's; there was that Memorial Day doubleheader when a gimpy Al Simmons beat them in two games they should have won; there was the series in Chicago in August when they lost three of four; and then there was Manush's injury.

"A winning streak of ten straight was stopped that day," said Johnson recalling the day Manush injured his leg. "And with the loss of Manush, we seemed to collapse completely."

Despite the problems, Johnson was satisfied that his was a strong team, not just a spirited one that played over its head.

"We had a mighty good team this year," Johnson reflected. "Just as good a one as the Mackmen except for two items—Lefty Grove and the ability of the Athletic clouters to pole out more extra base hits at timely moments." Johnson then paid tribute to the man who had inherited the Big Train's mantle as the best pitcher in the game. "Lefty Grove practically won the pennant for Connie Mack. He not only won his own games, he helped out the others two or three times a week. The A's practically won the flag with only four pitchers, and it was my belief that they could not last out the season that gave me hope of beating them out until the very last." A few days later, when asked to evaluate the A's chances in the World Series, Johnson again referred to the team's reliance on a few key players, but thought it a negative.

"They will be beaten," Johnson said. "Grove is the only pitcher they've got and outside of Simmons and Cochran, they are just an ordinary ball club."[21]

With the pennant race over, Johnson left the team in the hands of Joe Judge and returned home to rebuild his domestic life with his children.

The *Sporting News* took issue with Johnson's evaluation of the champions. "Managers who are rivals to Mack have declared this to be an ordinary team with great pitching. Some ... have gone to the extent of declaring that the A's only have two real players—Al Simmons and Mickey Cochran. But what has that to do with a team that can win a championship? We are sure that the same thing has been said of many other ball teams."[22]

If the pennant chase came to an early conclusion, the batting championship race between Lou Gehrig and Al Simmons went right down to the last at-bat of the season ... and then continued for a few days afterward.

Gehrig entered September leading Simmons by eight points. Slowly that lead dissipated as Gehrig struggled with a short slump and the affects of batting with a dislocated finger.

	Gehrig		*Simmons*	
	H/AB	AVG.	H/AB	AVG.
September 1	192/488	.393	180/468	.385
September 8	199/509	.391	190/493	.385
September 15	207/541	.383	194/511	.380
September 22	214/563	.3801	206/543	.3793

With four games remaining for both the Yankees and Athletics, Simmons had moved within a point of overtaking Gehrig. And fittingly enough, the two were about to go head-to-head in a three-game series at Shibe Park.

Gehrig got the duel off to a rousing start with a three-run first-inning home run, but that would be his only hit of the day. Simmons smashed a single and triple as part of a 13–3 mashing of the Yankees that was mercifully ended by weather and darkness after six innings. Gehrig went hitless in the second game while Simmons added another single and a game-winning double as the A's won, 7–6. With four hits in the series to Gehrig's one, Simmons edged ahead, .3792 to .3785. The Iron Horse recovered his footing in the third game with two singles (and two walks) as the Yanks salvaged a 10–8 win. Simmons answered with one single, just enough to keep him in front by the slimmest of margins—.3808 to Gehrig's .3800. The Athletics headed to Washington for one last game but Simmons did not play. Gehrig did play in the Yanks' last game— his 886th straight—and he collected three singles in five at-bats at Fenway Park to cross the finish line a wisp ahead of Simmons, .3819 to .3808.

Major newspapers covering the final day of the baseball season all headlined Gehrig as the unofficial American League batting champion—unofficial being the operative word since, in this age before computers and instant statistical updates, all of the season's statistics would have to be tallied and veri-

Lou Gehrig's swing resembled a lumberjack swinging an axe. He would hit 41 home runs, drive in 174 runs and battle Al Simmons for the batting title down to the last at-bat of the season—and beyond.

fied at the league office. When the league published its numbers a week later, the headlines changed. The number crunchers in the American League found that Gehrig had five more at-bats than had been reflected in the earlier statistics, and when those at-bats were added to his ledger, Gehrig's average dropped to .379, giving the batting title to Simmons at .381.

Even with this down-to-the-wire batting duel taking place, Babe Ruth found a way to make headlines through the last day of the season. In the game at Philadelphia on September 26, he launched a long one over the wall, only to have it hit the same protruding public address speaker that robbed the Bambino of a home run on Opening Day. He had to settle for a double again. He gained his revenge the next day when he swatted two more home runs, running his season total to 49. It was his fifth consecutive American League home run championship, seventh in eight seasons and eleven of the twelve he would win. The 1930 crown would be his last solitary one (in 1931, Gehrig tied him for the title). Gehrig finished behind Ruth with 41 home runs, followed by Foxx with 37 and Simmons with 36. Gehrig did win the RBI championship, amassing 174 while Simmons had 165, Foxx 156 and Ruth 153.

The Babe saved his most bizarre and incredible headline for the last day of the season. Egged on by the Red Sox, who wanted to pump up the gate for what would otherwise have been a mundane last game of the season, Ruth declared his desire to capture some of his youthful glory and pitch the Yankees' last game of the year in Boston. Ruth had come to the major leagues in 1914 as a pitcher, and was one of the league's best for five years, a fact often forgotten by fans enamored with his great slugging ability. With Bob Shawkey's approval, the 35-year-old slugger took the hill on September 29 against the team that had sold him to New York.

The Babe stretched a decade's worth of cobwebs out of his pitching arm and tossed a complete game, defeating the Red Sox, 9–3. He allowed only four hits in the first six innings of the game, one on an infield chopper and the other three on bloop hits to the outfield. When he finally surrendered a run in the bottom of the sixth, it was unearned. Twice in the game, he fielded hot smashes and started double plays. He walked two and struck out three in earning his 92nd career win.

He would not step on the pitching mound again until the Yankees' final game of the 1933 season when, incredibly, at the age of 38, he pitched another complete game victory, 6–5, over the Red Sox at Yankee Stadium.

American League Notes for September

Earl Averill of Cleveland joined the three-home-runs-in-a-game club against Washington in the lidlifter of a doubleheader on September 17. Averill

8 September

Babe Ruth takes fans and photographers back to his halcyon days as one of the game's great left-handed pitchers for Boston. Having not been on the mound in over a decade, Ruth agreed to start the Yankees' last game of the season. He pitched a complete-game victory, ironically, against the Red Sox.

made a bid for a fourth but his long drive curved foul. He added a fourth home run in his first at-bat of the nightcap.

Johnny Hodapp of Cleveland was not a factor in the batting race, but he surpassed both Lou Gehrig and Al Simmons to lead the American League with 225 hits. He also posted a league-high 51 doubles.

Earle Combs of the Yankees legged out a league-high 22 triples and Marty McManus of the Tigers had a relatively modest 23 stolen bases to lead in that category.

New York (.309), Washington (.304) and Cleveland (.302) finished with team batting averages above the .300 mark. The Yankees scored a major league-record 1,062 runs, besting the previous standard of 982 set by the Cubs in 1929.

Lefty Grove finished with a 28–5 record and teammate George Earnshaw went 22–13. Wes Ferrell posted an impressive sophomore year mark of 25–13 and Ted Lyons was 22–15. And in one of the most underrated feats of the season, Lefty Stewart won 20 games for the St. Louis Browns, going 20–12.

Milt Gaston and Jack Russell shared the distinction with both pitchers losing 20 games for the Red Sox—Gaston 13–20, Russell 9–20.

Final American League Standings

	W	L	PCT.	GB
Philadelphia	102	52	.662	–
Washington	94	60	.610	8
New York	86	68	.558	16
Cleveland	81	73	.526	21
Detroit	75	79	.487	27
St. Louis	64	90	.416	38
Chicago	62	92	.403	40
Boston	52	102	.338	50

The National League

"The team is just like a big ball rolling downhill and has gained a momentum that has made it hard to stop." warned St. Louis Cardinal manager Gabby Street after his team blazed through August with a 23–9 record and opened September by winning seven straight (the streak actually began with an 8–3 win over the Cubs on August 31).[23]

The Redbirds conquered all that they saw — taking a doubleheader from the Pirates on September 1 and then four straight from the Cincinnati Reds. Starters turned in solid performances in every game and were backed by a prolific and phenomenally balanced offensive attack. During this seven-game win streak, the Cardinals scored 61 runs. In the first six games of the streak, they banged out 18, 17, 18, 18, 15 and 14 hits, and in three of the games, every starter, including the pitcher, had at least one hit. Only in the last game were they held to a relatively modest seven hits, but because starter Jesse Haines allowed only five, the Cards won, 4–2.

L.H. Addington, who covered St. Louis for the *Sporting News* gushed at the Cardinals success. "While one of the most unrelenting fights in the history of the circuit is raging, the jaunty crimson banner of the St. Louis Cardinals can be seen in spots where the smoke is the thickest and where bats flash like bayonets amid a barrage of base hits."[24]

It was virtually inconceivable that a team could play better than St. Louis had since Gabby Street put his foot down in August and stomped out the Cardinals' apathy. Yet, incredibly, another of the contending teams was about to go on an even wilder September winning spree.

The Brooklyn Robins were left for dead after a 12–19 record in August and a September 1 doubleheader split with the Boston Braves that dropped them to fourth place. The Robins scored only seven runs in three games against the Braves and they looked exhausted and listless in doing so. Help arrived on September 6 in the form of the Philadelphia Phillies' pitching staff, which spent

Cleveland second baseman Johnny Hodapp was the brightest star in a crop of talent-packed but star-crossed players the Indians brought to the major leagues in the late 1920s. Hodapp would lead the league with 225 hits and post a .354 average in 1930, his third straight season hitting at least .320. Two years later a severe knee injury destroyed his swing and his career.

the season acting like smelling salts on the most dormant of offenses. Babe Herman (his 30th), Glenn Wright and Johnny Frederick all homered, and the Robins strafed the Phillies for 24 hits and a 22–8 win. The revival continued the next day against their inter-borough rivals. Herman and Frederick made sparkling defensive plays and Herman, Wright and Rube Bressler all had seventh-inning RBI singles to break a tie and earn the Robins a high-spirited 5–2 win over the Giants. Not wanting to lose any momentum, Uncle Robbie rushed his boys down to Philadelphia for more of the elixir that had given his team new life. This time the Robins swept the Phillies, 8–2 and 11–4, getting 15 hits in each game. The Robins had a second wind and it was about to carry them higher than they could have imagined.

The Giants were on a downward curve. Their September 7 loss to the Robins was part of a rough patch they were going through since the start of the month. They did enjoy an 18–5 hitting spree against the Phillies (who else?) on September 2, poking 25 safeties while Bill Terry drove in seven runs. Terry also pumped out four hits in the game, raising his season total to 222 and giving him a gaudy .411 average. The Giants managed to take two of three from Philadelphia, but they had a rougher time in Boston, where they blew two late leads and had to settle for a split of six games.

The Giants had a growing controversy in early September over the status of their manager. John McGraw had missed the team's long and successful Western swing and he continued to be absent in September. Because McGraw's contract expired at the end of the year, speculation began to run rampant that the Little Napoleon was about to sever his ties with the Giants and jump to the Bronx, where it was said the Yankees were not happy with Bob Shawkey. Before the questions about McGraw's status could embroil his club, owner Horace Stoneham acted and squelched them quickly. He announced on September 3 that McGraw had signed a new five-year deal as manager and president of the team and he would be paid a Ruthian salary of $70,000 a year. Stoneham also revealed that McGraw had been seriously ill with sinusitis and ordered by doctors to stay out of the dangerous summer heat. McGraw did not return to the dugout, but attended the Giants' September home games where he took a seat at the window of the center field clubhouse and relayed signs and instructions to acting manager Dave Bancroft. The Giants had dealt with the controversy over their manager expeditiously and before it became a distraction to the team.

The Cubs were not so deft. Rumors swirled all across Chicago that Cubs owner William Wrigley was disillusioned with McCarthy and was thinking of replacing him with Rogers Hornsby. Wrigley did nothing to quell the speculation. Persistent stories of a growing rift between Hornsby and Joe McCarthy dogged the team. News reports suggested fists flew in the Cubs' clubhouse in defense of one man or the other. The perception that the two men were feuding was intensified by the fact Hornsby sat in the bullpen rather than the dugout when he wasn't playing. Hornsby explained that he liked the bullpen because he could exercise as he watched the game.

Bill Corum of the *New York Journal* would have none of it. "Hornsby is not in McCarthy's good books," he reported. I talked to McCarthy ... before the last World Series and you would have thought the Lone Texan was the greatest guy ever. I talked to Joe at the Polo Grounds in June or July and you would have thought Rogers was just a crippled bush leaguer...."[25]

These distractions could not have come at a worse time. On September 1, the Cubs lost a doubleheader to the Reds, a team that gave them fits all season. They managed only eight hits in the two games. After beating Cincinnati on September 2, they lost the opener of a series to the Pirates a day later, making it four losses in five games (including the August 31 defeat by the Cardinals).

Hoping it might reverse the team's momentum, McCarthy inserted Hornsby back into the regular lineup on September 4 against the Pirates, and although the Rajah went hitless with two walks, his presence may have inspired his teammates to bludgeon Pittsburgh, 10–7. Gabby Hartnett continued his great season, smacking two homers and bringing home six runs, and Hack Wilson notched his 160th RBI to break his own National League record.

The next day Hornsby had a single in five at-bats with two RBIs, but he made an error as the Cubs lost, 8–7. In his third game back, Hornsby had two singles in four trips to the plate and again drove in two runs. Still looking slow and tentative in the field, however, Hornsby made two costly errors that led to six unearned Pittsburgh runs. Hack Wilson, meanwhile, hit his 47th home run and drove in four runs, and the Cubs, perhaps mistakenly thinking they were playing Pennsylvania's other team, outscored Pittsburgh, 19–14.

The two teams moved to Wrigley Field to continue their series the next day, but during pre-game warm-ups, Hornsby approached McCarthy on the Cubs' bench and complained that his legs were giving him difficulties. After a short conversation, the two agreed Hornsby should rest. Hornsby walked away glumly, his heralded return lasting all of three games. McCarthy turned to a newsman sitting near him and winked.

"I'm glad you were here to hear that," McCarthy said, "because in a couple of days I'll be reading stories that I kept him on the bench to embarrass him."

The final lap of the pennant contest began on September 9 with Chicago and St. Louis on the East Coast for one last showdown with the Robins and Giants. Three weeks remained and only four games separated the top four teams in the National League. It no longer mattered who was up and who was down or what had happened in the first five months of the season. All that mattered now was how the teams played down the stretch and how players

The undiluted power of Hack Wilson launching his 47th home run of 1930. Barely five years after rewriting the National League record book with 56 home runs and 191 RBIs, Wilson would be forced from the game due to alcohol abuse.

responded to the increasing pressure of knowing any one play could profoundly change the character of the race.

It began with the Cubs at Ebbets Field for three games and the Cardinals at the Polo Grounds for four.

September 9: The Robins relied on their two "babes" to conquer the Cubs. A 26-year-old rookie right-hander named Ray "Babe" Phelps mastered Chicago for a five-hit shutout, and Babe Herman knocked a two-run homer to seal a 3–0 Robins' win.

Over in Manhattan, New York's Clarence Mitchell out-pitched St. Louis' Burleigh Grimes, 2–1. Each team was limited to seven hits but the Giants managed to couple two of theirs in the seventh inning — a single by Travis Jackson and a double by Wally Roettger — and both scored on a ground ball out.

With the third- and fourth-place teams defeating the first- and second-place teams, the field was squeezed even tighter.

Chicago	80–57	–
St. Louis	77–59	2.5
Brooklyn	78–60	2.5
New York	77–60	3

September 10: The Robins settled matters early against the Cubs, bruising Charlie Root for five first-inning runs before a batter was retired. Dolph Luque grabbed the baton from Babe Phelps and threw his own five-hitter, blanking

the Cubs, 6–0. Brooklyn extended its winning streak to six and moved within one and one-half games of first place.

The Giants had the chance to squeeze the standings even tighter but they blew a 3–1 lead in the eighth inning. Andy High singled with one out for St. Louis, and with two away, he scored when Mel Ott just missed catching Taylor Douthit's line drive that went for a double. Frankie Frisch followed with an infield hit and Jim Bottomley arced one that just caught the façade of the upper deck in right field for a three-run home run and a 5–3 Cardinal win. Instead of closing within two games, the Giants remained three out.

Chicago	80–58	–
St. Louis	78–59	1.5
Brooklyn	79–60	1.5
New York	77–61	3

September 11: The Robins and Cardinals kept the pressure on the Cubs as both continued their phenomenal winning pace. The Robins won, 2–1, making it seven straight. Dazzy Vance fired the third consecutive five-hitter against the Cubs, striking out 13. Hack Wilson's 48th home run accounted for Chicago's only run in the series. Glenn Wright's two-run poke in the first inning was the margin of victory for the Flatbush flock who were now only a half-game out of first place.

The Giants blew a second straight opportunity to tighten the race as they wasted ten hits and six walks, leaving 14 men on base, including three in the bottom of the ninth. St. Louis broke a 4–4 tie in the eighth when Chick Hafey singled, went to third on Jimmy Wilson's single, and scored when Andy High hit a high bouncer to second that Howie Critz could not fling home in time.

The top three teams were now separated by one-half game.

Chicago	80–59	–
St. Louis	79–59	.5
Brooklyn	80–60	.5
New York	77–62	3

September 12: Fans in Flatbush had to be pinching themselves. The Robins won their eighth straight, riding Al Lopez's three-run homer and four RBIs to a 7–3 win over Cincinnati. Lopez's home run was the last of its kind. It bounced over the left field fence and into the seats, a hit that would today be a ground-rule double. In 1931, the National League adopted the rule change that was already in effect in the American League stating that home runs would only be awarded on balls hit over the fence on a fly.

St. Louis used a late rally to beat the Giants for a third time. This time they plated three ninth-inning runs as Chick Hafey, George Watkins and Jimmy Wilson singled for one run, Bill Terry made a throwing error on a grounder for a second tally, and pitcher Flint Rhem singled in the third one.

The Cubs took out their recent frustrations on the pitiable Phillies' pitching staff, 17–4, to maintain their hair-thin grasp on first place. Hack Wilson had another stellar game—five hits, a home run (his 49th) and six RBIs, raising his season total to 171 and moving him within four of Lou Gehrig's all-time RBI mark set in 1927.

It was status quo for the top three teams while the Giants slipped to four games out.

Chicago	81–59	–
St. Louis	80–59	.5
Brooklyn	81–60	.5
New York	77–63	4

September 13: The Cardinals culminated their long, steep climb by knocking the Cubs out of first place with an 8–2 win over Boston behind George Watkins' triple, home run and three RBIs.

The Cubs plummeted to third in the wake of a heartbreaking 7–5 loss in Philadelphia, incurred when Lefty O'Doul, on the bench because of an injured leg, pinch-hit a game-winning home run.

Brooklyn squeezed into second place, a few percentage points behind Chicago, by winning its ninth straight game, 4–3, on the strength of home runs by Babe Herman and Harvey Hendrick. The Giants were idle.

St. Louis	81–59	–
Brooklyn	82–60	–
Chicago	81–60	.5
New York	77–63	4

September 14: The Brooklyn Robins crowned their improbable resurrection by climbing past St. Louis and into first place, becoming the third team in three days to sit atop the National League. They made it ten wins in a row by erasing an early three-run deficit and easily beating Cincinnati, 8–3.

St. Louis split a doubleheader with Boston, with Burleigh Grimes scattering 11 hits and winning the first game, 9–2, before the team fell 7–4 in the nightcap.

The Cubs had an off-day scheduled and the Giants had an off-day on the field. They played a disastrous doubleheader, losing twice to the Pirates, 8–6 and 7–3, dropping them into a five-game chasm on the loss side while the top three teams were tied in the loss column.

Brooklyn	83–60	–
St. Louis	82–60	.5
Chicago	81–60	1
New York	77–65	5.5

September 15: The Robins may have put together an impressive ten-game winning streak, but this was still Brooklyn and these were still the Daffiness

Boys. With Wally Gilbert on second base and Babe Herman on first, Glenn Wright came up in the first inning against Cincinnati and drove a ball over the center field barrier. Gilbert scored but Herman lingered around second base to make sure the ball was not caught. Wright did not notice the loitering Herman and came around second base at full speed, passing his befuddled teammate. Wright was called out for passing Herman and his three-run homer was reduced to a two-run single. It was the second time this happened to Brooklyn in 1930 (Bissonette was victimized on a similar faux pas by Herman in May). In the past, everyone would have laughed, shook their heads and said "same old Brooklyn." Not this time. Despite the mishap, the Robins held their first-place position by skunking the Reds, 13–5, for their 11th consecutive win. Nobody was laughing at them now.

The Giants rebounded from their calamitous double loss to beat the Pirates, 6–1, and hang on the periphery of the race.

Meanwhile, the Cubs endured their second straight heartbreaker, losing the first game of a doubleheader, 12–11, when gimpy Lefty O'Doul came to the plate in the last inning and hit his second pinch-hit, game-winning home run in as many days. Chicago recovered to pull out the second game, 6–4, keeping them apace with St. Louis.

Brooklyn	84–60	–
St. Louis	82 60	1
Chicago	82–61	1.5
New York	78–65	5.5

The last thing Joe McCarthy needed was for Lefty O'Doul to beat his team not once, but twice in a row. O'Doul had been recruited and signed by Cubs owner William Wrigley some years earlier, but McCarthy cut O'Doul before the 1926 season, believing he was not ready for the big leagues.[26] O'Doul languished in the minors for two more years before the Phillies signed him and watched him light up pitchers for a record number of hits and a batting title in 1929.

As O'Doul circled the bases following his second pinch-hit home run against the Cubs on September 15, he made an obscene gesture directed at McCarthy, the culmination of a long resentment the former pitcher-turned-outfielder held against the Cubs' manager. One of the men sitting unhappily in the stands and watching O'Doul's antics was William Wrigley. He was still processing all of the critiques whispered to him by Rogers Hornsby, and now he had this humiliating reminder that his manager let his favorite talent (Wrigley always referred to him as "My O'Doul") get away.

The Cubs returned to New York for three games against the Giants with a team psyche that had disintegrated palpably. The rumors and the controversies were wearing them down; they had lost a four-game first-place lead in two

Phillies outfielder Lefty O'Doul, a converted pitcher, was the defending National League batting champion, having hit .398 in 1929. He hit a stellar .383 in 1930 and sealed Joe McCarthy's fate with some late-inning September home run heroics against the Cubs.

weeks and now they found themselves in third place chasing two teams playing world-class baseball.

"We'll beat all those guys regardless of what anyone else says," Hack Wilson proclaimed defiantly to the growing air of pessimism surrounding the club. "All this hooey about anybody stopping us makes me sick."

McCarthy's reaction was like a proud father's. "Nine fellows like that Wilson and we'd have never lost a ball game."[27]

The Giants were hoping to beat up on the reeling Cubs and pull themselves back into the heart of the pennant chase. Carl Hubbell did his part in the first game on September 16, holding the Cubs' lineup to three hits and winning, 7–0. Homers by Freddie Lindstrom and Ethan Allen socked the game away early for New York. In four September games in New York City, the Cubs had been shut out three times, stroked only 16 hits, and scored only one run on a Hack Wilson home run.

Wilson flexed his muscles the next day for two home runs (giving him 52) and four RBIs as the Cubs prevailed, 6–2. The four RBIs gave him 177 for the year, breaking Lou Gehrig's 1927 mark of 175.

The Chicago offense was mostly rendered impotent again the next day as Fred Fitzsimmons gave up only six hits in winning, 6–2. Mel Ott hit his 23rd home run. By winning two of three, the Giants remained five and one-half games off the pace while the Cubs, by losing two of the three, slipped to two and one-half games back.

If the excitement of the Giants-Cubs series was somewhat muted by the fact the Cubs were in a free fall and the Giants were trying to stave off elimination, there was no containing the excitement and buzz about the Cardinals-Robins series happening concurrently in Brooklyn. It was the premier series of the season between two teams separated by only one-half game and tied for first in the loss column. They were the two hottest teams in baseball—Brooklyn was 12–2 for the month and had won 11 straight. St. Louis was 11–2 for the month and 34–11 since hitting high gear in mid–August.

At least as many fans were turned away from the opening game at Ebbets Field on September 16 as attended the game. The 30,000 people shoehorned into the ballpark witnessed a game worthy of baseball's best teams. Dazzy Vance and Wild Bill Hallahan began exchanging zeroes early, Vance racking up strikeouts with a popping fastball and Hallahan retiring every batter.

The tension rose as the zeroes piled up. In the sixth inning, with Cardinals on second and third and two out, Taylor Douthit caught one of Vance's offerings and sent a frozen rope to deep right-center field that looked like the tie-breaker. Somehow Babe Herman lunged for it in full flight and snow-coned it into his glove for the third out. An inning later, Sparky Adams was on third base for St. Louis, and with Chick Hafey batting, Adams sprinted for home.

He had a great jump and looked like he had home plate stolen, but the clever Vance hit Hafey in the midsection with his pitch. The hit batsman resulted in a dead ball and sent Adams back to third where he was stranded.

Meanwhile, Hallahan gunned down the first 20 batters he faced. With two outs in the seventh inning, he induced Babe Herman to hit a slow roller back to the mound, but in his haste to field and throw, Hallahan booted the ball and Brooklyn had its first base runner. Hallahan emerged from of the inning without any trouble, but needed some luck to do the same in the eighth inning. Harvey Hendrick broke up the no-hitter with a clean single to center field. With Neal Finn at the plate, Hendrick took off for second base only to be nailed on a strong throw from Jimmy Wilson. It was a big defensive play because Finn swatted the next pitch to left-center for a single. Since two were out, Finn tried to stretch it into a double. He dove into second just as Wally Gelbert got the ball and reached back to tag Finn. The two collided heavily, the force of the blow knocked Gelbert dizzy, and the ball popped out of his glove to the delight of the Brooklyn faithful. However, Finn was knocked equally silly, and when he hit the ground, he rolled off the base semi-conscious. Hallahan, backing up the play, grabbed the loose ball and tagged out the limp Finn to end the inning.

Brooklyn came close again in the bottom of the ninth when Al Lopez banged a single to start the frame and advanced to second as Vance beat out a slow roller. Eddie Moore, an expert bunter, popped up his attempted sacrifice; catcher Ernie Mancuso caught it and ripped a throw to second base to double off Lopez. It was another key play for St. Louis because the next batter, Gilbert, slapped a single to center field for what could have been the game-winning hit.

In the top of the tenth, Vance struck out his 11th Cardinal before Andy High scorched a double and Taylor Douthit singled him home. As High scored the game's first run, he had to be feeling some of the same sweet revenge against Wilbert Robinson that Lefty O'Doul felt after beating Joe McCarthy. High had once been the property of the Robins, but Wilbert Robinson had released him some five years earlier.

The game came down to the bottom of the tenth. Glenn Wright led off and served notice that Brooklyn was not about to let its 11-game win streak die easily by rocketing a double to left-center field. All of Brooklyn was on its feet when Hallahan walked the next batter, Del Bissonette, to put the winning run on first base. Harvey Hendrick laid down a perfect sacrifice bunt to advance the runners, and Gabby Street decided Hallahan should walk Jake Flowers to set up a double play with Al Lopez at the plate. The already frenzied crowd reached hyper-decibel level when Lopez smashed a shot up the middle that appeared headed for center field. Shortstop Sparky Adams made a desperate dive and knocked the ball down, groped for and grabbed it, then zipped it to Frankie Frisch covering second. The Flash caught the ball and threw it to Bottomley at first in virtually the same motion, and Lopez was called out by a half-step. The Cardinals so quickly turning a game-ending double play on what looked like a game-winning hit stunned the crowd into a shocked and sullen silence. In just an instant, the game and Brooklyn's win streak were over, and the Cards had a 1–0 victory and were back in first place by percentage points.

Both managers praised the game as one of the best they had ever seen. Wilbert Robinson admitted he almost passed out from the strain, and Gabby Street said he had never seen so many dramatic plays in one game. The *Sporting News* called the game-ending twin killing "the play which may have won the pennant for the Cardinals."[28]

Cardinal centerfielder Taylor Douthit's .303 average and 201 hits ignited Cardinal rallies in 1930, especially late in the pennant drive. Traded to Cincinnati in 1931, he was never as prolific again.

The Robins came back the next day and gave the Cardinals another battle. The game was a 3–3 dogfight when the same Andy High who had helped beat Chicago in the 20-inning marathon two weeks ago and helped beat the Robins in the previous game, doubled home two ninth-inning runs, giving St. Louis a critical 5–3 victory and a one-game lead.

The next day, the Cards made it a clean sweep, scoring runs early as Frisch tripled home a run and Bottomley hit a two-run homer. Grimes stubbornly held the lead for the rest of the game and won, 4–3.

A deflated Brooklyn took stock of its team. After an ugly month of August that promised to make 1930 a very disappointing season, the Robins found life and went on a quixotic winning streak that actually carried them back to the top of the league. They then played three great games against St. Louis in the biggest series of the season, and even though they lost all of the games, they competed hard and well.

"The Robins took consolation from the fact that, for a change, they did not beat themselves, but were beaten by a good ball club," reported Tom Holmes in the *Sporting News*.[29] And all hope was not lost. The Robins were two games behind St. Louis and still had seven games to play.

"That good ball club" to which Holmes referred pulled out of New York in considerably better shape than when it arrived.

St. Louis	85–60	–
Brooklyn	84–63	2
Chicago	83–63	2.5
New York	80–66	5.5

St. Louis had nine games left to play and had a distinct advantage in that five of its remaining games were going to be against the Phillies at the Baker Bowl. They went right to work on Philadelphia, winning the first game, 7–3, despite two home runs by Chuck Klein (giving him 39). They won the second game, 9–3, as Mancuso (subbing for Jimmy Wilson, who hurt his ankle) hit two home runs and George Watkins hit one. They uncharacteristically blew a 3–0 lead in the third game and lost, 4–3, but came right back the next day to earn a 15–7 win. Mancuso had four more hits, and Bottomley and George Watkins produced three each (this was another of those games in which every St. Louis starter had at least one hit).

The Phillies hosted some special guests for the fifth and final game — Connie Mack's AL champs came to watch and scout the team they figured might be their World Series opponent. Mack had already authorized some scouting of St. Louis and the report he received said the Cardinals were in the best shape of the NL contenders and that "they were better than the Cubs in pitching but they were a lighter with the bats."[30] The Athletics were treated to a typical Baker Bowl blast — the Cardinals won, 19–16. Mack had to wonder about the validity of his scouting report after watching the usually reliable St. Louis pitchers get pummeled while the Cardinals' "lighter" bats churned out a National League season-high 26 hits. Wally Gelbert and Chuck Klein each had four RBIs for their respective teams and Frankie Frisch, Ernie Mancuso, Sparky Adams and Klein all had four hits.

The Giants did what they could to keep pace with the Cardinals. They beat Cincinnati four straight times. Willie Walker tossed a two-hit shutout in the first game, a 7–0 win. The next day, in a doubleheader sweep, Fred Lindstrom had one of his best days of the season, hitting two home runs in the first game and plowing a game-winning single through the infield in the bottom of the ninth to win the second game. On September 21, they had another twin bill and won the first game, 6–4, but ran into tough luck in the second game. After giving up six runs to the Reds in the second inning, the Giants were in the midst of fighting back (having closed the gap to 7–6 in the seventh inning) when the game was called by a combination of darkness and bad weather. With the loss, the Giants were one game away from elimination. They were off the next day, September 22, but with St. Louis' win at Philadelphia, John McGraw and his men were mathematically eliminated from the race.

The Robins only survived one day longer than the Giants. Unable to shake off the demoralizing effects of the St. Louis series, Brooklyn lost a pair of games to the Pirates, which put them within a game of elimination. On September 23, John McGraw got his last measure of revenge for the season as his minions defeated Wilbert Robinsons' crew, 8–2, officially driving a stake through the heart of Brooklyn's pennant chances. McGraw might have had the satisfaction of delivering the knockout blow to Brooklyn, but Robinson could take some solace in knowing his team defeated the Giants in 13 of the 22 games played between the two.

The events left the Cardinals and Cubs fighting for the pennant. Chicago showed some grit in a four-game series in Boston, pulling out the first game, 5–4, when Gabby Hartnett's double and George Kelly's single brought home a game-winning run in the ninth inning. After losing the second game, Chicago took the third game, 4–2, behind Hartnett's 34th home run of the year, a two-run shot that broke another ninth-inning tie. The next day, September 22, the Cubs rode Hack Wilson's 53rd home run and three RBIs (putting him at 182) to a 6–2 win.

Joe McCarthy did all he could to keep his team focused on playing baseball and not on the rumors enveloping the team, but apparently his boss had another agenda. William Wrigley finally broke his silence and gave an extensive interview to the *Chicago Tribune* that appeared on September 20. Wrigley first blamed the Cubs' shortcomings on bad luck and their many injuries before he made a less-than-veiled criticism of McCarthy while talking about his recent trip to Philadelphia and how he watched Lefty O'Doul beat the Cubs.

"In all my years in baseball I have bought only one player without consulting the experts. That player was Lefty O'Doul," Wrigley said. "Now the world knows we didn't keep him and now he turns up and beats us out of a pennant. My buy of him was a good one."[31] When asked to comment on the rumors regarding McCarthy's status, Wrigley poured fuel on the already blazing fire of speculation.

"I am a great admirer of Mr. McCarthy and as I said before, the team, injuries considered, did the best that it could. I will not say McCarthy will be manager next year. Neither will I say he will not be offered a contract for next year. We have no way of knowing what McCarthy might demand in the way of salary, or maybe McCarthy may not want the job any longer. He might feel that by failing to win the pennant, he has put me in an embarrassing position."[32]

While the Cardinals returned home to cheering throngs, Cubs fans had sunk into a bleak despair. As the Cardinals were preparing for their last series of the season against the Pirates and focusing on how to beat them and clinch the flag, the Cubs were surrounded and distracted by a media maelstrom ignited by Wrigley's comments. No one in Chicago seemed to notice that the Cubs had taken three of four from the Braves, and no one seemed to care that the Cubs were still alive in the race — they trailed by three games with four to play against Cincinnati.

Through all of the controversy, McCarthy never commented on the rumors and declined to respond to Wrigley's remarks. His work ethic and self-discipline allowed him to remain focused on his job — a job he continued to do right up until the moment he received a phone call just before leaving Boston.

William Veeck, Sr., was the president of the Cubs and his call with Joe McCarthy was short and to the point. McCarthy was being relieved of his duties when the season ended. He would not be offered a contract for 1931. That prize would go to Rogers Hornsby.

The headlines screamed across Chicago that McCarthy was out. Some questioned the timing with the Cubs still alive in the pennant race. Wrigley responded that he had to announce the change immediately because of "all the rumors flying around. I have always wanted a world championship team," he continued, "and I am not sure McCarthy is the man to give me that kind of team. There has been no misunderstanding with McCarthy. We simply decided to make a change and we plan to tender Hornsby a managers' contract at the end of the season."[33]

As described in Joe McCarthy's biography written by Alan H. Levy, Bill Veeck, Jr., would say in later years that his father had always been against firing McCarthy, but William Wrigley had never gotten over the loss in the 1929 World Series and in August made the decision to let McCarthy go.[34] Both Wrigley and Veeck encouraged McCarthy to finish the season, but McCarthy declined. He resigned and went home to Buffalo.

"I have no criticism of the Chicago club management," McCarthy stated. "I was treated fairly at all times.... If Mr. Wrigley wanted a new manager, that's perfectly all right with me. He is the one paying the freight."[35] Asked where he might go next, McCarthy shrugged. "In 24 years of baseball, I have never asked for a job and I don't intend to start now."[36] However, machinations were already underway to put McCarthy in touch with the leadership of the New York Yankees, who were interested in replacing Bob Shawkey.[37]

The stated reasons for firing McCarthy were that he did not do a good enough job scouting the Athletics for the 1929 World Series and that his pitchers paid a heavy toll for it; that he allowed his players to celebrate too much after clinching the 1929 pennant and they were not mentally ready for the World Series; and that he was slow to react to the need for changes in 1930 as his team faltered.[38]

"All I can say at this time is that I am happy to get a chance to manage the Cubs," Rogers Hornsby told the press, "and deny silly reports that I caused embarrassment to McCarthy. Of course I plan some changes for the interest of the club in 1931 but nothing is definite yet." The day after Hornsby's ascendancy, rumors began to fly that he wanted to get rid of Hack Wilson and Charlie Grimm, but Hornsby vehemently denied it.[39]

Joe McCarthy (right) just missed managing the Cubs to a second straight pennant in 1930 despite injuries, the death of a popular player, and a fractious clubhouse. He was fired and went on to manage the Yankees to eight pennants and seven world championships. Here McCarthy shakes hands with Chicago skipper Charlie Grimm before the 1932 World Series.

"It is Hornsby's ambition ... and temper always to be the boss," analyzed Dan Daniel in the *New York Telegram*. "Now he is to head the campaign for regeneration in Chicago which is more than lucky to be where it is after all its mishaps."[40]

With their new manager making his debut to a mixed greeting at Wrigley Field, the Cubs managed to defeat the Reds on September 25, but St. Louis shut down the Pirates, 9–0, in another well-pitched game by Burleigh Grimes. He allowed only seven hits and was backed up by Jim Bottomley's three-run homer and sacrifice fly. The Cubs were now three games out with three to play — they could do no better than earn a tie.

The next day, September 26, the Cubs won again for their new skipper, punching out the Reds, 7–5, as Hack Wilson drove his 54th home run through an unseasonably cold and omen-like wind.

Shortly thereafter, the news rolled in from St. Louis. The Cardinals had

Hall of Fame southpaw Dazzy Vance pitches to Cubs outfielder and Hall of Famer Kiki Cuyler during the teams' September showdown at Ebbets Field.

banged out 16 hits, and again every starter had at least one hit, and veteran Jesse Haines had pitched well enough to lead the Cards to a 10–5 victory and the 1930 National League pennant.

It was the end of an astounding comeback by St. Louis. It started on August 7 right after the Cardinals announced they had re-signed Gabby Street for the 1931 season. They were in fourth place on that day, 12 games out of first place. From that point on, they won 39 of 49 games, averaging 6.8 runs and 11.8 hits per game. They posted a mind-boggling 23–9 record in August and 21–4 record in September while winning 21 of their last 24 games.

When compared to other teams that made great comebacks, and where they were on Aug. 8, the 1930 Cardinals is equal to any of them:

1914: The miracle Boston Braves were in fourth place, but only 6½ games out of first place. They would skyrocket past the competition and win the pennant by ten games over the Giants.

1951: The New York Giants were 11½ games behind Brooklyn and fell as far as 13 back on August 11, but they were in second place, so they only had to leapfrog the Dodgers, which they did on Bobby Thomson's immortal home run.

1978: The New York Yankees were in third place, 8½ games behind a Boston Red Sox team they would eventually catch and defeat in a one-game playoff.

1995: Seattle's Mariners were in second place, 11 games behind the Angels—they would fall to third, as far as 12½ back on August 20 before a great charge won them the AL West.

"We beat out all those other clubs because every man on the team was hustling and giving his best," said Gabby Street. "It was team play and the fighting spirit of one of the gamest clubs I ever saw."

The Cubs won their remaining two games with the Reds, 13–8 and 13–11. Their four-game sweep over the Reds to end the season carried with it a certain irony. Apparently Rogers Hornsby had figured out a way to beat Dan Howley's team, something Joe McCarthy had trouble doing. McCarthy's Cubs won only seven of 18 games against the Reds, and it took Hornsby's end-of-the-season sweep to even their season record against Cincinnati at 11–11. St. Louis went 19–3 against the Reds.

Hack Wilson drove in seven runs in the final four games to end his astounding season with 190 RBIs. About 50 years later, diligent researchers found that an RBI mistakenly credited to Charlie Grimm should have been Wilson's and his record total became 191. He also hit his final three home runs of the season in the Cincinnati series, giving him a National League record 56 for the season and the Cubs a single-season team-record of 171. However, just like his RBI total, Wilson may have been shortchanged on his home run total as well.

"Hack really hit 57," admitted Clyde Sukeforth in *Baseball When the Grass Was Real*. "He hit one up into the Crosley Field seats so hard that it bounced right back. The umpires figured it must have hit the screen and called it a double. I was in the Reds bullpen and didn't say a word."[41]

Chuck Klein was runner-up to Wilson in both home runs (40) and RBIs (170). Wally Berger, Cincinnati's slugging rookie, finished third with 38 home runs (a record for rookies), Gabby Hartnett had 37 and Babe Herman 35. Kiki Cuyler finished behind Wilson and Klein in the RBI parade with 134. Babe Herman had 130.

Klein's 40 homers, 170 RBIs and .386 average would have won the Triple Crown in 24 of the National League's 20th century seasons, but in this hyperinflated year, he led in none of the three categories, although his RBI total remains the second highest in National League history. He did set records by scoring 158 runs, hitting 59 doubles and totaling 107 extra-base hits. Klein had two 26-game hit streaks in 1930, at one point hit safely in 71 of 75 games, and hit safely in a record 135 games. Little remembered is that Klein also set a still-standing defensive record in 1930 with 44 assists.

The National League batting race in September became less a contest between Bill Terry and other hitters and more a contest between Terry and the .400 mark. Three times during September his average dipped to, or just below, the hallowed mark and each time he responded with a big offensive performance the following day.

After peaking at .411 on September 2, Terry went hitless for three straight

The sweet swing of Giants first baseman Bill Terry. Terry beat back the challenge of Babe Herman and Chuck Klein in the 1930 National League batting race, then chased the vaunted .400 mark right down to his last at-bat of the season.

games and recorded only one hit in five games. His average dropped to .402. The next day, September 9, he got three hits in four at-bats, jumping his average back to .405.

A mild week-long slump followed and his average tanked to .399. The next day he responded with four hits in five at-bats to restore it to .404.

When Terry only managed three hits in his next three games, his average sunk to .398, but in a doubleheader the next day, he racked up five hits in seven tries to raise his average to .405.

That left him with three games to play—one against the Robins and two against the Phillies.

On September 23, against Brooklyn, he went one-for-four and the average took a downtick to .404.

After the team enjoyed three days off, they resumed against Philadelphia on September 27 and Terry went one-for-four. His average slipped another point to .403.

It came down to the last game of the season. In his first four plate appearances, Terry drew a walk and went hitless in three at-bats. In his fifth plate appearance, he hit a sacrifice fly in the bottom of the ninth to tie a game the Giants eventually won in ten innings. Although hitless in three official at-bats, he brought the average over the finish line at .401; no National League batter has surpassed the .400 mark since. His 254 hits tied the National League record set by Lefty O'Doul a season earlier and missed by three George Sisler's then-standing major league record of 257 (since surpassed by Ichiro Suzuki).

The dust had settled on one of the most extraordinary and exciting seasons in major league baseball history.

A total of 13,695 runs were scored in 1930, smashing the record set a year earlier by a whopping 946 runs. The mark would last until baseball added more teams and more games with its expansion in 1961. Until that point, the closest baseball came to its 1930 run production level was 1936, when 12,846 runs were scored — still 846 runs short of the record.

The National League set its own milestone with 7,025 runs scored, a mark that held until expansion in the 1960s. The American League also set a record by scoring 6,670 runs, but that was eclipsed in 1936 (7,009).

On average, more than 11 runs were scored per game in 1930. By contrast, during baseball's modern offensive explosion, the highest run-per-game average was 10.2 in the 2000 season.

The Yankees (1,062) and Cardinals (1,004) became the first teams to score more than 1,000 runs in a season, and 1930 remains the only campaign in which more than one team managed to do accomplish the feat (only seven teams scored 1,000 or more runs in 20th century seasons).

A record total of 1,565 home runs were hit, a mark that would last a decade before larger home run totals were achieved on a frequent basis.

To some observers of the game, this accelerated and inflated offensive performance was already wearing thin.

"Remember when The Babe rose to fame by setting a record 29 home runs in a season?" asked John Kieran in the *New York Times*. "There are 10 big league batters who have equaled or surpassed that mark this season. The home run has lost it kick."[42]

In late September, an intoxicated Grover Cleveland Alexander sat in a Grand Island, Nebraska, jail charged with eight separate violations of the state's liquor laws after he caused an auto accident and then led police on a six-mile chase before surrendering.

National League Notes for September

Wally Berger slugged three home runs for Cincinnati in a doubleheader on September 17, and ten days later hit his 38th of the season, a National League record for home runs hit by a rookie. He also set an NL record for RBIs by a rookie with 119.

Boston (.281) and Cincinnati (.280) are the only National League teams that failed to post a .300 team batting average. The Giants led the way at .319, the Phillies .315, the Cardinals .314 and the Cubs .309. Brooklyn and Pittsburgh were both at .304.

The Cardinals set a National League record by scoring 1,004 runs, besting the mark of 982 established by the Cubs in 1929. The Yanks, however, scored 54 more runs in the AL.

Adam Comorosky of the Pirates led the league with 23 triples and Kiki Cuyler was the stolen base leader with 36.

Pat Malone of the Cubs (20–9) and Ray Kremer of the Pirates (20–12) were the only 20-game winners in the National League.

Final National League Standings

	W	L	Pct.	GB
St. Louis	92	62	.597	–
Chicago	90	64	.584	2
New York	87	67	.565	5
Brooklyn	86	68	.558	6
Pittsburgh	80	74	.519	12
Boston	70	84	.455	22
Cincinnati	59	95	.383	33
Philadelphia	52	102	.338	40

9

October and the World Series

After the kind of season that 1930 proved to be, many believed every offensive mark in the World Series record book to be in jeopardy. But in a season defined by the unexpected, the World Series was about to serve up one of the biggest surprises of the year.

Three days after completing their regular seasons, the Cardinals and Athletics converged in Philadelphia along with reporters from almost every major newspaper, radio network commentators, ticket scalpers, marching bands, celebrities, politicians, souvenir hawkers and fans of every ilk to share in the excitement of major league baseball's 27th World Series.

The first two games would be played at Shibe Park (October 1–2), followed by a travel date. Sportsman's Park would be the venue for the next three games (October 4–5–6), and after another travel date, the teams would return to the City of Brotherly Love for the final two games (October 8–9). Ticket prices remained the same as the past few years—box seats were $6.60, grandstand admission $5.50, general admission $3.00 and bleacher seats $1.00.

The A's were installed as 7–10 favorites. There was a general perception that the Athletics had a better offensive club, this despite the fact St. Louis scored 53 more runs and had 159 more hits than its opponent on the season. While the Athletics hit more home runs, 125 to 104, the Cardinals had more extra-base hits, 566 to 518, and more total bases, 2,595 to 2,415. The Athletics did have a measurable advantage in two areas. They had baseball's best pitcher in Lefty Grove, and they had Connie Mack, who brought almost three full decades of managerial experience to this—his eighth World Series, while Gabby Street was a rookie manager in his first World Series.

Gabby Street (left) and Connie Mack exchange the traditional pre–World Series handshake in 1930. Street's team engineered an incredible comeback to get him to his first World Series. For Mack, it was the second of three straight World Series appearances, the last he would make in the Fall Classic.

The First Game — October 1

Burleigh Grimes' impact on the St. Louis pitching staff was made evident when Gabby Street tabbed "Old Stubblebeard" to pitch the first game. The pugnacious Grimes turned in 13 wins for the Cardinals after they traded for him in mid–June. More important than the wins was Grimes' gritty, take-no-prisoners attitude that rubbed off on the rest of the pitching staff.

"It seemed Street was handed the short end of the stick in picking up Grimes, but Burleigh's brilliant work in recent weeks had justified Gabby's faith in him," Joe Vila reported in the *Sporting News*. "Burleigh is loaded to the brim with fighting spirit and he must have passed some of it along to the rest of the club."[1]

On the Philadelphia side, there were some questions as to whether Mack would use Lefty Grove to open the series. In 1929, Mack shocked the baseball world by shelving Grove for the first game and turning to a 35-year-old journeyman right-hander named Howard Ehmke to face the powerful Cubs' lineup. Ehmke, who appeared in only 11 games for the A's that year, used a repertoire of off-speed stuff to handcuff the Cubs, 3–1, and make Mack look like a genius. Grove only made two appearances in the series, both in relief. However, Mack decided not to tempt fate this time, and named his southpaw ace to start the first game.

Grove separated himself from the rest of baseball's pitchers in 1930. Using what was already a legendary fastball, Grove won the first of his two pitchers' Triple Crowns, leading the American League in wins (28), ERA (2.54) and strikeouts (209). His was the only ERA in the American League below 3.00, and he was the only pitcher to break the 200-strikeout threshold in either league.

Philadelphia did not play the role of the warm and genial host on October 1. It was a gray and windy day more typical of late November than early October. A full house packed Shibe Park and gave President Herbert Hoover a polite reception when he and five cabinet members arrived just before the start of the game. Unlike Opening Day, when the president wore a topcoat on an unseasonably warm day, Hoover arrived at this game wearing only a jacket and tie. Early on, however, he acceded to the blustery Philadelphia conditions and donned a borrowed topcoat.

There were the usual pre-game ceremonies, including a flag-raising and a marching band. The Athletics took the field just after 1 P.M., and following an uneventful first inning, they nicked Grimes in the bottom of the second. Jimmie Foxx blasted one that got by right fielder Ray Blades and bounded to the wall. Foxx was able to lumber his way to third base, and he scored when Bing Miller lifted a sacrifice fly to Blades a moment later.

The Cardinals responded in the next inning when Ernie Mancuso, still subbing for the hobbling Jimmy Wilson, singled and advanced on Charlie Gelbert's single. Grimes then bunted, reaching safely when Grove lost his footing while fielding the ball. Taylor Douthit and Sparky Adams hit consecutive sacrifice flies to give St. Louis a 2–1 lead.

In the fourth inning, the Athletics' catalyst struck again — Al Simmons

homered over the right field wall to tie the game. Two innings later, his team took the lead when Joe Boley drew a two-out walk off Grimes and circled the bases on a double by Jimmy Dykes. In the seventh, Mule Haas tripled and came home on a perfect squeeze bunt by Boley. Mickey Cochran closed out the scoring in the game when he parked a Grimes pitch over the right field wall in the eighth inning to make it 5–2. The home run was especially sweet for Cochran, as he and Grimes had engaged in some sharp verbal sparring after Cochran struck out in the sixth. It would not be the last conversation between the two during the series.

Cochran guided and cajoled Grove to a complete-game victory on a day when he did not have overpowering stuff. Grove scattered nine hits and needed some excellent defensive plays by shortstop Boley and second baseman Bishop to escape a seventh inning in which the Cardinals pounded him hard. By contrast, Grimes allowed only five hits. After the game, the teams continued sparring in the newspapers.

"We never thought we'd hit Grove's fastball as hard as we did," said an unimpressed Frankie Frisch. "If that's the greatest speed that we'll see in the series we're going to do a lot of hitting."[2]

Street agreed with his second baseman that Grimes out-pitched Grove and blamed the loss on bad breaks, referring to the A's great seventh-inning defensive plays and some hard-hit balls driven right at A's defenders.

Grove did not say anything either way about his performance, instead heaping praise on the defensive play of his shortstop, Joe Boley. "[Without him] we might still be out there," Grove said.[3]

The Second Game — October 2

Gabby Street surprised baseball pundits by selecting Flint Rhem to pitch Game Two. Well known as a free spirit with an equally free attitude toward alcohol, Rhem had showed tremendous promise when he went 20–6 for the 1926 world championship Cardinal team. He never reached those heights again, trudging through an up-and-down career (105–97 over 12 seasons). He started poorly in 1930, finally getting into a good rhythm just as the Cardinals caught fire in August. He finished the year 12–8, although not without a bit of curious controversy. During the Cardinals' three-game September mega-series in

Opposite: Two views of Shibe Park during the 1930 World Series. The three games in Philadelphia were sellouts, but reporters noted a decided lack of enthusiasm among Philly fans, speculating the town had become bored with the A's constant winning. Fan indifference, coupled with the onset of the Depression, would set the A's on a downward spiral from which they would never recover.

Manager Gabby Street (right) discusses the World Series with Frankie Frisch, the heart and soul of the Cardinal team. Traded to St. Louis in a blockbuster deal for Rogers Hornsby, Frisch's aggressive play and spirited leadership earned him a special place in the hearts of St. Louis fans.

Brooklyn, Rhem disappeared on the day of the game he was scheduled to pitch. When he resurfaced that night at the team hotel, a staggering Rhem explained to Manager Street that he had been kidnapped by a group of Brooklyn fans who tied him to a chair and poured whiskey down his throat until he was flat-on-his-back drunk. Whether Street was just in a great mood because of his team's sweep of Brooklyn, or because he admired Rhem's imaginative if not plausible explanation, he did not fine or suspend Rhem. General manager Branch Rickey shrugged off Rhem's Brooklyn incident as well.

"You couldn't disprove his story by the way he smelled," Rickey deadpanned.[4]

Rhem's mound opponent was George Earnshaw, and the lanky right-hander retired the first two batters he faced before surrendering a double to Frankie Frisch. It was a milestone for the Fordham Flash — his 43rd career World Series hit, giving him sole possession of the record for career World Series hits that he had shared with Eddie Collins. Frisch made it no farther than second as Jim Bottomley popped out.

Rhem also retired the first two batters he faced in the game but ran into trouble when Mickey Cochran reached him for a home run, his second clout of the series. Al Simmons followed with a screaming single and scampered around to score on a long double by Jimmie Foxx.

George Watkins halved the lead in the second inning with his first home run of the series, but that would be the only highlight of the day for the Cardinals.

In the third inning, the usually dependable Frisch flubbed Cochran's two-out grounder to open the door to two unearned runs. Simmons followed with a double that brought Cochran home, and after Foxx drew a walk, Bing Miller slapped a base hit to score Simmons. The score was 4–1 and Rhem was out of the game. Street's gamble did not pay off. Later he blamed Rhem's problems on a poor breaking ball. The Athletics were a little less generous in their assessment of Rhem.

"We've got right-handers in our league faster than him who can't get a chance to start a game," one Athletic player said anonymously.[5]

The A's reached the Cardinal bullpen for the last two runs of the game in the fourth inning when Joe Boley singled, Max Bishop walked, and both scored on Jimmy Dykes' double. The final score was 6–1. A very efficient Philadelphia offense had scored eleven runs on twelve hits in sweeping the first two games. After allowing Watkins' second-inning home run, Earnshaw allowed only five more hits and finished with eight strikeouts while walking one. Proclaiming that he felt best on only one day's rest, Earnshaw said he hoped Mack would use him in the third game as well.

Mack's biggest concern as the teams headed to St. Louis was to guard his team against the overconfidence that can permeate teams that waltz through the first two games of a championship series.

The Third Game — October 4

The scene shifted to baseball-crazy St. Louis, where the hometown fans cheered every move by their Redbird heroes, even during batting and infield practice. It was a marked contrast to the staid Philadelphia crowds.

"There is more enthusiasm to the square inch here than to the square mile in Philadelphia," wrote John Kieran of the *New York Times*.[6]

The Athletics were a confident and cocky bunch as they arrived in St. Louis. With two wins in hand, they were purveyors of the notion that no team in the National League could compete with teams in the American League.

Since the Cardinals won the 1926 championship, the American League had utterly dominated the Fall Classic, starting with the Yankees' consecutive sweeps of the Pirates in 1927 and the Cardinals in 1928, followed by the Athletics easily dispatching the Cubs in five games in 1929. The American League had won 14 of the last 15 World Series games.

Burleigh Grimes did not care. On the 20-hour train ride to St. Louis, he declared, "If Hallahan starts tomorrow ... and if they start Grove against me in the fourth game, this series will be tied by Sunday night."[7]

Wild Bill Hallahan was the starting pitcher for the Cardinals in the third game and Connie Mack countered with Rube Walberg. Both pitchers had similar careers, similar talents and similar weaknesses. At times they looked like the best pitchers in their respective leagues, but both were plagued by an infuriating inconsistency and streaks of wildness that relegated them to middle-of-the-rotation status. Because of Walberg's erratic pitching, this would be the only start he made in the Athletics' 18 World Series games from 1929 to 1931. Hallahan had his own inconsistencies as he led the National League in both walks (126) and strikeouts (177) in 1930 and again in 1931 (while winning 15 and 19 games, respectively).

The Athletics looked to bury the Cardinals right out of the starting gate when they loaded the bases in the first inning with two outs before Hallahan squeezed out of trouble by striking out Bing Miller. Walberg retired the first nine Cardinals he faced, but when he left a pitch too far out over the plate against Taylor Douthit in the fourth inning, the Cardinals' speedster jumped all over it, lining it into the bleachers.

"You have to hit one sometime if you just keep swinging,"[8] a sheepish Douthit said afterward about his home run that gave St. Louis a 1–0 lead. He hit only seven during the season.

The Cards doubled the lead to 2–0 and chased Walberg with a fifth-inning run produced on consecutive singles by Ray Blades, George Watkins and Charlie Gelbert. The Cardinals could have made it a bigger inning but Al Simmons threw Wilson out at third base on Gelbert's hit. Wilson slapped a two-run single in the seventh inning to open up a 4–0 lead, and in the eighth inning, Jim Bottomley, struggling mightily in the series, produced his first hit by lining a double down the right field line. He scored the Cards' fifth run when Chick Hafey doubled behind him.

After closing down the Athletics' threat in the first inning, Hallahan cruised through the rest of the game to earn the 5–0 win. He wound up scattering seven hits and five walks and he struck out seven, pitching the first World Series shutout since his teammate Jesse Haines closed down the Yankees in Game Three of the 1926 series. The win also broke a six-game World Series losing streak for the franchise.

Taylor Douthit crosses home plate after his fourth-inning home run in Game Three sent Cardinal fans into a frenzy and gave St. Louis a lead in the game it would never relinquish.

The same anonymous Athletics' source that derided Rhem after the second game sung a different tune about Hallahan. "That kid showed us something," the unidentified player said. "With him out of the way we'll take the next two."[9]

Gabby Street confided to reporters that he did not unpack his bag upon arriving home, convinced the Series would have to go back to Philadelphia.

The Fourth Game — October 5

One surprising trend was evident in this World Series—it was nothing like the regular season just completed. In three games, the Cardinals had an unimpressive .250 team average; their cleanup hitter, Jim Bottomley, was hitting an embarrassing .083 (one-for-twelve with four strikeouts). The Athletics had a positively anemic .217 team average, with their offense concentrated on Al Simmons (.456), Max Bishop (.333), Jimmie Foxx (.300) and Mickey

Cochran's two home runs. For the moment, the World Series record book seemed safe.

Jesse Haines was tabbed to start Game Four for St. Louis, and the 36-year-old right-hander took the mound four years to the day since his shutout of the Yankees in the 1926 World Series. Haines was the elder statesman of the Cards' pitching staff, winning 24, 20 and 13 games in the last three seasons. Normally a mild-mannered man, Haines was a stormy competitor on the field, known to get steamed at defensive or mental lapses that ruined his pitching efforts. He would eventually become a master of the knuckleball, allowing him to pitch until he was 43. Known as "Pops" for both his longevity and taking young Cardinal pitchers under his wing, Haines pitched a total of 18 years for the Cards (no one has pitched longer) and he held the franchise record for victories (210) until Bob Gibson came along.

An angry Philadelphia team went right at Haines in the first inning, determined to prove St. Louis' win in Game Three was a fluke. Max Bishop began the game with a single, moved to second on a Jimmy Dykes sacrifice, and came home on Al Simmons' base hit.

Grove held the Redbirds at bay in the first two innings, but in the third, Charlie Gelbert banged one deep to right field that hit the wall. Bing Miller had trouble fielding it and by the time he recovered, Gelbert had stretched his hit

into a triple. Moments later Jesse Haines delighted the hometown crowd with an RBI single to tie the game, 1–1.

The next inning, Grove retired the first two batters before Chick Hafey stung one of Groves' slants for a double and came around to score on a costly Jimmy Dykes throwing error. Gelbart added an RBI single and the Cardinals

Opposite and above: Two plays at first base capture the competitive heat of the World Series. In the first play, Jimmie Foxx prepares to whip the ball home after retiring Frankie Frisch. In the second play, Al Simmons beats the throw despite a big stretch by Sunny Jim Bottomley.

had two unearned runs, which proved to be the margin of victory in a 3–1 win. Both pitchers were magnificent. Haines allowed Philadelphia only two more hits after the first inning and finished with a nifty four-hitter, while Grove allowed only five hits and one earned run. The series was tied, 2–2 although the efforts of Grove and Haines did little to help the puny offensive statistics put together by both teams. "Scientists with high powered microscopes are now engaged in trying to find the averages of the Cardinals and the Athletics in this World Series," joked John Kieran of the *New York Times*.[10]

The Fifth Game — October 6

"We're the fellows who come from behind to win," said Sam Breadon, wearing a proud smile that contrasted the day's gray and threatening skies and signaled the Cardinals' new-found confidence. "We spotted the Athletics a lead just to fool them."[11]

The Athletics were in no mood for humor or to concede the Cardinals were their equals on the playing field. "The Cardinals shouldn't be close to us," growled an ornery Al Simmons. "We were rotten in those last two games. ... We weren't hitting hard enough to dent a paper bag."[12]

To right the ship, Connie Mack again turned to George Earnshaw. A formidable figure on the mound at 6 feet 4 inches and 210 pounds, Earnshaw was probably the best number two starter on any pitching staff at the time. He was one of four 20-game winners in the American League in 1930, and he averaged 22 wins for the A's three straight pennant winners (1929–31). He and Grove made an effective tandem — they were the only two pitchers to each win 20 or more games during that three-year stretch.

The Cardinals pinned their hopes on Burleigh Grimes and he did not disappoint. Grimes shut down the Athletics completely, allowing no runs and only four hits through seven innings. However, Earnshaw was doing the same to the Cardinals. He allowed a first-inning single to Sparky Adams and then absolutely nothing until Jimmy Wilson hit a harmless double in the seventh inning.

Not having any luck swinging against Grimes, Mule Haas dropped a bunt on him with one out in the eighth and beat it out. He took off for second base on the next pitch and Jimmy Wilson's throw to Frankie Frisch appeared to have Haas beat, but after Frisch slapped down the tag, the ball came out of his glove. The umpire ruled Haas safe, much to the ire of Frisch and his teammates, who pleaded the case that Frisch had control of the ball long enough for the putout. When play resumed, the umpire's ruling prevailed and Haas was safely stationed at second base. He moved to third quickly when Grimes unsuccessfully tried to throw him out on Joe Boley's comebacker. With runners at the corners and one out, Earnshaw was the scheduled batter, and Mack had an extremely difficult decision to make. Should he keep his dominating right-hander in the game to pitch, even though it probably meant giving up a good chance to get a run? Or should he pinch-hit and try to capitalize on one of the few scoring chances either team had generated in the game? Mack elected to pinch-hit. He sent up Eddie Moore, who drew a walk to load the bases. It went for naught as Max Bishop hit a grounder to Jim Bottomley, which Sunny Jim deftly turned into a force play at home. Dykes then grounded out to end the threat.

One of the key factors in Mack's decision to lift Earnshaw from the game was the fact he had Lefty Grove. Mack brought in his ace to pitch and the south-paw surrendered only a single to Frisch in the eighth, which he negated by striking out Bottomley. It was Sunny Jim's third consecutive strikeout of the day and his eighth in 20 series at-bats.

In the top of the ninth inning, Grimes and Mickey Cochran continued their verbal jabs during and between pitches. Cochran won this skirmish, drawing ball four on a very close pitch. Not at all ruffled, Grimes kept the ball in on Al Simmons and induced him to pop to shortstop. That brought up Jimmie Foxx. In what was probably the series' decisive moment, Foxx decided to go after Grimes' first offering. The distinctive crack of the ball meeting Foxx's bat echoed throughout Sportsman's Park, and by the time the echo ebbed away, the ball was descending into the left field seats and the Athletics had a 2–0 lead. Almost immediately after Foxx finished his jog around the bases, the gray skies opened up and the rest of the game was played in a heavy drizzle, almost as if the collective tears of the city were falling on the Cardinals as they went quietly against Grove in the bottom of the ninth.

"It was a curve ball," Foxx said about the game-winning hit. "I thought he [Grimes] would try and fool me with a curve, so I decided to have my cut at the first pitch ... and the ball was right there for me."[13]

"It was a perfectly pitched ball," an unapologetic Grimes said. "I struck Foxx out with the same pitch in the seventh inning.... So I gave it to him again. It was just one of those things."[14]

The win resurrected the Athletics' bluster.

"The only thing that can save the Cards from a terrible licking Wednesday is rain," Jimmy Dykes said in the clubhouse after the game.[15]

While Connie Mack would not be as cocky as Dykes, he was more direct than usual in his statements to the press after the game, not allowing Grimes or Street to make excuses about bad breaks as they had after the first game. "One pitched ball tells the whole story," Mack said. "The mistakes and the breaks had nothing to do with it."[16]

With five games in the books, it was evident this was a pitcher's World Series and the offensive carnage of the regular season seemed a distant dream-

Jimmie Foxx slapping one of his seven hits in the World Series. His ninth-inning, tie-breaking home run in Game Five would turn the tide inexorably for the Athletics.

like memory. "What became of that lively ball they used during the summer?" asked John Kieran of the *New York Times*. "The two teams went into the game with sickly batting averages and in the first four innings, the eighteen men in action piled up the enormous total of two hits."[17]

The Sixth Game — October 8

"I don't know why our chances aren't as good as they have ever been," reasoned Gabby Street before the start of Game Six. "This is a team that fights best with its back to the wall...."[18]

Street sent Bill Hallahan to the mound hoping his gunslinger of a southpaw had his best stuff as he did in Game Three. When the Athletics took the field to start the game, the familiar presence of George Earnshaw was on the mound again after one day of rest. Street also tried to shake up his batting order by moving Jim Bottomley, hitting a microscopic .050 for the series, down to the number six spot, while moving George Watkins to the third slot and Frankie Frisch to the fourth slot.

It did not help. The Cardinals were as baffled by Earnshaw in this game as they were in the earlier one. Meanwhile, for the fifth time in the six games, the Athletics scored first, bringing home two runs in the first inning. Jimmy Dykes walked with one out and Mickey Cochran drilled a double to move Dykes to third. After Al Simmons struck out, Jimmie Foxx walked and Bing Miller cracked a two-run double. Simmons launched his second home run of the series—a solo shot in the third inning to make it 3–0—and the Cardinals, helpless against Earnshaw, had to feel the series slipping from their grasp. In case they did not, the Athletics forcibly grabbed it from them in the fourth inning when Max Bishop walked and Dykes slammed a two-run homer to increase the score to 5–0. Mule Haas drove in another run in the fifth with a sacrifice fly, and Cochran did the same in the sixth inning to make it 7–0. Earnshaw effortlessly clipped the Redbirds through eight innings, allowing only three hits. In the ninth, he was within an out of a shutout when Chick Hafey doubled home Andy High with the Cardinals' only run. The next batter, Jimmy Wilson, lofted a routine fly ball to center field, and at 3:15 P.M., Bing Miller snared it to end the game and the World Series. The A's had a convincing 7–1 victory and a six-game series win, their second consecutive world championship.

Before the start of the World Series, Ira Thomas, a long-time coach for Connie Mack, scoffed when the Cardinals said they were not worried about the Athletics' pitching staff, saying Philadelphia had only two good pitchers in Grove and Earnshaw.

"How many do they think we need?" he asked at the time. The answer, as it turned out, was the two were more than adequate. Earnshaw and Grove started five of the six games for Philadelphia and pitched every single inning of the World Series other than the eight innings of Game Three.

Earnshaw went 2–0, pitched 25 innings, and struck out 19 while allowing only 13 hits, seven walks and two runs (0.72 ERA). Lefty Grove was equally impressive. In three games, he went 2–1, striking out 10 while allowing 15 hits, three walks and two runs (1.42 ERA).

In this the year of the hitter, the 1930 World Series turned out to be a surprising pitchers' series. Philadelphia's team ERA was 1.73, while the Cardinals' was 3.35. The Athletics mustered a team average of .197, the Cardinals .200. The teams combined to average only 5.5 runs per game—the A's scored 21, the Cardinals only 12. No more than two runs were scored in any inning of the series.

"Naturally I am glad we won," Connie Mack said afterward, "for as ... the test of a real championship team is if it can repeat."[19] The Athletics did indeed repeat, handing their distinguished manager his fifth and final world championship. It was the team's second straight, answering the challenge Mack had set down for his team in spring training. Now Connie Mack could call his boys a great team.

A happy throng of Philadelphia fans took to the streets after the game to celebrate their team's win, the Cardinals solemnly boarded a train for home, and the Athletics hung up their uniforms for another winter. Figuratively if not literally, Connie Mack shut off the lights and was the last one out. Shibe Park became the last of baseball's parks to go silent in 1930.

AFTERWORD

While baseball had not yet established a formal MVP Award, the Associated Press voted Joe Cronin the honor in the American League and the Baseball Writers Association of America knighted Hack Wilson as the National League winner. The *Sporting News* tabbed Cronin the MVP of the American League and Bill Terry the MVP of the National League.

The offensive tsunami subsided after 1930 and the drop-off in offensive production made 1931 a normal year by most standards. In 1931:

- the American League batting average dropped from .288 to .278;
- the National League average plummeted from .303 to .276;
- run production dropped by 13 percent — the American League scored 316 fewer runs; the National League an incredible 1,488 fewer, making for an unprecedented reduction of 1,804 runs in 1931;
- home run production dropped by almost one-third: from 1,565 to 1,069; the American League total dropped from 673 to 576, the National League total dropped an astounding 45 percent from 892 to 493;
- the runs-per-game average dropped to 9.7;
- American League average runs per game dropped 5 percent;
- National League runs per game dropped 21 percent.

Philadelphia Athletics

Connie Mack took his team to the World Series for a third straight year in 1931, earning his ninth and final pennant. The Cards gained revenge and won the series in seven games. As his team's financial position deteriorated, Mack sold his great stars, ensuring that his team's competitive position deteriorated just as badly. The Athletics rarely contended during their remaining years in Philadelphia, and attendance reflected the city's apathy. The Athletics waved goodbye to Philadelphia and moved to Kansas City after the 1954 season, spending nine abysmal campaigns in the Midwest before moving to their present home in Oakland, California.

Afterword

Shibe Park was renamed Connie Mack Stadium and became the home of the Phillies through the end of the 1970 season. The last game at Shibe Park took place on October 1, 1970. After the Phillies left, the park became a neighborhood dumping ground until it was finally torn down in 1976. A church now occupies the site.

Al Simmons changed his home-field address to Comisky Park after the 1932 season. He played three years for the White Sox and then did stints with Detroit, Washington, Boston's Braves, and the Cincinnati Reds before returning to Philadelphia, where he retired as a player in 1944 and became one of Connie Mack's coaches. In 1953, Simmons devoted virtually his entire Hall of Fame induction speech to Mack. Three years later, he was dead of a heart attack, dying only three months after Mack passed away.

Jimmie Foxx played four more seasons for the Athletics and then pounded baseballs for the Red Sox for another six years. He retired in 1944 having hit more home runs than any batter in history except Babe Ruth. He was elected to the Baseball Hall of Fame in 1951. After his playing days, he was a minor league manager and coach, spending some time with the Ft. Wayne Daisies of the All-American Girls Professional Baseball League. Foxx suffered a number of failed business ventures that resulted in money problems later in life. At age 59, he choked to death while dining with his brother in Florida, less than a year after Willie Mays passed him to become the most prolific right-handed power hitter in the game's history.

Mickey Cochran was sold to the Tigers in 1933. It was no coincidence that the Athletics spiraled downward immediately and Detroit rose to the top of the American League. Hired as a player-manager, he led the Tigers to two straight pennants in 1934-35 and a world championship in 1935. Cochran added the responsibilities of general manager to his portfolio; by 1936, it proved too much for the high-strung catcher. He had a breakdown and was out of the game until 1937. He rejoined the team only to have his playing career come to a shocking and sudden end when he was hit in the face by a Bump Hadley fastball at Yankee Stadium on May 25. He was carried off the field on a stretcher and nearly died. He was never the same player again and retired to a ranch he bought in Montana in 1938. He died of cancer in 1962 at age 59.

Lefty Grove said goodbye to Philadelphia after the 1933 season and headed to Boston, where he proceeded to win more than 100 games for the Red Sox, retiring after winning his 300th game in 1941. He won 68 percent of his career decisions, the fourth highest success rate in baseball history. He joined the Cooperstown immortals in 1947, five years after retiring to his hometown of Lonaconing, Maryland, where he operated a bowling alley until his death in 1975 at age 75.

Washington Nationals

Clark Griffith continued to own and run the business operations of the Washington franchise until his death in 1955. At that time, his adopted son Calvin took over. Like Philadelphia, Washington's deteriorating economic situation made it difficult for the team to operate there. Calvin Griffith moved the franchise to Minnesota for the 1961 season and a new expansion Washington franchise replaced it in the nation's capital, but it too floundered both competitively and financially. This version of the Senators only lasted until the 1971 season, when it moved to Texas to become the Rangers.

Walter Johnson managed the Nationals for two more seasons, both times finishing third, 16 games behind Philadelphia in 1931 and 14 behind the Yankees in 1932. He was reluctantly let go by Clark Griffith and moved to Cleveland, where Johnson replaced Roger Peckinpaugh for two years. He had two third-place finishes with the Indians as well. Johnson became involved in local politics, winning a county commissioner position but losing a run for Congress in 1940. A brain tumor claimed Johnson in 1946 at the age of 59.

Joe Cronin replaced Johnson and became the Nationals' player-manager in 1933, leading the franchise to what turned out to be its last pennant in Washington (they lost the World Series to the Giants). After being traded to Boston by his father-in-law (Griffith) in 1935, Cronin was also player-manager for the Red Sox, winning one pennant in 1946 but losing the World Series to the Cardinals in seven games. He retired as a player in 1945 and as a manager in 1947. He was elected to the Baseball Hall of Fame in 1956. After serving a stint as Boston's general manager, he was elected president of the American League, a position he held until retiring in 1973. He died 11 years later.

Joe Judge lost his starting job to Joe Kuehl in 1931 and was disappointed when Griffith turned to Joe Cronin as the team's new manager in 1933. He went on to play one season with Brooklyn and two partial seasons with the Red Sox before calling it quits. He then served at baseball coach at Georgetown University from 1936 until 1958. While shoveling snow in March of 1963, Judge suffered a heart attack and died at age 68.

Heinie Manush continued to be a solid hitter for Washington through the 1933 pennant-winning season, after which he finished his career with Brooklyn and Pittsburgh.

Goose Goslin gave the Browns two solid offensive seasons before returning to his beloved Nationals for the 1932 campaign when he shared the outfield with Manush. Goslin then spent four seasons with the Detroit Tigers, where he helped the Tigers to two pennants and a world championship. Manush was elected to the Baseball Hall of Fame in 1964 and Goslin in 1968. The two outfielders were inextricably linked in baseball history by their scintillating batting race in 1928, the blockbuster trade for each other in 1930 and their shared season in Washington in 1932. Therefore, it was particularly poignant that they died within three days of each other — Manush in Florida on May 12, 1971, and Goslin in New Jersey on May 15, 1971.

New York Yankees

Joe McCarthy signed to manage the Yankees only days after returning to his home in Buffalo. After a second-place finish in 1931, he led the club to the 1932 World Series and got the immense satisfaction of watching his Yankees pummel the Chicago Cubs in four games. The man William Wrigley doubted could bring Chicago a championship team would go on to win eight pennants and seven world championships for the Yankees, including four straight from 1936 to 1939 (the 1938 team also swept the Cubs in the World Series). McCarthy retired with the most wins in Yankee franchise history. From 1948 to 1950, he managed the Boston Red Sox, and while he did not win a pennant, the 1948 team tied Cleveland for first place, only to lose a one-game playoff, and the 1949 team lost the pennant on the last day of the season to the Yankees. His career winning percentage of .615 in regular-season play and .698 in post-season play remain the best in baseball history. McCarthy retired to his farm after his time with the Red Sox and lived a quiet retirement until his death of pneumonia at the age of 90 in 1978.

Bob Shawkey was angry at the way the Yankees brought McCarthy on board before relieving him of his duties, but he eventually got over it and maintained a lifelong affection for and affiliation with the pinstripes. He managed and coached in the Pittsburgh and Detroit farm systems and later became the baseball coach at Dartmouth University. Shawkey was the starting pitcher in the first game the Yanks ever played at Yankee Stadium in 1923, and 53 years later, he threw out the ceremonial first pitch at the refurbished Yankee Stadium in April, 1976. He died four years later.

Babe Ruth played four more seasons with the Yankees before moving on to the Boston Braves, for whom he played part of the 1935 season before hanging up his spikes. While he never got a job as a manager, he did coach with Brooklyn for a short time. He was one of the original five members of the Baseball Hall of Fame named in 1936 and spent the rest of his days as a national celebrity, raising money for charities and for the United States war effort in World War II. He died of cancer in 1948, his legacy and fame as vibrant today as it was when he passed away.

Lou Gehrig became the captain of the Yankees and continued his amazing slugging. He hit four home runs in a game in 1932 and won the Triple Crown in 1934. But after Ruth left, the team went into a three-year stretch without a pennant until Joe DiMaggio joined the lineup in 1936. For the rest of the decade, the team was all but invincible. Gehrig, on the other hand, proved to be very mortal. After 2,130 consecutive games over 14 seasons, his career ended when he was diagnosed with Amyotrophic Lateral Sclerosis (ALS), a fatal disease that condemns the afflicted to a slow wasting away. Gehrig was voted into the Baseball Hall of Fame in a special election in 1939 and died just a few weeks short of his 38th birthday in 1941.

Tony Lazzeri was often overshadowed by Ruth, Gehrig and DiMaggio, but he took a back seat to few hitters as a run producer — he once had two grand slams and 11 RBIs in one game (an American League record), six home runs in three consecutive games, seven in four games, and he averaged 85 RBIs per season over a 14-year career. The acknowledged on-field leader of both the Huggins Yankees of the 1920s and the McCarthy Yankees of the 1930s, Lazzeri had one well-kept secret. Like Grover Cleveland Alexander, with whom he is forever linked for their showdown in the 1926 World Series, Lazzeri was an epileptic. In 1946, two years after his retirement, and while his wife was away on a vacation, Lazzeri died after falling down a staircase and hitting his head. It is thought Lazzeri took the fall after suffering a seizure.

Cleveland Indians

Roger Peckinpaugh managed the Indians into the 1933 season. He was fired after 51 games and replaced by Walter Johnson. Eight years later, he was back to manage the team for one year and finished with an overall 500–491 record as a manager. In all those games, he was thrown out of a game only once. He died in 1977 at the age of 86.

Wes Ferrell was felled by shoulder trouble after four 20-game winning seasons in his first four years with Cleveland. He resurrected his career with the Red Sox, where he won over 20 games twice in three seasons. Overall, his 193 wins in 15 years were considered insufficient for the Baseball Hall of Fame by the Baseball Writers Association of America and the Veterans Committee. His brother Rick, however, was admitted via the Veterans Committee in 1984. Wes Ferrell died in Florida in 1976 at the age of 68. His brother outlived him by 19 years.

Detroit Tigers

Bucky Harris managed the Tigers for three more seasons and was then replaced by Mickey Cochran in 1934. Harris, who started his managerial career in Washington, returned to pilot the Senators from 1935 to 1942 and also 1950–

54. He also directed the Red Sox, Phillies and Yankees, with whom he won a world championship in 1947. He spent the last decade of his life as a special assistant to the new Washington Senators during the 1960s. The Veterans Committee welcomed him to Cooperstown in 1975 and he died two years later on his 81st birthday.

Charlie Gehringer enjoyed three trips to the World Series with the Tigers (1934, 1935, 1940), winning only in 1935. He was elected to the Baseball Hall of Fame in 1949 and had his number retired by the Tigers. He spent a few years as Detroit's general manager and was one of their vice presidents until 1959. He was active on the Hall of Fame Veterans Committee for almost four decades. He died in January of 1993 at the age of 89.

St. Louis Browns

Bill Killefer had no more luck managing the Browns than anyone else. He managed them to two sixth-place finishes and was let go in 1933 as the Browns brought up the rear of the American League. It was his last managerial job. Rogers Hornsby replaced Killefer and managed them through 1937, never getting them out of the second division. Luke Sewell did what neither Killefer nor Hornsby could do—he became the only man to ever lead the Browns to a pennant as they beat out the Tigers by a single game in 1944, only to lose the World Series in six games to the Cardinals. The Browns packed their bags after the 1953 season and moved to Baltimore to become the Orioles.

Chicago White Sox

Donie Bush managed the White Sox to a last-place finish in 1931 and was let go by Charles Comisky. He managed only one more year in the major leagues, finishing last with the Cincinnati Reds in 1933. He managed in the minor leagues and later scouted for the Red Sox and White Sox until his death in 1972 at the age of 85.

Ted Lyons closed out his pitching career with the Chisox in 1942, then came back to manage them in 1946. During his three-year tenure, the Sox won only 43 percent of their games. He was elected to the Baseball Hall of Fame in 1955 and continued in the game as a coach and scout until 1966, when he retired to help his sister run a rice plantation in Louisiana. He died in 1986.

Boston Red Sox

Heinie Wagner was the only other pilot besides Joe McCarthy not to survive his performance in 1930. After the Red Sox went 52–102, Wagner was fired.

It turned out to be his only season as a major league manager. He moved to New Rochelle, New York, where he lived out the last 13 years of his life as a coach for local baseball teams and was a supervisor in a lumberyard.

St. Louis Cardinals

Gabby Street took his Cardinals back to the World Series in 1931 and this time they beat the Athletics in seven games. Following two consecutive disappointing seasons, Street lost his job to Frankie Frisch, who became player-manager. Street also managed the St. Louis Browns for an unmemorable season in 1938. After a few years managing in the minor leagues, Street gained a new level of recognition as a radio broadcaster for the Cardinals. He survived a cancer condition in 1949, but succumbed to heart failure in 1951 at the age of 68.

Frankie Frisch led the immortal "Gas House Gang" Cardinals to a world championship in 1934 after replacing Street. He finished his playing career in 1937 and was elected to the Baseball Hall of Fame ten years later. In addition to managing the Cardinals, Frisch had stints managing the Pirates and the Cubs, but 1934 proved to be his only first-place finish. He worked as a coach and broadcaster for the New York Giants and remained active on the Hall of Fame Veterans Committee, serving as its chairman for several years. During that time, many of Frisch's former teammates were elected in some of the most controversial selections to the Hall of Fame made by the committee. Frisch died in 1973 from injuries sustained in an automobile accident. He was 74.

Chick Hafey won the batting title in 1931 but a protracted salary dispute the next winter led to his being traded to the Cincinnati Reds. He hit well for the Reds and holds the distinction of getting the first hit in the history of the All-Star Game. He retired in 1935, only to attempt a comeback in 1937, which ended after 89 games. He was only 34. He spent the rest of his life in the sheep and cattle business in California and died in 1973, just a few months after Frisch. He was 69.

Jim Bottomley played two more years for St. Louis, but his best years were behind him and neither campaign was particularly productive. He managed to hang on for five more seasons, three with Cincinnati and two with the St. Louis Browns. Like Hafey, he went into the cattle business after his playing days. Bottomley died in 1959 in Missouri and was elected to the Baseball Hall of Fame by the Veterans Committee in 1974.

Burleigh Grimes helped the Cardinals to the 1931 championship with a 17–9 record but he was soon on the move again, playing for the Cubs, Pirates and Yankees before ending his career in 1934. He remained in the game as a minor league manager and scout. His only major league managing job was in

Brooklyn for two unsuccessful seasons in 1937–38. He lived to the ripe old age of 92, dying of cancer in 1964.

Sam Breadon sold the Cardinals in 1937 for $3 million and died of cancer 18 months later at the age of 72.

Chicago Cubs

Rogers Hornsby managed the Cubs to a third-place finish in 1931, a full 17 games out of first place. By the middle of the 1932 season, he had worn out his welcome in Chicago, his blunt arguments with William Wrigley creating friction with the front office and his oppressive managing style creating a group of angry and disgruntled players. Hornsby was fired on August 2, despite the fact the Cubs were in first place. He was replaced by "Jolly Cholly" Grimm, who loosened up the clubhouse and helped the team capture the pennant (although they were swept four straight in the World Series by the Joe McCarthy–led New York Yankees). In a demonstration of their ill will toward Hornsby, when the team voted shares of its 1932 post-season money, they awarded their former manager nothing. Hornsby went on to manage the St. Louis Browns and the Cincinnati Reds with no distinction and spent time managing minor league teams as well. His last job was as a scout for the New York Mets. He died in 1963.

Gabby Hartnett continued to be one of the National League's best catchers. He was named NL MVP in 1935 and was runner-up in 1937. In 1938 he replaced Grimm in the manager's chair halfway through the season and sparked an underachieving Chicago club to the pennant. They again lost to Joe McCarthy's Yankees in four straight in the World Series. Hartnett then came to the New York Giants for one final season as a player in 1941 and later as a coach. He also coached in the minor leagues and for the Kansas City Athletics. He died on his 72nd birthday in 1972.

Hack Wilson, who flourished under Joe McCarthy, chafed under Rogers Hornsby. Contemptuous of Wilson's drinking, Hornsby benched Wilson when he got off to a bad start in 1931, and the slugger responded by hitting only 13 homers and driving in 61 runs for the entire season. The next year he was traded to Brooklyn, where he rebounded to hit .297 with 23 home runs and 121 RBIs. His constant carousing and drinking caught up to him and he never had another productive season. Only four years removed from his spectacular, once-in-a-generation season of 1930, Wilson was out of baseball while doing menial jobs like managing a public swimming pool and working for Baltimore's municipal parks department. Four years after leaving the game, Wilson was dead, the victim of his uncontrolled drinking. He was destitute and forgotten, his body unclaimed for three days after he died. The Hall of Fame Veterans Committee finally remembered enough of Wilson to elect him to the Cooperstown shrine in 1979.

New York Giants

John McGraw attended the National League meetings in November of 1930 in New York City and when he ran into Wilbert Robinson, the two shook hands and finally ended their 17-year feud. McGraw returned to the Polo Grounds' dugout to manage the Giants for one more complete season and then 40 games into the 1932 campaign. Bothered by his health, burned out by thirty years on the job and unhappy with the trends he saw in the game, McGraw handed the reins of power to Bill Terry. McGraw finished with 2,763 wins as a manager (second to Connie Mack) and posted a winning percentage of .586. Only twice in 33 years did his teams have losing records. He won ten pennants, had 11 second-place finishes and earned three world championships. McGraw had little time to enjoy retirement. In February of 1934 he died of internal hemorrhaging at age 60. He was buried in Baltimore.

Bill Terry managed the Giants to a world championship in 1933, his first full year as manager. He had the Giants back in the series again in 1936 and 1937, although in both instances they lost to the Yankees. As a player, Terry delivered five more exceptional seasons to the Giants, never hitting below .310. Ever the businessman, Terry left baseball and made a good living on an automobile distributorship and in oil and cotton speculation. He died in 1989 at the age of 90.

Mel Ott remained a beloved Giant throughout his 22-year career. He retired in 1946 with 511 home runs, good for third on the all-time home run list at the time. Ott succeeded Bill Terry as manager of the Giants with minimal success. He was replaced by Leo Durocher during the 1948 campaign. He spent much of the 1950s as a broadcaster. On a foggy November night in 1958, Ott and his wife were involved in a terrible head-on car crash. His wife pulled through but Ott died a week later on November 21.

Carl Hubbell became one of the National League's premier pitchers during the 1930s and lasted until 1943. After 16 years in a Giants' uniform, he retired from the playing field and spent 35 years in the team's front office, serving as a scout and later as the team's director of minor league operations and director of player personnel. Like his lifelong friend Mel Ott, an auto mishap claimed his life at the age of 85 in 1988.

Fred Lindstrom left the Giants rather than play for Bill Terry. He spent his remaining seasons with the Pirates, Cubs and Dodgers. He played well enough for the Veterans Committee to open the doors to Cooperstown for him in 1976. He coached baseball at Northwestern University for 13 years, and for 17 years he was the postmaster in Evanston, Illinois, until his death in 1981 at the age of 75.

Brooklyn Robins

Wilbert Robinson managed Brooklyn for only one more season after burying the hatchet with John McGraw. After a second straight fourth-place finish in 1931, Robinson retired with 1,375 managing victories which, at the time, placed him third on the all-time list behind McGraw and Fred Clarke. Robinson moved to Atlanta and became president of a minor league team. On August 8, 1934, the 71-year-old Robinson slipped and fell in his hotel room, breaking an arm. While being tended to at the hospital, he joked with friends and reporters that they ought to make the story funny by saying he had slipped on a banana peel. A few hours later, he was dead of a cerebral hemorrhage. He was buried in Baltimore in the same cemetery with John McGraw.

Babe Herman played only one more year with Brooklyn, batting .313 before being traded to Cincinnati. He did two tours of duty with the Reds, and then bounced around with the Cubs, Tigers, and Pirates before one final stop back in Flatbush. He had the distinction of hitting the first home run in a night game in 1935 when he connected for the Reds against the Dodgers. After his playing days concluded, he was a scout for a number of teams. Pneumonia claimed him in 1987 at the age of 84.

Dazzy Vance was traded from Brooklyn to St. Louis in 1933, giving the Cardinals a pitching rotation with Dizzy, Daffy and Dazzy—the two Dean Brothers and Vance. He appeared in the 1934 World Series with the Cardinals to earn his only World Series ring. After a brief tour with Cincinnati and Brooklyn again, Vance retired to Florida, where he operated a hunting and fishing lodge until his death from a heart attack in 1961. He had been elected to the Baseball Hall of Fame five years earlier.

Pittsburgh Pirates

Jewel Ens managed only one more season in Pittsburgh before being replaced by George Gibson. Gibson and the long string of managers that followed him had little luck managing the Bucs—the team would not win another pennant until 1960.

Paul and Lloyd Waner played for Pittsburgh until 1940 and 1941, respectively. Paul finished his last few years with the Dodgers, Braves and Yankees while Lloyd bounced around with the Reds, Braves and Phillies before winding up back in Pittsburgh. Paul moved to Florida where he occasionally worked as a hitting instructor and opened up his own batting practice range in Sarasota. He was elected to the Baseball Hall of Fame in 1952 and died in 1965 at the age of 62. Lloyd scouted for the Pirates and Orioles and worked for the Oklahoma City government until his retirement in 1967. He joined his brother in Cooperstown in 1967 and died of emphysema in 1982 at the age of 76.

Boston Braves

Bill McKechnie had three more seasons with the Braves before moving them up to fifth place in 1934 and to fourth place in 1935. They crashed back into the basement the following year. McKechnie was replaced by Casey Stengel in 1938 and proceeded to guide the Cincinnati Reds for nine years, first moving them to fourth place in 1938, then winning consecutive pennants in 1939–40. After Cincinnati, he signed with the Indians to coach and play the role of "advisor" to the young player-manager Lou Boudreau. He retired in 1953, was named to the Baseball Hall of Fame in 1962 and died of pneumonia in 1965 at the age of 78.

Wally Berger played ten more seasons after his impressive rookie campaign but never again matched the 38 home runs he hit his first year. He twice hit 34, and in 1935, that total was good enough to lead the National League. After retiring as a player, he scouted and managed in the minor leagues for the Yankees. He retired to California where he died of a stroke at the age of 83 in 1988.

Cincinnati Reds

Dan Howley had a promising managerial career when he came to Cincinnati, but it came to a screeching halt after the Reds finished seventh in 1930 and last in 1931 and 1932. The franchise fared no better under Donie Bush in 1933 or Bob O'Farrell in 1934, again finishing last both years. Chuck Dressen was able to manage the club to one decent season in 1936 but they crashed back to the cellar in 1937. It was the arrival of Bill McKechnie in 1938 that led to the Reds' revival and back-to-back pennants in 1939–40, including a world championship in the latter season.

Harry Heilmann ended his career after 17 seasons in 1932 and then developed a new generation of fans as he broadcast Detroit Tiger games on radio for

18 years. He died in 1951 from lung cancer at the age of 56; the next year was voted into the Baseball Hall of Fame.

Philadelphia Phillies

Burt Shotton managed the Phillies through the 1933 season, reaching as high as fourth place in 1932. Shotton made his name managing the Brooklyn Dodgers for Branch Rickey from 1947 to 1950, winning two pennants and integrating Jackie Robinson onto the team. He died in 1962 at age 77.

Chuck Klein posted huge numbers for the Phillies in his remaining years with the team, leading the National League in home runs and RBIs in 1932 and winning a Triple Crown in 1933. He also hit four home runs in a game in 1936 during a second tour of duty with Philadelphia. After his Triple Crown season, the Phils traded him to Chicago, and the Cubs sent him back to Philadelphia in 1936 when Klein could not match the slugging numbers in Wrigley Field that he posted at the Baker Bowl. After hanging up his spikes in 1944, Klein worked as a coach. In 1958, he died of a cerebral hemorrhage, 22 years before the Veterans Committee voted him into the Baseball Hall of Fame.

Lefty O'Doul was traded to the Brooklyn Dodgers for the 1931 season and hit .336 prior to batting .368 to win a second batting crown in 1932. He only played one more full season, retiring in 1934 after partial seasons with the Dodgers and New York Giants. He returned home to San Francisco and managed one of the game's most prominent minor league teams, the San Francisco Seals, where he took an active hand in developing a young player named Joe DiMaggio. He died of a stroke in 1969 at age 72.

Chapter Notes

Chapter 1

1. Robert W. Creamer, *Babe: The Legend Comes to Life* (New York: Pocket Books, 1976), 349–350.
2. Ibid., 6.
3. Creamer, *Babe*, 349–350.
4. Creamer, *Babe*, 351.
5. Ibid., 350; *New York Times*, March 8, 1930, 18.
6. *New York Times*, March 9, 1930, 161.
7. Kingwood College Library Online, "American Cultural History 1930–1939," available at http://kclibrary.nhmccd.edu/decade30.html.
8. Philadelphia Athletics Historical Society website, "Tribute to the 1930 Championship Team"; Quote taken from R. Warrington speech saluting the 1930 world champion A's at a reunion held in 2005; www.philadelphiaathletics.org/history/1930speech.html.
9. Lawrence Ritter, *The Glory of Their Times* (New York: Perennial Books, 1984 edition), 279.
10. *Washington Post*, March 9, 1930, M19.
11. Walter Johnson website, quote from Ty Cobb; www.cmgworldwide.com/baseball/johnson/quotes.html.
12. Baseballlibrary.com website, Walter Johnson profile; www.baseballlibrary.com/baseballlibrary/ballplayers/J/Johnson_Walter.
13. Ibid.
14. Baseball-Almanac.com website, quotations about Walter Johnson; www.baseball-almanac.com/quotesquojhns.shtml.
15. *Washington Post*, April 19, 1930, 15.
16. Ibid., April 4, 1930, 13.
17. Ibid., March 17, 1930, 13; March 18, 1930, 18; March 19, 15; March 27, 15.
18. Ibid., April 3, 1930, 13.
19. Ibid., 13 and 14.
20. *Washington Post*, August 23, 1908, 2. Some contemporary accounts credit Charley Snyder with having successfully caught a ball tossed from the top of the Washington Monument before Street, but in this contemporaneous story, the reporter, who evidently knew Snyder (still living at the time), reported he failed in his attempt.
21. The 135 feet-per-second estimate is a modern one; at the time the estimate was 161 feet-per-second.
22. There are varying numbers used in stories as to how many attempts Street had before he caught the ball. The contemporaneous *Washington Post* story of August 23, 1908, states he caught the thirteenth ball thrown.
23. *Washington Post*, August 23, 1908, 2.
24. Ritter, *The Glory of Their Times*, 214.
25. Ibid., 214–215; Baseballlibrary.com website, Wilbert Robinson profile; http://www.baseballlibrary.com/baseballlibrary/ballplayers/R/Robinson_Wilbert.stm.
26. Baseball-Almanac.com website, quote of McGraw attributed to Douglass Wallop, *Baseball: An Informal History*, (1970).
27. SABR website, Wilbert Robinson biography by Alex Semchuk; www.bioproj.sabr.org/bioproj.cfm?a=v&v=l&bid=933&pid=12082.
28. Ibid.
29. Baseball-Almanac.com website, quote of Christy Mathewson from Noel Hynd, *The Giants of the Polo Grounds* (Taylor Publishing, 1988).
30. Ibid.
31. Charles C. Alexander, *John McGraw* (New York: Viking, 1988), 4.

32. Ibid., 171.
33. Thomas Gilbert, *The Good Old Days: Baseball in the 1930s* (New York: Franklin Watts, 1996), 121.
34. *Washington Post*, April 13, 1930, 19.

Chapter 2

1. For consistency's sake, the author chose to refer to the Washington team by its official name of the Nationals throughout the book. Occasional quotes by players or managers in the text that referred to the team as the Senators remain unchanged.
2. Mark Gallagher and Walter LeConte, *The Yankee Encyclopedia, 5th Edition* (New York: Sports Publishing), 287.
3. Baseballlibrarywebsite, Clark Griffith profile; http://www.baseballlibrary.com/baseballlibrary/ballplayers/G/Griffith_Clark.stm.
4. Jack Kavanagh, *Walter Johnson, A Life* (South Bend: Diamond Communications, 1995), 64. All quotes from Baseball-Almanac.com website, "Baseball and Presidents," http://www.baseball-almanac.com/prz_menu.shtml.
5. Baseball Hall of Fame website, Al Simmons page; http://www.baseballhalloffame.org/hofers_and_honorees/hofer_bios/simmons_al.htm.
6. Baseballlibrary.com website, Al Simmons profile; http://www.baseballlibrary.com/baseballlibrary/ballplayers/S/Simmons_Al.stm.
7. Ibid.
8. Baseball-Almanac.com website, "Baseball and Presidents Quotations," http://www.baseball-almanac.com/quotes/quomack.shtml.
9. Wikipedia Online Encyclopedia, Herbert Hoover; http://en.wikipedia.org/wiki/Herbert_Hoover.
10. Baseball-Almanac.com website, "Baseball and Presidents Quotations," http://www.baseball-almanac.com/prz_qhh.shtml.
11. *Sporting News*, April 24, 1930, 1.
12. Honig, *Baseball When the Grass Was Real*, 82.
13. Ibid., 54.
14. Gilbert, *The Good Old Days*, 42–43.
15. Ibid.
16. Ibid.
17. Honig, *Baseball When the Grass Was Real*, 44–45.
18. Gilbert, *The Good Old Days*, 54.
19. Honig, *Baseball When the Grass Was Real*, 121.
20. Ibid, 31.
21. *Sporting News*, April 24, 1930, 1.

Chapter 3

1. *Sporting News*, May 1, 1930, 1.
2. *New York Times*, April 29, 1930, 30.
3. *Washington Post*, April 28, 1930, 11.
4. The Baseball Hall of Fame website, Lou Gehrig page; http://www.baseballhalloffame.org/hofers%5Fand%5Fhonorees/hofer%5Fbios/gehrig%5Flou.htm.
5. *New York Times*, April 29, 1930, 30.
6. *Sporting News*, May 1, 1930, 1.
7. *New York Times*, May 14, 1930, 32.
8. *New York Times*, April 26, 1930, 20.
9. Ibid.
10. www.brainyquote.com website, Bill Terry quotes; http://www.brainyquote.com/quotes/authors/b/bill_terry.html.
11. Baseball-Almanac.com website, Bill Terry quotes; http://www.baseball-almanac.com/quotes/quotrry.shtml.
12. Ibid.
13. Ritter, *The Glory of Their Times*, 256.
14. Allegheny County (NY) local history website, "John McGraw Visits Wellsville," http://www.usgennet.org/usa/ny/county/allegany/InterestingStoriesFiles/John%20J%20McGraw%20to%20Wlsv/JohnMcGrawVisitsWlsv.htm.
15. Baseball-Almanac website, Carl Hubbell quotes; http://www.baseball-almanac.com/quotes/carl_hubbell_quotes.shtml.
16. Alexander, *John McGraw*, 308.
17. *Sporting News*, May 1, 1930, 1.
18. Wikipedia Online Encyclopedia, Babe Herman entry; http://en.wikipedia.org/wiki/Babe_Herman.
19. Ritter, *The Glory of Their Times*, 206.
20. *Sporting News*, May 1, 1930, 1.
21. Wikipedia Online Encyclopedia, Babe Herman entry; http://en.wikipedia.org/wiki/Babe_Herman.
22. The Baseball Page website, Babe Herman; http://www.thebaseballpage.com/players/hermaba01.php.
23. Ibid.
24. Ibid. *Sporting News*, March 9, 1933.
25. Ritter, *The Glory of Their Times*, 210–213.

26. Ibid., 206–207.
27. Ibid., 216.
28. The Diamond Angle website, "The Other Babe" by Bob Brigham; http://www.thediamondangle.com/archive/jan02/otherbabe.html.
29. Baseball Library.com website, Babe Herman page; http://www.baseballlibrary.com/baseballlibrary/ballplayers/H/Herman_Babe.stm.
30. The Baseball Page website, Fred Fitzsimmons biography page; http://www.thebaseballpage.com/players/fitzsfr01.php.
31. *New York Times*, April 30, 1930, 28.

Chapter 4

1. SABR website, SABR Biography project: "Grover Cleveland Alexander," by Jan Finkel; http://bioproj.sabr.org/bioproj.cfm?a=v&v=l&bid=945&pid=140.
2. Ibid.
3. Jack Kavanagh, *Old Pete: The Grover Cleveland Alexander Story* (New York: Diamond Communications, 1996).
4. Ritter, *The Glory of Their Times*, 194.
5. Mr. Baseball.com website, Grover Cleveland Alexander page; http://www.mrbaseball.com/aAlexander.php.
6. Baseball-Almanac.com website, "Quotations," Rogers Hornsby; http://www.baseball-almanac.com/quotes/quohorn.shtml.
7. Ibid., "Quotations," Grover Cleveland Alexander; http://www.baseball-almanac.com/quotes/quoalex.shtml.
8. Ibid.
9. Baseball-Almanac website, Grover Cleveland Alexander biography by Dennis Yuhasz; http://www.baseball-almanac.com/players/grover_alexander_biography.shtml.
10. Kavanagh, *Old Pete*, 65.
11. Ibid., 105.
12. *New York Times*, June 4, 1930, 31.
13. *Sporting News*, August 7, 1930, 4.
14. SABR Website, The SABR Biography Project, Grover Cleveland Alexander by Jan Finkel; http://bioproj.sabr.org/bioproj.cfm?a=v&v=l&bid=945&pid=140.
15. *Sporting News*, May 22, 1930, 4.
16. Ibid., 1.
17. *New York Times*, May 24, 1930, 21.
18. *Sporting News*, May 29, 1930, 4.
19. Ibid.
20. Ibid, June 5, 1930, 4.
21. The SABR website, the SABR Biography Project, Pie Traynor Biography; http://bioproj.sabr.org/bioproj.cfm?a=v&v=l&pid=14330&bid=1101.
22. Ritter, *The Glory of Their Times*, 305.
23. Wikipedia Online Encyclopedia, Paul Waner; http://en.wikipedia.org/wiki/Paul_Waner.
24. Ibid., also Baselllibrary.com website, Pie Traynor profile; http://www.baseballlibrary.com/baseballlibrary/ballplayers/T/Traynor_Pie.stm; *New York Times*, March 17, 1972, 52, reference to Traynor being the manager trying to "reform one of his best players" and the fact that he gave up after the star player went into a slump.
25. Ibid., Paul Waner profile, http://en.wikipedia.org/wiki/Paul_Waner.
26. The Baseball Page website, Paul Waner page; http://www.thebaseballpage.com/players/wanerpa01.php.
27. SABR Website, The SABR Biography Project, Pie Traynor biography; http://www.thebaseballpage.com/players/wanerpa01.php.
28. Ritter, *The Glory of Their Times*, 338.
29. SABR Website, The SABR Baseball Biography Project, Pie Traynor Biography; http://bioproj.sabr.org/bioproj.cfm?a=v&v=l&pid=14330&bid=1101.
30. Alexander, *John McGraw*, 294.
31. *Sporting News*, May 1, 1930, 1.
32. Alan Levy, *Joe McCarthy, Architect of the Yankee Dynasty* (Jefferson, NC: McFarland Press, 2005), 1.
33. Baselllibrary.com website, Joe McCarthy profile; http://www.baseballlibrary.com/baseballlibrary/ballplayers/M/McCarthy_Joe.stm.
34. Alan Levy, *Joe McCarthy: Architect of the Yankee Dynasty*, 2.
35. Ibid., 3.
36. Ibid., 2.
37. Gilbert, *The Good Old Days*, 123.
38. *Baseball Digest*, "Joe McCarthy Ranks Among Baseball's Greatest Managers," by Randy Schultz, August 2005.
39. Baseball Hall of Fame Website, Joe McCarthy page; http://www.baseballhalloffame.org/hofers_and_honorees/hofer_bios/McCarthy_Joe.htm.
40. Baselllibrary.com website, Gabby Hartnett page; http://www.baseballlibrary.com

com/baselllibrary/ballplayers/H/Hartnett_Gabby.stm.

41. Baseball Hall of Fame Website, Gabby Hartnett page; http://www.baseballhalloffame.org/hofers_and_honorees/hofer_bios/Hartnett_Gabby.htm

Chapter 5

1. *New York Times*, May 14, 1930, 32.
2. *Sporting News*, July 24, 1930, 1; Alexander, *John McGraw*, 294–295.
3. Alexander, *John McGraw*, 294.
4. Ibid., 295.
5. *Sporting News*, May 22, 1930, 4.
6. Ibid.
7. Ibid., July 31, 1930, 4.
8. Honig, *Baseball When the Grass Was Real*, 109–110.
9. Ted Williams and John Underwood, *My Turn at Bat*, (New York: Fireside, 1988), as excerpted on Baseballibrary.com website, Ted Lyons profile; http://www.baselllibrary.com/baselllibrary/excerpts/ted_williams.stm.
10. *Chicago Tribune*, May 30, 1930, 19.
11. Ibid., 20.
12. The Baseball Page website, Wes Ferrell page; http://www.thebaseballpage.com/players/ferrewe01.php.
13. Honig, *Baseball When the Grass Was Real*, 27.
14. Baselllibrary.com website, Wes Ferrell profile; http://www.baselllibrary.com/baselllibrary/ballplayers/F/Ferrell_Wes.stm.
15. Honig, *Baseball When the Grass Was Real*, 45–46.
16. Ritter, *The Glory of Their Times*, 284.
17. *Washington Post*, June 15, 1930, M17.
18. *Sporting News*, June 19, 1930, 1.
19. *Washington Post*, June 15, 1930, M17.
20. Ibid.
21. *Washington Post*, June 15, 1930, M17.
22. *Sporting News*, June 19, 1930, 2.
23. *New York Times*, May 31, 1930, 18.
24. The Baseball Page website, Wes Ferrell page; http://www.thebaseballpage.com/players/ferrewe01.php.
25. Ritter, *The Glory of Their Times*, 284.
26. *Washington Post*, June 15, 1930, M17.
27. *New York Times*, June 10, 1930, 31.
28. Baselllibrary.com website, Burleigh Grimes profile; http://www.baselllibrary.com/baselllibrary/ballplayers/G/Grimes_Burleigh.stmhttp.
29. Baseball-Almanac website, Burleigh Grimes quotes; www.baseball-almanac.com/quotes/quogrime.shtml.
30. Baselllibrary.com website, Bill McKechnie profile; http://www.baselllibrary.com/baselllibrary/ballplayers/M/McKechnie_Bill.stm.
31. National Baseball Hall of Fame website, Bill McKechnie page; http://www.baselllibrary.com/baselllibrary/ballplayers/M/McKechnie_Bill.stm.
32. Honig, *Baseball When the Grass Was Real*, 243.
33. *Sporting News*, June 19, 1930, 4.

Chapter 6

1. *New York Times*, July 13, 1930, 128.
2. Ibid., July 20, 1930, S2.
3. *Washington Post*, July 10, 1930, 15.
4. *Washington Post*, July 10, 1930, 15.
5. Ibid., July 23, 1930, 12.
6. Ibid., July 19. 1930, 11.
7. Ibid., July 24, 1930, 13.
8. *New York Times*, July 27, 1930, 124.
9. *Washington Post*, July 31, 1930, 12.
10. Ibid., August 2, 1930, 1.
11. *New York Times*, August 10, 1934, 22.
12. *New York Times*, June 6, 1930, 114.
13. Ibid., November 30, 1977, 95; Baselllibrary.com website, Bob Meusel profile; http://www.baselllibrary.com/ballplayers/player.php?name=Bob_Meusel_1896.
14. *Chicago Tribune*, July 10, 1930, 19.
15. *New York Times*, July 27, 1930. 124.
16. *Chicago Tribune*, August 27, 1930, 19.
17. Levy, *Joe McCarthy*, 141.
18. Ibid., 142.
19. Ibid.
20. Ibid., 141.

Chapter 7

1. Baselllibrary.com website, Eddie Collins Profile; http://www.baselllibrary.com/ballplayers/player.php?name=Eddie_Collins_1887.
2. *Sporting News*, August 7, 1930, 4.
3. Kavanagh, *Walter Johnson*, 254.
4. Ibid., 264.
5. Baselllibrary.com website, Charlie Gehringer profile; http://www.baselli-

brary.com/baseballlibrary/ballplayers/G/Gehringer_Charlie.stm.
6. Honig, *Baseball When the Grass Was Real*, 31.
7. Ibid., 55–56.
8. *Washington Post*, August 9, 1930, 11.
9. Ibid., August 27, 1930, 13.
10. *Sporting News*, September 11, 1930, 4.
11. Ibid.
12. *Washington Post*, August 27, 1930, 3.
13. Levy, *Joe McCarthy*, 142–143.
14. *Chicago Tribune*, August 3, 1930, A1.
15. *Sporting News*, July 17, 4.
16. *New York Times*, August 31, 1930, S2.
17. Ibid, August 26, 1930, 25.
18. SABR Website, the SABR Biography Project, Dave Bancroft; http://bioproj.sabr.org/bioproj.cfm?a=v&v=l&pid=560&bid=951.
19. Ibid.
20. *Chicago Tribune*, August 20, 1930, 21.
21. Ibid., August 27, 1930, 19.
22. *Sporting News*, August 7, 1930, 1.
23. *Chicago Tribune*, August 30, 1930, 14; *Sporting News*, August 7, 1930. 1; *Sporting News* August 14, 1930, 3–4.
24. *New York Times*, May 11, 1949, 29.
25. Baseballlibrary.com website, Frankie Frisch profile; http://www.baseballlibrary.com/baseballlibrary/ballplayers/F/Frisch_Frankie.stm.
26. National Baseball Hall of Fame website, Chick Hafey page; http://www.baseballhalloffame.org/hofers_and_honorees/hofer_bios/Hafey_Chick.htm.
27. The Baseball Page website, Chick Hafey page; http://www.thebaseballpage.com/players/hafeych01.php.
28. *Sporting News*, August 21, 1930, 1.
29. *Chicago Tribune*, August 27, 1930, 19.
30. *New York Times*, August 31, 1930, S1.
31. Levy, *Joe McCarthy*, 143.

Chapter 8

1. *Sporting News*, August 21, 1930, 4.
2. Baseballlibrary.com website, John Heydler profile; http://www.baseballlibrary.com/baseballlibrary/ballplayers/H/Heydler_John_A.stm. Heydler and others referred to the DH as "the tenth regular."
3. *Washington Post*, September 3, 1930, 11.
4. *Sporting News*, September 11, 1930, 3.
5. *Washington Post*, September 7, 1930, M19.

6. Honig, *Baseball When the Grass Was Real*, 121–122.
7. Ibid.
8. *Chicago Tribune*, September 19, 1930, 23.
9. Honig, *Baseball When the Grass Was Real*, 197.
10. *New York Times*, September 22, 1930, 23.
11. Explorepa.com Website, Connie Mack; hiscmhttp://www.explorepahistory.com/hmarker.php?markerId=9 also bb library; *Baseballlibrary.com website*, Connie Mack profile; http://www.baseballlibrary.com/ballplayers/player.php?name=Connie_Mack_1862.
12. Honig, *Baseball When the Grass Was Real*, 80.
13. Gilbert, *The Good Old Days*, 45.
14. Philadelphia Athletics Historical Society website, "A Tribute to Connie Mack," http://www.philadelphiaathletics.org/history/macktribute.htm.
15. Gilbert, *The Good Old Days*, 45.
16. *Chicago Tribune*, September 19, 1930, 23.
17. *Sporting News*, September 11, 1930, 4.
18. The Philadelphia Athletics Historical Society website, "Tribute to the 1930 World Champions," by Bob Warrington; http://www.philadelphiaathletics.org/history/1930speech.htm.
19. Baseball Hall of Fame website, Connie Mack page; http://www.baseballhalloffame.org/hofers_and_honorees/hofer_bios/Mack_Connie.htm.
20. *Washington Post*, September 21, 1930, 15.
21. *Sporting News*, September 18, 1930, 1.
22. Ibid., September 25, 1930, 4.
23. Ibid., September 11, 1930, 1.
24. Ibid., September 18, 1930, 1.
25. Ibid., September 18, 1930,1.
26. Levy, *Joe McCarthy*, 143.
27. Ibid.
28. *Sporting News*, September 25, 1930, 1.
29. Ibid., 1.
30. Ibid., September 25, 1930, 4.
31. *Chicago Tribune*, September 20, 1930, 1.
32. Ibid.
33. *Chicago Tribune*, September 23, 1930, 1.
34. Levy, *Joe McCarthy*, 144–145.
35. *Sporting News*, October 2, 1930, 2.

36. *Chicago Tribune*, September 23, 1930, 17.
37. Levy, *Joe McCarthy*, 147–148.
38. *Chicago Tribune*, September 23, 1930, 1.
39. *Chicago Tribune*, September 25, 1930, 21.
40. *Sporting News*, October 2, 1930, 2.
41. Honig, *Baseball When the Grass Was Real*, 179.
42. *New York Times*, September 7, 1930, S2.

Chapter 9

1. *Sporting News*, September 25, 1930, 4.
2. *New York Times*, October 2, 1930, 18.
3. Ibid.
4. Gilbert, *The Good Old Days*, 71.
5. *New York Times*, October 3, 1930, 22.
6. Ibid., October 5, 1930, S2.
7. Ibid., October 4, 1931, 21.
8. Ibid., October 5, 1930, S8.
9. Ibid.
10. Ibid., October 8, 1930, 23.
11. *New York Times*, October 7, 1930, 34.
12. Ibid.
13. Ibid., October 7, 1930, 33.
14. Ibid.
15. Ibid.
16. Ibid.
17. Ibid., October 7, 1930, 34.
18. Ibid., October 8, 1930, 20.
19. Ibid.

BIBLIOGRAPHY

Newspapers and Periodicals

The Associated Press
Baltimore Herald
Baltimore News
Baseball Digest
Boston Globe
Brooklyn Eagle
Chicago Tribune
Cleveland Plain Dealer
International News Service
Los Angeles Times
Milwaukee Journal
Minneapolis Tribune
New York Journal
New York Times
New York World Telegram
Philadelphia Record
St. Louis Post Dispatch
The Sporting News
Time Magazine
Washington Post

Books

Alexander, Charles C. *Breaking the Slump: Baseball in the Depression Era.* New York: Columbia University Press, 2002.
_____. *John McGraw.* New York: Bison Books, 1995.
Bevis, Charles. *Mickey Cochran: The Life of a Baseball Hall of Famer.* Jefferson, NC: McFarland, 1989.
Browning, Reed. *Baseball's Greatest Season, 1924.* Boston: University of Massachusetts Press, 2003.
Creamer, Robert, *Babe: The Legend Comes to Life.* New York: Simon & Schuster, 1976.
Curran, William. *Big Sticks: The Batting Revolution of the Twenties.* New York: Morrow, 1990.
Daniel, W. Harrison. *Jimmie Foxx.* Jefferson, NC: McFarland, 1997.
Deutsche, Jordan, Richard Cohen, Roland Johnson, and David S. Neft. *The Scrapbook History of Baseball.* New York: Bobbs-Merrill, 1975.
Gallagher, Mark, and Walter LeConte. *The Yankee Encyclopedia.* Champaign, IL: Sports Publishing, 2001.
Gilbert, Thomas. *The Good Old Days: Baseball in the 1930s.* New York: Franklin Watts, 1996.
Goldman, Steven. *Forging Genius: The Making of Casey Stengel.* Washington, DC: Potomac Books, 2005.
Greenberger, Matthew, Dick Johnson, David Nemec, Dan Schlossberg, and Mike Tully. *Players of Cooperstown: Baseball's Hall of Fame.* Lincolnwood, IL: Publications International, 1994.
Honig, Donald. *Baseball When the Grass Was Real.* New York: Coward, McCann & Geoghegan, 1975.
Hynd, Noel. *The Giants of the Polo Grounds.* New York: Taylor Publishing, 1988.
James, Bill. *The Baseball Book, 1991.* New York: Villard Books, 1991.
Johnson, Lloyd. *Baseball's Book of Firsts.* Philadelphia: Courage Books, 1999.
Jordan, David M. *The Athletics of Philadelphia.* Jefferson, NC: McFarland, 1999.
_____. *Occasional Glory: The History of the Philadelphia Phillies.* Jefferson, NC: McFarland, 2003.
Kavanagh, Jack. *Old Pete: The Grover Cleveland Alexander Story.* South Bend, IN: Diamond Press, 1996.

_____. *Walter Johnson: A Life*. South Bend, IN: Diamond Press, 1995.
_____, and Norman Macht. *Uncle Robbie*. Cleveland: The Society of American Baseball Research, 1999.
Koppett, Leonard. *Baseball's Top Managers and How They Got That Way*. Philadelphia: Temple University Press, 2000.
Levy, Alan H. *Joe McCarthy: Architect of the Yankee Dynasty*. Jefferson, NC: McFarland, 2005.
Mead, William B. *Two Spectacular Seasons: 1930—The Year The Hitters Ran Wild; 1968—The Year the Pitchers Took Revenge*. New York: Macmillan, 1990.
Neft, David S., Richard M. Cohen and Michael L. Neft. *The Sports Encyclopedia: Baseball*. New York: St. Martin's Griffin, 2005.
Parker, Clifton Blue. *Fouled Away: The Baseball Tragedy of Hack Wilson*. Jefferson, NC: McFarland Press, 2000.
Pepe, Phil. *An Authorized History of the New York Yankees*. Dallas: Taylor Publishing, 1998.
Reidenbaugh, Lloyd, *Take Me Out to the Ball Park*. St. Louis: The Sporting News Publishing Co., 1987.
Ritter, Lawrence S. *The Glory of Their Times*. New York: Perennial/HarperCollins, 2002.
_____, and Donald Honig. *The Image of Their Greatness*. New York: Crown Publishers, 1979.
Robinson, Ray. *Lou Gehrig in His Time*. New York: HarperCollins, 1990.
Stout, Glenn, and Richard A. Johnson. *The Dodgers: 120 Years of Dodger Baseball*. New York: Houghton Mifflin, 2004.
Stump, Al. *Cobb*. Chapel Hill, NC: Algonquin Books, 1996.
Tofel, Richard. *A Legend in the Making: The New York Yankees in 1939*. Chicago: Ivan R. Dee, 2002.
Williams, Ted, and John Underwood. *My Turn at Bat*. New York: Simon & Schuster/Fireside Publishing, 1988.

Websites

Baseball Almanac: The Official Baseball History Site. www.baseball-almanac.com.
Baseball Library: The Home of Baseball History. www.baseballlibrary.com.
Baseball Page. www.thebaseballpage.com.
Baseball Reference: Statistics and History. www.baseball-reference.com.
Brainy Quotes. www.brainyquote.com.
Diamond Angle: The Eclectic Baseball Magazine. www.thediamondangle.com.
Encyclopedia Britannica. www.brittanica.com.
Explore Pennsylvania. www.explorepahistory.com.
History of Allegheny County (NY). www.usgennet.org.
Kingwood College Library, Kingwood, TX. http://kclibrary.nhmccd.edu.
Major League Baseball. www.mlb.com.
Mr. Baseball. www.mrbaseball.com.
National Baseball Hall of Fame and Museum. www.baseballhalloffame.org.
Official Website for Walter Johnson. www.cmgworldwide.com.
Philadelphia Athletics Historical Society. www.philadelphiaathletics.org.
Retrosheet. www.retrosheet.com.
Society for American Baseball Research. www.sabr.org.
Wikipedia, the Online Encyclopedia. www.wikipedia.com.

INDEX

Adams, Earl "Sparky" 149, 183, 184, 186, 197, 206
Alexander, Dale 2, 89, 140
Alexander, Grover Cleveland 2, 54–59, 92, 193, 215
Allen, Ethan 102, 126, 127, 148, 183
Averill, Earl 2, 62, 85–86, 172

Bancroft, Dave 44, 81, 152, 154, 176
Barrow, Edward 6, 8, 20, 65
Bartell, Dick 74, 76
Benton, Larry 76–77
Berger, Wally 98, 160, 191, 193, 221
Biddle, John 14
Bishop, Max 34, 40, 64–65, 67, 113, 116, 118, 142, 166, 199, 201, 203–4
Bissonette, Del 50, 71, 101, 125, 126, 148, 149, 150, 181, 184
Blair, Clarence "Footsie" 125, 128, 146, 153
Blake, John "Sheriff" 21, 36, 76, 124, 160
Bluege, Ossie 23, 69, 116, 118, 143, 144, 164, 165
Boley, Joe 199, 201, 206
Bottomley, Jim 2, 14, 100, 127, 149, 158, 159, 179, 184, 185, 186, 189, 200, 202, 203, 207, 208, 217
Braxton, Garland 29, 70, 94
Breadon, Sam 14, 155, 206, 218
Bressler, Raymond "Rube" 46, 48, 51, 148, 149, 176
Bush, Donie 9, 84, 216, 221
Bush, Guy 3, 21, 36, 52, 125, 154

Carlson, Hal 76, 100, 129
Cochran, Gordon "Mickey" 2, 9, 27, 30, 31, 32, 37, 39, 40, 79, 95, 113, 115, 116, 138, 141–45, 164, 168–70, 199, 201, 203, 207, 209, 212, 215
Collins, Eddie 131–33, 201

Collins, Phil 54, 105
Combs, Earle 39, 40, 119, 173
Comorosky, Adam 2, 74, 194
Critz, Howie 77, 99, 103, 120, 126, 153, 179
Cronin, Joe 2, 23, 24, 38, 64, 65, 67, 86, 115, 116, 138, 142, 164, 165, 211, 213
Crowder, Alvin "General" 89
Cuyler, Hazen "Kiki" 2, 21, 73, 77, 79, 84, 100, 101, 103, 105, 106, 123, 126, 127, 129, 150, 153, 154, 159, 191, 194

Dickey, Bill 2, 9, 39, 78, 95, 119, 135, 164
Douthit, Taylor 80, 100, 158, 159, 179, 183, 184, 197, 202
Durocher, Leo 51, 124, 219
Dykes, Jimmy 34, 65, 67, 78, 115, 116, 118, 142, 144, 168, 199, 201, 204, 205, 207, 209

Earnshaw, George 3, 114, 116, 118, 141, 142, 165, 173, 200, 201, 206–9
English, Woody 101, 126, 150, 153, 154, 159
Ens, Jewel 13, 72, 220

Ferrell, Rick 93, 215
Ferrell, Wes 3, 33, 62, 63, 85, 88, 93, 140, 141, 165, 166, 173, 215
Finn, Neal 101, 106, 120, 122, 184
Fitzsimmons, Freddie 3, 51, 76, 120, 148
Flowers, Jake 50, 53, 71, 101, 148, 149, 184
Fonseca, Lou 2, 60, 63
Ford, Horace "Hod" 81, 123
Foxx, Jimmie 2, 9, 26, 27, 32–34, 43, 64, 65, 67, 69, 88, 89, 109, 111, 113–15, 119, 123, 132, 138, 141, 142, 144, 145, 162, 164, 166, 168, 169, 172, 197, 201, 203, 207, 209, 212
Frederick, Johnny 49, 71, 101, 122, 176
Frisch, Frankie 2, 14, 95, 99, 100, 126, 127,

231

149, 155, 156, 179, 184–86, 199, 200, 201, 206, 209, 217
Fuchs, Emil 97

Gaston, Milt 66, 173
Gehrig, Lou 2, 9, 34, 39, 67, 69, 70, 78, 79, 86–89, 95, 119, 123, 132, 141, 145, 164, 170, 170–73, 180, 183, 214, 215
Gehringer, Charlie 2, 30, 31, 85, 132, 139, 140, 145, 216
Gelbert, Charlie 2, 80, 95, 158, 184, 186, 197, 202, 204, 205
Genewich, Joe 51, 74, 77, 106
Gibson, Preston 14–16
Gilbert, Wally 52, 101, 122, 150, 181
Gomez, Lefty 33
Goslin, Leon "Goose" 2, 10–13, 23, 29, 30, 38, 64, 69, 88, 89, 91, 93, 94, 142, 145, 213, 214
Grantham, George 74
Griffith, Clark 11, 12, 23–26, 28, 29, 89, 114, 137, 213
Grimes, Burleigh 3, 58, 95–97, 99, 100, 126, 178, 180, 185, 189, 196, 197, 199, 202, 206, 207, 217
Grimm, Charley 72, 77, 79, 101–3, 127, 129, 153, 188, 191, 218
Grove, Robert "Lefty" 2, 9, 27, 30, 31–32, 34, 39, 40, 65, 71, 86, 88, 114, 116, 118, 119, 132, 141, 142, 144, 164, 165, 168–70, 173, 195, 197, 199, 202, 204–7, 209, 212

Hadley, Bump 38, 116, 142, 212
Hafey, Chick 2, 14, 95, 127, 149, 155, 156, 161, 179, 183, 184, 202, 205, 209, 217
Haines, Jesse 3, 14, 127, 174, 202, 204–6
Hallahan, Bill 3, 14, 53, 58, 100, 160, 183, 184, 202, 203, 208
Harder, Mel 2, 62, 71
Harnett, Charles "Gabby" 2, 21, 76, 77, 79, 80, 100–2, 106, 124, 125, 153, 159, 177, 187, 191, 218
Harris, Bucky 10, 111, 139, 215
Hauser, Joe 162
Heilmann, Harry 2, 91, 106, 123, 221
Hendrick, Harvey 51, 127, 180, 184
Herman, Floyd "Babe" 2, 45, 46, 48, 49, 51, 52, 71, 72, 101, 105, 106, 120–22, 125, 126, 130, 148–50, 152, 176, 178, 180, 181, 183, 184, 191, 220
Heving, John 29, 77
Heydler, John 163
Hodapp, John 2, 60, 86, 173
Hogan, Shanty 102, 103, 120, 127

Hoover, Herbert 8, 28, 29, 108, 114, 197
Hornsby, Rogers 2, 21, 36, 53, 56, 76, 77, 79, 80, 81, 97, 100, 105, 129, 139, 146, 154–56, 160, 176, 177, 181, 189, 191, 216, 218
Howley, Dan 13, 92, 123, 191, 221
Hoyt, Waite 3, 39, 65, 132
Hubbell, Carl 2, 42, 43, 52, 74, 76, 100, 102, 103, 122, 123, 126, 148, 183, 219

Jackson, Travis 42, 43, 51, 76, 77, 99, 102, 106, 120, 122, 126, 127, 153, 178
Jamieson, Charley 166
Johnson, Hazel 114, 135, 137
Johnson, Walter 11–14, 25, 29, 37, 38, 69, 86, 88, 91, 110–14, 116, 118, 119, 131, 135, 137, 138, 140, 141, 144, 145, 164, 165, 169, 170, 213, 215
Johnson, Walter, Jr. 13, 23, 24, 114, 116
Jolley, Smead 84
Jones, "Sad Sam" 2, 71, 110, 138, 164
Judge, Joe 23, 29, 64, 69, 110, 116, 118, 135, 137, 138, 142, 213

Kelly, George 109, 153, 159, 187
Killefer, Bill 9, 91–93, 98, 216
Klein, Chuck 2, 36, 50, 69, 71, 72, 103, 105–7, 122, 123, 126, 128–30, 147, 150–52, 161, 186, 191, 193, 222
Klem, Bill 82, 83, 125
Kremer, Ray 2, 122, 130, 161, 194
Kress, Ralph "Red" 91, 93

Landis, Kenesaw Mountain 8, 22, 31
Lazzeri, Tony 9, 56–58, 67, 88, 215
Leach, Freddie 76, 99, 100, 102, 122, 127, 148, 153
Lindstrom, Fred 2, 44, 76, 77, 99, 100, 122, 126, 129, 148, 153, 154, 160, 183, 186, 219, 220
Liska, Adolph 69, 85, 143, 144
Lopez, Al 50, 51, 71, 101, 106, 148, 179, 184, 185
Luque, Dolf 102, 125, 127, 178
Lyons, Ted 3, 32, 83, 165, 166, 173, 216

MacFayden, Danny 133
Mack, Connie 9, 13, 19, 20, 21, 26–28, 30, 31, 38, 64, 70, 78, 113, 118, 131, 133, 142, 162–64, 166–70, 186, 195, 197, 201, 202, 206, 207, 209, 210–12
Malone, Pat 3, 21, 53, 106, 127, 161, 194
Manush, Henry "Heinie" 2, 10, 89, 91, 93–95, 110, 111, 113, 115, 135, 137, 169, 170, 213, 214

Index

Maranville, "Rabbit" 98
Marberry, Fred "Firpo" 29, 69, 86, 164, 165
McCarthy, Joe 19–21, 56, 76–80, 101, 102, 104, 122, 129, 146, 147, 153, 154, 160, 176, 177, 181, 183, 184, 187, 188, 191, 214–16, 218
McGraw, John 2, 17–20, 42, 44, 51, 52, 76–78, 82, 83, 97, 99, 106, 119–22, 126, 133, 148, 152, 156, 157, 163, 176, 186, 187, 219, 220
McKechnie, Bill 13, 41, 97, 221
Meusel, Bob 123
Miller, Ed "Bing" 34, 38, 40, 69, 88, 109, 111, 113, 116, 141, 144, 197, 201, 202, 204, 209
Morgan, Eddie 2, 60, 63, 86, 89
Myer, Buddy 23, 29, 38, 65, 110, 116, 142, 143

O'Doul, "Lefty" 2, 103–5, 107, 122, 128–30, 161, 180, 181, 184, 187, 193, 222
O'Farrell, Bob 41, 102, 120, 126, 153, 154, 221
Ott, Mel 2, 42, 51, 52, 76, 77, 99, 100, 104, 126, 153, 160, 179, 183, 219

Peckinpaugh, Roger 59, 85, 86, 88, 110, 213, 215
Pennock, Herb 39, 65, 87, 110, 132
Pipgras, George 3, 34, 40, 65, 67
Porter, Dick 2, 62, 86, 166

Quinn, Jack 94, 131–33

Reynolds, Carl 84, 109
Rhem, Charles "Flint" 126, 179, 199, 201, 202, 203
Rice, Sam 2, 23, 29, 38, 67, 70, 71, 89, 95, 110, 116, 118, 140, 143, 165
Rixey, Eppa 2, 124
Robinson, Wilbert 16–19, 36, 44, 46, 48, 51, 52, 72, 101, 105, 106, 119, 120, 150, 176, 184, 185, 187, 219, 220
Roettger, Wally 51, 120, 126, 153, 178
Root, Charlie 3, 21, 52, 101, 105, 106, 125, 160
Ruel, Muddy 69, 164, 165
Ruffing, Charles "Red" 2, 26, 65, 132, 137
Ruppert, Jacob 6
Russell, Jack 66, 137, 173
Ruth, Babe 2, 5, 6, 8–10, 34, 39, 40, 43, 58, 62, 65–68, 70, 87–89, 109, 110, 119, 123, 132, 137, 138, 145, 158, 162, 172, 193, 214

Sewell, Joe 70
Sewell, Luke 86, 216
Shawkey, Bob 6, 8, 9, 34, 38–40, 86, 11, 172, 176, 188, 214
Sherid, Roy 40, 110
Shires, Art 94, 110, 165
Shotton, Burt 54, 222
Simmons, Al 2, 9, 13, 26–28, 30, 32, 34, 36–38, 64, 65, 67, 69, 70, 88, 89, 95, 109, 111, 113, 115, 116, 119, 123, 132, 138, 141, 142, 144, 145, 164–66, 168–73, 197, 201–4, 206, 209
Sisler, George 98, 160, 193
Spencer, Roy 86, 110, 116, 142, 143
Stephenson, Riggs 2, 53, 76, 77, 79, 100–3, 105–7, 126, 129, 150, 159
Stewart, Lefty 93, 173
Stone, John 70, 138
Stoneham, Horace 176
Street, Charles "Gabby" 14–16, 95, 155, 174, 184, 185, 190, 191, 195, 197, 199, 200, 201, 203, 207, 208, 217
Sweetland, Les 50, 105, 152

Terry, Bill 2, 41, 42, 44, 51, 52, 76, 99, 100, 102, 106, 107, 120, 122, 126, 127, 130, 148, 152–54, 161, 176, 179, 191–93, 211, 219
Todt, Phil 29, 66
Traynor, Harold "Pie" 2, 72–74, 76, 128

Vance, Arthur "Dazzy" 3, 45, 48, 49, 52, 101, 105, 120, 148, 179, 183, 184, 220

Wagner, Heinie 9, 66, 110, 111, 216
Walberg, Rube 3, 37, 40, 67, 88, 202
Walker, Willie 51, 74, 76, 99, 186
Waner, Lloyd 2, 73, 74, 220, 221
Waner, Paul 2, 53, 73–76, 78, 107, 220, 221
Webb, Earl 66
West, Sam 29, 64, 116, 138, 142
Whitehill, Earl 138, 139
Williams, Dib 69, 113, 114, 118, 129
Wilson, Hack 2, 21, 36, 66–68, 71, 76–80, 100–3, 105, 106, 122, 124, 126–28, 130, 147, 149–54, 158, 160, 162, 177, 179, 180, 183, 187–89, 191, 211, 218
Wright, Glenn 49, 51, 74, 100, 125, 148, 176, 179, 181, 184
Wrigley, William 81, 129, 146, 176, 181, 187, 188, 214, 218

Zachary, Tom 38, 39

www.ingramcontent.com/pod-product-compliance
Ingram Content Group UK Ltd.
Pitfield, Milton Keynes, MK11 3LW, UK
UKHW041944140426
5217IPUK00014B/650